ANZACS BETRAYED

ANZACS BETRAYED
The Story of the 2nd D&E Platoon

Don Tate

©2013 Donald William Tate
All Rights Reserved

The moral right of the author has been asserted.

No part of this publication may be reproduced, stored in a retrieval system or transmitted in any means or by any means, electronic, mechanical photocopying, recording or otherwise without prior permission of the author.

To contact Don, email at: warvet_69@yahoo.com

For further information:
Web: http://warvet69yahoo-com.webs.com/
Facebook page: Donald William Tate
Facebook: *'Anzacs Betrayed'*
Facebook: *'MEMOIR-THE WAR WITHIN'*

Original cover photograph by Adam Rainford, Raining Films

Cover design by Steve Guest at: www.sgraphics.com.au

Book design by: www.finitepublishing.com

ISBN: 978-0-9875860-0-1

DEDICATION

    To my family, who must endure the slings and arrows that fighting a war like this has brought upon us by a corrupt Australian Defence Force.

    Especially to my dear wife– Carole, who has had to contend with the consequences of marrying a man who not only fought in the nation's most unpopular war and who was wounded in it, but who also happened to be part of one of the war's most unsavoury matters.

    And to my grandchildren for whom I will ultimately only be part of history– Jordan Isaac; Madison Isaac; Elliot Rainford; Georgia Tate; Oliver Rainford; Emmerson Isaac; Hannah Tate; Theodore Rainford; and Lachlan Tate.

    I trust that along with my films from the war, and my memoir– *The War Within*, this book will tell the full story of one of the most controversial events from the Vietnam War, my part in it, and what damage was done to me and so many others who pursued it.

*'You know– we all died in that fookin' war.
Some of us are just taking longer to stop breathing.'*

Cpl James B. Riddle
Platoon Commander, 2nd D&E Platoon
1 Australian Task Force
South Vietnam, 1969

CONTENTS

DEDICATION 6
INTRODUCTION 11

Chapter 1	MAKING HISTORY 15
Chapter 2	THE DOGS OF WAR 20
Chapter 3	CORNERSTONES 29
Chapter 4	THE QUEST 39
Chapter 5	THE HORNET'S NEST 48
Chapter 6	STIRRING THE POT 57
Chapter 7	FULL THROTTLE 65
Chapter 8	THE WALK 72
Chapter 9	THE CRUX OF THE MATTER 83
Chapter 10	MANIPULATING MANPOWER 92
Chapter 11	IN ACTION 101
Chapter 12	THE CORRUPTIONS 108
Chapter 13	THE COLLECTIVE 114
Chapter 14	ASSAULT TROOPERS 121
Chapter 15	THE MONEY SHOTS 132
Chapter 16	THE RIDDLE 143
Chapter 17	THE CONTENTIONS 160
Chapter 18	PSY OPS 166

Chapter 19	THE WAR WITHOUT	180
Chapter 20	NOW THE SQUEEZE	191
Chapter 21	PUTTING UP	201
Chapter 22	THE CORRUPTIONS	206
Chapter 23	THE LEVER	213
Chapter 24	THE WAR WITHIN	225
Chapter 25	APPEAL TO THE MIGHTY	239
Chapter 26	THE LISTENING POST	248
Chapter 27	THE END GAME	259
Chapter 28	RUN, RABBITS	272
POSTSCRIPT The Legal Situation		282
ATTACHMENTS		293

INTRODUCTION

This is a story of many parts, but at its heart, it is a story of betrayal.

Not only the betrayal of the thirty-nine men who formed the *ad hoc*, 2nd D&E Platoon in Vietnam for about six weeks in 1969, and who were then discarded into the waste-paper bins of history, but betrayal of all that stuff about 'mateship' and the Anzac spirit.

Because what has been done to those thirty-nine men, not only in Vietnam but in the four decades hence, is a sordid part of the nation's military history. It is the story the gatekeepers of our military heritage don't want told– the 'red hats' of the military establishment, and the historians and directors of the Australian War Memorial.

And there is good reason why they don't want it told. Because it turns on its head the romanticised image of *Anzac* and the noble traditions that goes with it.

The irony being that technically, all thirty-nine men from this particular platoon were truer 'Anzacs' than most, all having served initially in the 4th RAR/NZ Battalion.

It is a story the Australian Defence Force has done its best to keep a lid on all these years since the Vietnam War ended, irrespective of the damage done to those men who served in it.

It is a story of military deception and political intrigue, of atrocities committed in the field, of corruption of service records and military documents, and of the vainglorious pursuit of gallantry medals by officers. It is also about the abrogation of all sense of responsibility by senior officers to those men at the time, and afterwards.

And it is a story that was ignored by recalcitrant politicians of all persuasions for almost four decades– who preferred the option of turning a blind eye till their arms were twisted and their eyes prised open.

But even more, it is a story of unscrupulous senior army officers of the highest ranks who were not only prepared to deceive governments as to operational matters, and maintaining a military cover-up after a series of contentious events, but who stood quietly by while those men they had once led were shredded by an incredulous army of former veterans from the same war who knew nothing of the matters, and sided with the 'establishment'. They sat on their hands while a braying ex-service community poured scorn on those seeking to bring this story to light– a battle that led to character assassination, death threats, and actual physical violence.

In the end though, those same officers were brought undone (but not yet called to account) by those very same men who had been used and discarded back in June of 1969, and who were destined to wander in an administrative no-man's-land for the rest of their lives.

They were brought undone because the one thing the military 'establishment' hadn't counted on was that some of those men pursuing the validation of the 2nd D&E Platoon – ex-privates for the most part – still retained that fighting spirit drummed into them at infantry training at Battle Wing, Ingleburn in 1968.

These were men who had seen combat against a ruthless enemy in the harshest of terrains. Men, not necessarily psychologically sound (as indeed, most men from that war aren't) but men for whom the 'fight' switch had never been turned off. Men who were still at war.

So this is also the story of how a platoon of men that 'disappeared' from the history books for almost forty years was born again– against all the odds.

It was a battle that pitted veteran against veteran, mate against mate, Corps against Corps, and veterans against entrenched stupidity and corruption within the government and the military.

Above all, it is the story of my quest to ensure that the 2nd D&E Platoon went from being 'one man's fantasy', to formal recognition by a recalcitrant government.

THE HISTORICAL PERSPECTIVE

Sydney Morning-Herald, 31st May 1969

Australians kill 16 Vietcong

SAIGON, Friday. — Australian troops killed at least 11 Vietcong in a three-hour battle 12 miles north-east of Nui Dat last night.

The same troops late today killed another five Vietcong in another clash as they were on their way to make temporary camp at a village 14 miles away.

There were no Australian casualties.

Armoured personnel carriers and infantry last night surprised 50 Vietcong on a road in a clearing.

The Vietcong are believed to be from the D445 Bn., a long-standing enemy of the Australians in Phuoc Tuy Province.

The trap was sprung at 10.30 p.m. Sydney time during a 48-hour Vietcong cease-fire for Buddha's birthday, which Allied forces did not recognise until their own 24-hour cease-fire began at 8 a.m. today.

Only two armoured personnel carriers opened up on the main body of the Vietcong company after the Australians had let four scouts through their position.

Five carriers were grouped in a circle in a small clump of low trees 20 yards from the road. Another 650 yards further up the road, hidden in thick scrub, were 10 infantrymen of the defence platoon of the Task Force HQ.

Late today, as the troops were on their way to Xuen Moc to make camp, they were hit by small arms fire and rocket grenades.

Five more Vietcong were killed in this clash.

(A.A.P.)

THE SERVICE RECORD OF Pte DON TATE

23rd December 1968: Arrives in Vietnam- <u>Reinforcement to 1ARU</u>

27th Jan 1969: <u>joins 4RAR (10 Platoon, 'D' Company)</u>

30th Jan: platoon fired on (no result)
30th Jan: platoon engaged 2 VC from rear (2VC KIA)
31st Jan: contact 1 VC (no result)
31st Jan: platoon contacts 5-10 VC in a bunker system (2 Aust KIA; 2 Aust WIA)
5th Feb: contact 1 VC (no result)
15th Feb: ambush 4-5 sampans with 12-15 VC (6VC KIA poss)
18th Feb: D Coy fire on movement and sounds (weapons and equipment found)
20th Feb: platoon fires on one enemy (no result)
22nd Feb: platoon fires on one enemy (no result)
<u>10 Platoon at The Horseshoe (2-3 weeks?)</u>
10th Apr: platoon contacts 2-5 VC in bunkers (no result)
17th Apr: 10 Pl (together with 12 Pl) assault bunker system (5 Aust WIA)
21st Apr: platoon contacts 3 VC (unknown results)
22nd Apr: platoon engages 1 VC at rear (no result)
28th Apr: platoon engaged by 2 VC (no result)
30th Apr: platoon ambushed (1 VC KIA)

14th May 1969: Joins <u>HQ Company 1ATF: (placed into 2nd D&E Platoon)</u>

22nd May: APC hits a mine (3 Aust WIA- 1 trooper; 2 engineers)
25th May: section ambush against about 20 VC (7 VC KIA)
29th May: combined force ambush large enemy force, Thua Tich (11 VC KIA)
30th May: combined force ambushed en route to Xuyen Moc (5 VC KIA)

15th June 1969: Joins <u>9RAR (7 Pl 'C' Company)</u>

19th July: platoon ambushed (1 Aust KIA, 8 WIA- Don Tate wounded in action)

- **Note:** Don Tate never went on R&R. When it was offered in July, he opted to remain in his platoon on *Operation Hat Dich*. The platoon was undermanned at the time.

22nd July 1969: Returned to Australia as a battle casualty

25th July 1969: now in <u>1 Military Hospital</u>, Yeronga until discharged

CHAPTER 1
MAKING HISTORY

On May 29th 2008, an event occurred which was regarded by investigative journalist Frank Walker as being 'unparalleled in Australian military history'. There was a serendipitous aspect to the date.

The event didn't happen on a battlefield.

And none of the major players involved were in the military at the time.

But it was a day when the official histories of the Vietnam War were altered to accommodate a platoon of men that had been unceremoniously excluded from those histories for almost four decades.

It happened around a large table in a small office at Parliament House, Canberra.

Four of us – all former infantry privates who had been members of the Australian Regular Army and fought in the Vietnam War across more than one unit – had been invited down to a meeting with the Parliamentary Secretary for Defence, the Honourable Dr Mike Kelly MP.

Mike Kelly was a former soldier, as well– a peacekeeper. He'd served in Somalia and had been forced to fix a bayonet at one point. But more importantly, he'd also been a Legal Officer in the army.

So, he was a man who knew his way around both the military and political jungles.

Also present was Ms Jennie George MP, the local Member for Throsby. At my instigation, she had set the wheels in motion for what was about to transpire, despite her and I being on opposite sides of the political divide and her knowing it would make no difference to how I voted in the future. The thing was, she was regarded as a tough-asteak politician from the even tougher steel town she represented– Wollongong, on the picturesque south coast of New South Wales, and was representing one of her constituents to the best of her ability.

Also at that meeting, uninvited, was a former senior officer from the Vietnam War– Brigadier Neil Weekes AM, MC. He had taken a keen interest in the matter about to be decided, both as a former army officer, and as a man who respected the true notions of *Anzac*. He had received a Military Cross for conspicuous gallantry in Vietnam at the Battle of Fire Support Base Coral – one of the more genuine gallantry medals awarded – and was known as a man who genuinely cared about the traditions of the army as well as the welfare of former soldiers of that war.

He had recently been elected to the Prime Minister's Advisory Council (PMAC) on veteran affairs and was aware of the vitriol that had surrounded this issue– so this was a matter of particular interest to him.

It said a lot about Neil Weekes as a man that he attended that meeting. First, because he was still grieving the loss of his beloved wife who had died suddenly; and secondly, because the matter had stirred the emotions of fellow veterans in a vicious debate that had swirled around the veteran community for years, polarising it.

That question was whether or not a platoon called the '2nd D&E Platoon' had even existed in the war, let alone it be a matter of any consequence. And even if it *had* existed, there were contentions being spruiked about it that had splintered the fragile veteran community and threatened to reflect poorly on the Australian Defence Force which he had proudly served.

Truth was, those of us seeking to validate the platoon's existence weren't in the mood for taking prisoners, and allying himself with rabble-rousing ex-privates like us wasn't a good look for a man who had ended his career as a Brigadier. But it says much about Neil Weekes that he put himself at odds with the military 'establishment' simply to get at the truth of the matter.

Later, he was to say, half-jokingly, that he only attended the meeting to make sure decorum was maintained– a couple of the players had reputations as hot heads. But he also wanted to validate what was said, what Dr Kelly was about to decide.

Like me, Neil Weekes had also been a teacher– and truth was of the essence in matters like this, though I think, later, that he might have regretted that decision when the lynch-mob element in the Australian veteran community bared its fangs and attacked him as ruthlessly as it did the rest of us.

Whatever the reason, we other four were glad to have him there because it was a daunting prospect knowing that years of battling a recalcitrant military and political bureaucracy were finally coming to a conclusion.

And as it turned out, Neil Weekes was privy to the making of history.

It was a rather informal meeting, I must say.

Dr Kelly welcomed us and went through the process of discussing why we were there.

Then, as if he hadn't bothered to watch it beforehand, we watched an extract of a statement made by Major George Pratt during an interview he had given to a documentary-maker. I thought watching it at that point was more for show than anything else, although the substance of what George Pratt had to say was of the highest importance.

Major George Pratt had been the Officer Commanding Headquarter Company of the Australian Task Force in Vietnam during 1969. It had been *he* who had created the 2nd D&E Platoon.

Locating Major Pratt had been a coup for my son-in-law, Adam Rainford. A budding documentary-maker, Rainford was also the son of a Vietnam veteran– a sailor. He had become interested in the 2nd D&E Platoon matter after years of watching me try to prove that it had existed.

To date, he had already recorded interviews with a number of individuals intimately involved.

None were as important as the one with Major George Pratt. Not only was Pratt the prize interview, but likely to provide the keys to the puzzle, so when Rainford was invited to interview him, I volunteered to go with him.

But Rainford was keen to 'own' the interview so to speak– an exclusive, and even though it had been me who had driven the fight to validate the platoon for years, he refused to let me tag along. It was a critical error on Rainford's part that had ramifications for the documentary, and our relationship thereafter.

Simply, not having served in the military himself, and not realising just how important a cog Major Pratt was in the greater scheme, he failed to ask the specific questions that needed answering– like *why* was the platoon formed and disbanded, and was he aware of the atrocities that had been committed, and what role did he play in the corruptions of the service documents of the infantrymen who had formed that platoon, and the like.

It is the arrogance of youth that precluded Rainford allowing his father-in-law to ask those questions– so they never got asked at all.

Similarly, in a later interview on the run with Major General C. Pearson up in the Blue Mountains in 2007 (Pearson had been the Task Force Commander at the same time as Major Pratt, and was at the pointy end where the buck stopped) Rainford was unable to ask the hard questions of him, off the cuff.

So, just like Pratt, Major General Pearson escaped the full glare of intelligent, investigative interrogation as well.

And, it's probably why the documentary was never taken up by any television station. It lacked both the journalistic integrity required to tell the story, and the necessary focus on the more contentious elements of the story, to sell it.

But Rainford did manage two coups. First, he secured the most significant admission from Major George Pratt we could get– an admission that he had formally created the '2nd D&E Platoon'. And secondly, quite by accident, he had located a vital piece of evidence by looking in the wrong place for information about infantry units– in the *Engineers' Narratives* of all places, and I'll come back to that point later.

So that's what Dr Kelly and Ms George and the rest of us listened to at that meeting– a formal admission from a senior officer that he had created the 2nd D&E Platoon. And, as well, an interesting comment by Pratt that the soldiers in the *other* D&E Platoons were men he considered to be *'best suited to kitchen duties'*– a revelation that earned him no friends, and caused quite a ruckus among veterans.

Afterwards, Dr Mike Kelly advised us that he would be declaring that the 2nd D&E Platoon *had* existed, and would issue a formal statement to that effect later in the day and email it to the interested parties.

He kept his word.

On May 29th 2008 – exactly thirty-nine years to the day since the platoon had fought its most significant battle at a place called Thua Tich – a statement issued under the name of the Hon Dr Mike Kelly MP was released by his office at Parliament House, Canberra.

It was titled: "COMBAT HISTORY OF THE 2nd D&E PLATOON IN THE VIETNAM WAR"

One might have thought that that would be the end of the matter.

But it wasn't the case.

It didn't explain *why* the platoon had been erased from the record books.

Nor did it explain the extraordinary personal attacks that we had had to endure for all those years in pursuing that question.

The veterans who were called to Parliament House by the Hon Dr Mike Kelly MP on the 29th May 2008 to hear his announcement.
From left: Brigadier Neil Weekes AM MC;
Richard Bigwood; Edward Colmer; Don Tate; and Kevin Lloyd-Thomas

CHAPTER 2
THE DOGS OF WAR

In a battle being fought between alienated veterans who were attempting to highlight endemic corruption in the military, and a military establishment clinging to the noble virtues of the 'Anzac tradition', there were going to be casualties.

I suppose I was damaged the most, but others also came in for their share. These included a couple of decent, very senior ex-officers– Brigadier George Mansford AM, and Brigadier Neil Weekes AM MC, as I said. They became collateral damage.

For the most part, I was the focus of the vitriol because as time went by, most of my mates from the 2nd D&E Platoon who had begun the battle with me, turned and fled when the blowtorch was applied by a foul, cowardly group of veterans.

And I was never one to turn tail like they had. I returned fire as best I could.

But if battling to validate the 2nd D&E Platoon wasn't a tough enough assignment, I found myself fighting on two other fronts.

First– having to defend my own service as a soldier; and secondly, defending myself against character assassination.

'Liar!'; 'Dog!'; 'Fraud!'; 'Wannabee!'; 'Vermin!'; 'Judas!', they trumpeted.

Yes, *'Judas'*, for Christ's sake. Only those who knew me could've seen the irony in that.

But on and on it went. Apparently, I was a:

> ……*'bumbling excuse for a soldier; I'd left my bolt out of my rifle; I hadn't gone outside the wire, except on the day I got shot; I didn't serve in 9RAR; I had*

served in 4RAR but not in 10 Platoon, or 12 Platoon; I hadn't seen any combat whatsoever; no '2nd D&E Platoon' ever existed but if it did, I was just a 'dixie-basher' in it; my colour films are fake; the still shots of me in the Australian War Memorial are 'posed' because I'm wearing clean greens; I wasn't even at the Thua Tich ambush; there were no atrocities committed; I was responsible for men being killed and wounded on the night I was shot; I compromised the safety of my fellow soldiers by taking movie film; I wasn't as badly wounded as some, so stop whining; I shot myself in the hip, or was shot by other members of the 9th Battalion; I falsified documents and photographs to validate the existence of the 2nd D&E Platoon, and the Army History Unit was too stupid to realize it; I bullied and confused politicians into formally recognizing the 2nd D&E Platoon; I dishonoured the Australian Defence Force with my allegations, and poured scorn on the notion of Anzac; the Yanks didn't carry out the dustoff when I was wounded, it was the good ol' boys of 9 SQN; I have a ghost writer; I'm a *criminal;* I'm a *fake TPI'*, and so on, and so on. . . . .'

My crime to deserve that slander? Other than pursuing a matter of a platoon having been edited out of the historical records, it was writing my memoir, *The War Within* in which the *2nd D&E Platoon* first saw the light of day.

Didn't *that* get some noses out of joint.

That– and the fact that I exposed certain Australian Army officers as *liars, frauds, wannabees, dogs,* and *vermin* and a lot more besides, in the process.

Although I wrote about my experiences in the war from the limited perspective of the naïve, nineteen-year old boy, it wasn't appreciated by sections of the Vietnam veteran community– particularly not by the 'establishment'. There are those who regard my voice, and my perspective, as derogatory– tarnishing the image of our 'proud' military traditions.

And we can't have that, because those traditions have been carefully crafted over the decades so as to show our military history and our officers, in particular, in the very best light.

So when I dared raise the matter of an infantry platoon having disappeared from all histories of the war for almost four decades, and spoke about its involvement in the atrocities that occurred at Thua Tich on May 30th 1969, the officer ranks erupted.

The process of discrediting that voice, and the message, then began in earnest.

It wasn't unexpected though.

I've never had any great love for officers, and they certainly have none for me. Mostly, I saw them as incompetents chasing 'gallantry' medals who almost got me killed on a number of occasions– and badly wounded, eventually. Spend a couple of years in hospitals, end up permanently disabled from it, then find your service records corrupted, and believe me, one's perspective on the military becomes coloured.

Not that all officers are like that. There *are* some genuine men in the officer ranks who were competent and efficient and courageous, and who respected those lesser ranks who served under them. And there were also those who earned gallantry medals legitimately.

Nevertheless, they are all part of the brotherhood. And blood is thicker than water.

The brotherhood will protect itself at all costs.

Particularly when a lowly infantry Private starts whistle-blowing about wrongdoings, and contentions in the field. It casts a slur over all.

So yes, when I began talking about the platoon of infantrymen who had operated on armoured personnel carriers for a month or so as part of a combined infantry/armoured force under the leadership of Capt Tom Arrowsmith back in Vietnam in 1969, and of those atrocities that occurred during that time and which were covered-up by the military all these years since, I put a target fair on my forehead.

Allegations of atrocities was one thing; alleging that they were covered-up at the expense of ordinary servicemen's histories and reputations, is altogether another.

The last thing the military 'establishment' ever wants is negative press. Promotion within the military and civilian employment afterwards (not to mention appointments to various offices of high esteem like Governors-General, and on Boards of business and the like) depend solely on the positive comment earned on the battlefield: battles won; body counts; bravery medals pinned to chests.

All that jazz.

So the military 'establishment' *will* fight back to protect its image, and the reputations of their own– and they have the resources, the networks, subservient and acquiescent low-life at their disposal, and generally speaking, the expertise, to do a good hatchet job on any critic they need to silence.

Men like me.

But I would *not* be silenced. The issues surrounding the 2nd D&E Platoon are so significant, and reveal so much about the ethos of the Australian army officer ranks, that the general public needs to be made aware of it.

Why?

Because the stench is a microcosm of all the deception, the distortions, and the guff that compromises the true accuracy of our military history– ever since Charles Bean's dodgy diaries from Gallipoli during World War 1 were accepted as military 'truth'.

You see, what this matter is really all about, are the actions of certain senior military officers deceiving politicians back there in Australia during the war, safe and snug in their comfortable beds. It's about man-power ceilings, and budget limitations imposed by government – and the fudging thereof by those senior officers in order to get the job done – regardless of the legalities. And it's about selective memory from junior officers when it comes to 'after-action' accounts, and the very careful wording of documents so as to project the best version possible. And it's about protecting the reputations of fellow officers and the 'Corps' when the shit hits the fan– as it invariably does when truth is compromised.

It's also about having a cavalier attitude towards the safety of the private soldiers – the fodder of war – who do the dirty work for those officers in the battles orchestrated from the safety of command posts and tents back behind the wire. And it's about dereliction of duty, negligence and maladministration.

But worse, it's about the corruptions of military history.

These are things I dared to write about in just one chapter of *The War Within*– the chapter titled: 'The Orphan Platoon'.

But even worse than writing about it, was *proving* that the Australian military had 'edited-out' that platoon from the histories of the war to cover-up that series of atrocities committed in 1969.

The best way to divert attack is to bring the critic to heel. And the best way to do that is to vilify him. Do so effectively, and you destroy his credibility. Trash his service history. Humiliate him. Attack his character. Make up any old story about him and force him to respond.

Attack, attack, attack– from every angle. Use any means, and every low life you have at your disposal to carry it out, and bring as much firepower as possible to bear.

In my case, with compromised service records, I was an easy target.

Because not only was the second unit I served in (the 2nd D&E Platoon) 'missing' from the official records, but according to the Army, I had never been posted to the 9th Battalion either. This was the third and last unit I served in, and the one in which I was eventually wounded in action.

So there I was in a hospital bed, not knowing at the time that there wasn't any record of my having served with two of the three units I had served in.

When I *did* learn of the omissions, I was devastated. It was as if my entire service for my country had been invalidated.

These twin errors also cost me dearly as far as my credibility was concerned.

If I said I served in the 9th Battalion and there was no record of it, I could (and was) called a liar; and if I also claimed to have served in a platoon like the 2nd D&E Platoon of which there was no official record, not only was there a profound psychological impact to deal with on a personal level, but it was regarded as a lie as well, so the damage to my credibility was proportionally compounded.

On top of that were my admissions in *The War Within* with respect to my relative failings as a soldier. Modest though they may have been, I had given my critics ammunition.

And they used it effectively.

There is one simple fact about my service in the war that shuts up every critic when I present the evidence– and that is, that on the day I was wounded (about day 211 of my tour) I *was* serving as an infantryman with the 9th Battalion, and doing so as a forward scout.

One can argue that there is no greater degree of responsibility in an infantry platoon than that placed on the shoulders of the forward scout. No incompetent is given the task.

As well, the fact is, ever since I had joined the real war in the 4th Battalion on January 27th 1969, I had served every single day in the war as a rifleman.

The point is– if I had been as poor a soldier as one man in particular had claimed I was (for his own malicious reasons) or if I had ever let my fellow soldiers down any time in the 210 days previously, I would *not* have been in the position I found myself in on the day I was wounded.

I would have been spirited out of 7 Platoon "C" Company of 9RAR faster than working out what 'WTFRW' means.

I'd have been filling jerry cans with water back at Nui Dat, or painting rocks, or washing dishes and the like in the generic 'D&E Platoon' of HQ Company where rejects and sad sacks ended up, according to Major George Pratt.

But no– now into my third unit after almost seven and a half months 'in country', there I was, still serving as an infantryman in an infantry battalion.

Proof that I was serving as an infantryman for the whole of my time in the 4th Battalion between January and May can be found in my colour films at:

https://www.youtube.com/watch?v=c35VLlZmIk4

And proof as to *when* I reinforced 4RAR is obvious in the document below:

AUSTRALIAN MILITARY FORCES HBE	RESTRICTED ROUTINE ORDERS PART 2		AF—O 1810—5 Reprinted Oct. 66
COMPILED FOR RA INF		ISSUE No: INF 1236	
DISTRIBUTION: LIST 'A' plus Aust Records Det VIETNAM		DATE OF ISSUE: 19 FEB 69	
RO2	51306 400 1236	69 V	

EDP LINE No.	CORPS SHEET	PERSONAL PARTICULARS	KEYWORD	PARTICULARS OF OCCURRENCE	ENTRY No
		1 AUST RFT UNIT RFT STR	UNIT	the following personnel now 4 RAR 27 Jan 69 AND	
		1201907 Pte D.W. TATE	POSTING	Rfn ECN 343 27 Jan 69	18,19.
		2789401 Pte R.T. BRADY			12,13.
		2789973 Pte J.A. SILLENCE			16,17.
		2790080 Pte G.W. SULLIVAN			12,13.
UNIT SERIAL		Checked by n.		RECORDS OFFICER	

As well, I received a personal reference from Pte Bryan Holborow, the machine-gunner in 10 Platoon of 4RAR (I was his 'number-two' on the M60 for most of the time) which meant a great deal to me. He became a NSW detective after the war. He said, (sic):

> 'Don, Holby here, who is taking you to task now, yes you were there, yes you were my no2, yes you took film of us and we (mainly me or 'Bear') took film of you, yes you assisted with the clean up after Joe and Sammy got hit, (they left for the patrol from our gun piquet if you remember), I can still recall giving Sammy a bollocking as they left, cheeky little shit he was and I certainly remember, although I don't really want to, that shit fight in the bunker system what a nightmare. Why is this an issue 40 years on??? You know what you did, we know what you did, sod the

rest of them.... You certainly have a gift for tilting at windmills, anyway good luck in whatever you are involved in hope it works out well for you, look after yourself, fly under the radar and stay safe my old mate. Regards Holby'

(**Note:** The matters Holborow referred to were the deaths of Sam Graham and Joe Ramsay in one contact on January 29th 1969, and a bunker assault in April 1969).

And in all that that time, I'd never accidently killed any fellow soldier, like some did; not murdered anyone, like some did; not gone AWOL like some did; not assaulted anyone; not been insubordinate; was never charged with drunkenness, or stealing from fellow veterans like some had been; not bashed anyone, or been bashed; not used any excuse to get out of the jungle like some cowards had; not lost a rifle; nor faked injury or malingered, like some had; not tripped over a twig and hurt myself like at least one fool in 4RAR did; not tried out for officer school as an excuse to escape the war for a month like at least one other, egotistical fool did; not tripped a mine or booby-trap and injured others; not had an accidental discharge, like some did; and not let any man down when the bullets were flying like some did.

Played up a bit on leave in Vung Tau once, but there wasn't any harm done.

And as for what sort of soldier I was– let the history show that on my *first* day in the war with the 4th Battalion, I prevented the Viet Cong from attacking my platoon from the rear with RPG's, as recorded in Brian Avery's *In the Anzac Spirit*):

' ...the rear elements of 10 Pl noticed two VC following the platoon, one of a number of occasions that this happened to 4RAR/NZ platoons. They fired at the two, killing one and capturing an AK47 and a RPG2 launcher...'

...and on my *last* day in the war, I ran to the assistance of my fellow soldiers in the forward section of 7 Platoon who had all been wounded. I wasn't called upon to do that. Only the machine-gunner (Pte Greg Salmon) and his 'number 2' (Pte John Walker) were ordered to do so.

I went with them though (and led the way in fact) because that's what I was there for. That required me to run uphill through mud into a Viet Cong killing field knowing that I was most likely going to get shot when I breasted the rise on that jungle track.

Want to talk about courage– try that one on.

The only time I ever heard from the platoon commander of 7 Platoon that night – Lt Brian Osborne – in all the years since, was for him to shut one particularly obnoxious critic up by stating publicly that my actions on that night had been 'exemplary'.

The national historian – Ashley Ekins – who favoured no man, and stated no fact that wasn't verified and validated, wrote a brief account of the action in which I was wounded in the final volume of his trilogy, *'Fighting to the Finish'* (Allen & Unwin) on p. 295:

He wrote (sic):

'At 3.30 pm (July 19th 1969) in a brief contact with two Viet Cong near a creek, 7 Platoon C Company (9RAR) killed one of the enemy. They then began following blood trails. For two hours, soldiers struggled up a muddy hill through thick jungle and under a building monsoonal downpour. Daylight was fading and many soldiers were weary. There were few signs of enemy until suddenly the platoon was ambushed. Within seconds, the leading section was cut down by heavy fire from machine-guns, RPGs and small arms. Forward scout Ray Kermode was wounded along with several other soldiers. The lead section and platoon headquarters found themselves pinned down by a platoon-sized enemy force in a large enemy bunker system. Private Don Tate, in the following section, believed the enemy was waiting for them...Tate's section was ordered forward to provide covering fire. He and two other soldiers (Pte Greg Salmon and Pte John Walker) took an M60 machine-gun to the top of a slope and then assaulted into a storm of enemy fire……an enemy bullet smashed into his hip...'

'...assaulted into a storm of enemy fire...'!

Those words will live on, long after I am gone.

Not many other infantry privates got a mention in those volumes.

So the criticisms about my soldiering ability have to be seen for what they were. Absolutely baseless. They'd been the words of men who had done a great deal less than me and who had been soured by life, is all– and others had run with it.

And as for the character assassination, well, all I can say is that I taught English and History in High Schools for a dozen years, and in 2000 was awarded a national honour by the Prime Minister of Australia – the Australian Sports Medal – for services to my community in the area of sport over three decades.

Such prestigious awards are *not* made to persons of contention.

Don Tate, as forward scout with the 9th Battalion, July 1969

CHAPTER 3
CORNERSTONES

One cannot possibly understand all the intrigue surrounding the disappearance of the 2nd D&E Platoon from all records of the Vietnam War, or of the ferocious battle that ensued as we attempted to have it reinstated, or to come to terms with all the controversies, unless I make certain points quite clear at the outset.

The first relates to my personal motivations. After all, although others came along for the ride at times, some lasting longer than others, I was fundamentally the driver of the campaign.

And my motivation was two-fold– to correct the historical accounts relating to my overall service in the Vietnam War, and particularly in relation to the 2nd D&E Platoon. They were inextricably linked.

There was good reason for wanting to do this.

As well as becoming a History teacher in my later years, and appreciating the intrinsic importance of truth when it comes to military matters, I had embarked upon a military career as a boy holding forth those values Australians hold so dear when it comes to men who go to war.

I cannot emphasise that enough.

Because, and make no mistake about this– I'm one of those men who went to the war of my time, willingly. I believed there was nothing nobler a man could do in his lifetime than to fight for his country, and nothing grander than risking life itself on a battlefield on its behalf.

Somehow, despite a rough upbringing, I had become imbued with the spirit of patriotism– the belief that one's country was of such importance that a man should risk everything, and lay down his life for it, if necessary, in time of war.

And I believed that the greater nobility still, came from enlisting in the infantry– the fighting arm of the services. The way I saw it, bearing arms against the enemy was a greater expression of the preparedness to sacrifice all. To face an enemy soldier on his own turf and engage him in armed combat, face to face, that's what it was all about.

No offence to other veterans, but I wanted none of that paper-shuffling nonsense, or bottle-washing, or floating around the ocean out of harm's way.

No sir. I wanted the full war experience.

But I was also naïve enough to believe that my country would honour such patriotism, and that for the rest of my days I could wear my war service as a badge of honour. And even more so if I happened to be wounded in action– and got some scars to prove it.

Such was the height of my passions, and my stupidity, when I was just an eighteen-year old boy.

As it turned out, I was wrong on all counts, because I served in the wrong war– Vietnam. There was no honour in it for me.

Nor for many others.

But in my case, I suffered at the hands of the military I'd trusted:

- in having the misfortune of volunteering as a 'reinforcement' and serving in *four* different units within seven and a half months, thereby being denied the true sense of ever *belonging* to any of them;
- of being wounded in an assault against a Viet Cong bunker complex during a monsoonal storm when more astute leadership might have realised the enemy held all the advantages at that moment, and adopted a wiser strategy than sending men straight into the heart of it;
- of a cavalier attitude by the military towards my particular wound in a military hospital which created a permanent disability out of what might have been otherwise;
- from finding out that my name was missing from the unit I was wounded with– the 9th Battalion;
- and being a member of the 2nd D&E Platoon– a platoon that 'disappeared' from military records of the war altogether for the best part of four decades.

One cannot minimise the individual or cumulative effect of those things on a man's psyche.

In total, these things served to invalidate the integrity of my war service and of the sacrifice of my health– and forced me into a war all over again to correct the wrongs.

It was a war that would last all my life.

The two years I spent in that military hospital in Yeronga after being wounded – which included a year in a chest-to-toe plaster cast – was just a layer of the Anzac *shit-sandwich* as some called it.

Only about 5% of men got to experience that 'sandwich'.

But without doubt, the greater psychological damage was done by the erasure from official histories of the war of all details of the formation and activities of the 'discrete infantry force' known as the 2nd D&E Platoon.

Nothing has caused me more angst. And nothing ever provided me with a greater challenge in life than to prove that it *had* existed. But not only to *prove* its existence, but record the fact that it had engaged the enemy in a particularly extraordinary and successful ambush at an abandoned village called Thua Tich in the best traditions of the Australian Army, even though it was spoiled by being part of a series of atrocities that followed.

These were things which the military 'establishment' did its best to cover-up for almost forty years.

It was a cover-up that reached into the highest levels of the government and the military.

It is a truism that one cannot argue a case with any degree of surety unless he does so from a position of strength, and where there is no doubt as to his authority to do so– and in that respect it would be remiss of me to not provide proof of my *bona fides* at the outset.

This is a critical factor, especially since the 'establishment' ensured that their best method of defence was to shoot the messenger– and if the 'messenger' had only been a lowly private who spent the last half of his career in a military hospital, he was an easy target.

And the best way to go about that was to discredit what little there was of his service.

So, it would seem to me that the most appropriate course of action here would be to validate one particular aspect of my service that is the most significant. And that is, the fact that I was one of that very small percentage of men who feels the real steel of war– wounds earned in combat.

Believe me – and it's not a vanity thing either – but being wounded inside a Viet Cong bunker system is a vastly different thing to injuries received from falling off a truck, or tripping over a log, or getting stung by a scorpion, or some such thing.

Only men who were genuinely wounded in the war can appreciate that.

Yet, to *be* so wounded, and then find your name missing from that battalion's Roll Call, has two quite significant consequences.

First, it denies you that historical validation which has some positive, psychological advantage in life as time goes by. And secondly, the omission allows any critic to call you a 'liar' or a 'wannabee'– a person claiming to have done something, or have belonged somewhere he didn't.

Omission from an historical record has a grievous effect on the soldier.

In 2009, I took the matter of how my name came to be omitted from the battalion record directly to one of those two officers who had put the record together– Michael Mummery. Mummery had been a platoon commander at the scene of the ambush on the night when I was wounded. His 9 Platoon had eventually moved up through difficult terrain to provide covering fire for those of us already wounded in 7 Platoon.

He and other officers had compiled that record of the 9th Battalion's tour.

He replied:

> *'G'day Don,*
> *Most of it came from Guy (Bagot) or myself. At the time we had no access to any "official" reports such as the Commanders Diary and everything was from memory. All those who we had contact with at the time where asked to contribute. Unfortunately we did not have contact with them all, such as yourself, and most chose not to contribute. As you know the book was written 25 years after the event and despite the best efforts a number of mistakes were made. The one thing I can assure you of Don, there was nothing deliberate in your part in the 19th July 1969 being left out. I don't know how we could have forgotten those details but that's what happened... Regards, Mick'*

Later, on behalf of the battalion, Michael Mummery apologised for that error and the impact it had had on my life.

He wrote:

> *'G'day Don,*
> *Can I say that there is no doubt in my mind that...*

- *You served in 7 Pl C Coy 9RAR from June 1969 until the 19th July 1969*

- *That you were severely wounded on the 19th July 1969 whilst in action with 7Pl C Coy 9RAR.*

- *That whilst I was not in the same Platoon as you on that day/night, I was with 9Pl and I was very aware of the difficulties that 7 Pl were in*

- *I am now aware that the description of the C Coy action on the 19th of July 1969 on pages 82 & 83 in the book "9th Battalion Royal Australian Regiment, Vietnam Tour Of Duty, 1968 - 1969, On Active Service", was inaccurate in that it did not include all those members of 7 Pl that were wounded in that action and that along with you Don, John Walker and Dave Jeffrey should also have been mentioned as having been wounded in that action.*

- *I also acknowledge that, (due to the deployment of 9 Pl up on the left flank of 7 Pl), until the mid-1990s, I was unaware of the evacuation of you and three others, on the night of the 19th, by jungle penetrator. It was my understanding that all evacuations took place the following morning, by USAF helicopter landing at a landing zone, prepared by members of C Coy.*

- *I would also like to provide to you a quote from the preface of the book that may assist you in answering some of those who continue to insist that the book was the "Official" record of 9RAR in Vietnam. The 5th paragraph of the "Preface" by Ted Chitham on page XI of the book states, "We have tried to include as much detail of operational activities as possible but have been restricted by access to official information and book size limitations. Therefore, not all actions are recalled nor all casualties named. To those who carry the physical scars and are unnamed, we offer our apologies."*

I hope that the details above are of some help for you in clearing the smears that have occurred to your name.'

Michael Mummery was very gracious. It said much about him as a man that he had made a public apology. But nothing he could say could ever compensate for the slander and 'smears' that the omission of my name from that Battalion's records had generated for more than a quarter of a century.

The worst of it though, was that there always *had been* ample evidence available of my service with 9RAR, particularly after I was wounded. Here are just two examples:

- in an official Signal sent from the Task Force in Vietnam to Australia on the night I was wounded

```
VV  EHA214                                    1969 JUL 19  16:22

OO RATAFA

DE RAMARL 083 1971680Z

ZNR UUUUU

O P 191545Z JUL

FM AUSTFORCE VIETNAM

TO RATWAA/ARMY CANBERRA

RATAFA/CENARMYREC MELBOURNE

RAYDAL/MILCOMD BRISBANE

INFO RAMABC/9 RAR

RAMABC/1 ATF                                      NO 1 TF

RAMAAK/1 AUST FD HOSP

RAMAAK/1 ALSG

BT                                                  6RAR.

UNCLAS PA 11659  IN CONFIDENCE. NOTICAS . WOUNDED.

ONE. 1201907  PTE TATE DW 9 RAR R AUST INF RC.

TWO. BATTLE CASUALTY CMM WOUNDED IN ACTION.

THREE. LONG KHANH PROVINCE YS389907  CMM 190915Z JUL 69.

FOUR. CONTACT WITH ENEMY IN BUNKER SYSTEM CMM GUN SHOT WOUND TO RIGHT
HIP AND UPPER THIGH CMM CONDITION SATISFACTORY.

FIVE. NOK CMM FATHER MR WH TATE 100 BAGNALL STREET INAL CMM QLD
NOK NOT ADVISED.

SIX . LOCATED 1 AUST FD HOSP.

SEVEN. NO MORE TO FOLLOW. ACK
```

That Signal not only provides the exact military information pertinent to the wound (what I was doing, and where) but also clearly states *who* I was serving with at the time.

The Signal is significant to this narrative, because when the first Nominal Roll of Vietnam veterans was published, there was no record of my having served in the 9th Battalion in it– yet here was the official Army Signal recording my wounding and clearly showing '9RAR' as my unit.

- The second instance is the media account of the wounding– in Queensland's premier newspaper, The Courier-Mail. The information had been provided by the Army's Public Relations Service:

Then, there was about eight minutes of colour movie footage that I shot during my time with the 9th Battalion.

I placed an extract of that film on Youtube at:

https://www.youtube.com/watch?v=zxN3RM9-LPA

Any which way one looks at this issue, one must conclude that such an error is evidence of sheer army maladministration and/or negligence at best, and allowed my enemies a free kick.

Veterans who didn't know any better, had no option but to accept what the military record had to say– that I *hadn't* served in the 9th Battalion. When it comes to the crunch, the bureaucracy rules.

For the individual to stand against the machine and argue otherwise is the most daunting of tasks.

But locating that Signal (as well as the intervention by fellow soldiers of the platoon I served with who contacted CARO with validating statements) allowed that contention to be finalised in 1998.

It had taken me just twenty-eight years to prove I had served in that battalion.

Proving that I had also served in a '2nd D&E Platoon' though, was a different kettle of fish.

But because the fight to prove the existence of the platoon was linked to the maladministration (or corruption) of my service records (and indeed to the service records of *all* who fought in it) it went into the same crucible.

There is an old army saying all old soldiers well recall because we were reminded of it often– 'Keep it simple, stupid!'

This isn't necessarily as easy as it sounds– especially dealing with the relatively complex nature of the issues surrounding the 2nd D&E Platoon.

But it is an historical imperative that a framework of the military situation be established here, at the get-go.

The irony of course, is that the platoon was made up of infantry odd-bods and only graced the war for about six weeks. Hardly the stuff of legend– though the ambush it was involved in on May 29th 1969, was worthy of much acclaim.

But when actual historical events are interwoven with allegations of atrocities, military intrigue and political deceptions, and where the unravelling of those things takes place across a forty year time span by amateur sleuths, the matter takes on a powerful dynamic.

Still, while there is so much information that has 'gone missing' or been deliberately corrupted, or blatantly purged from the official records, there are certain undeniable facts concerning this matter which are on the public record in various documents held within the Australian War Memorial's Collections– and which serve as the cornerstone of validating the existence of the 2nd D&E Platoon.

They are:

- that Maj George Pratt had begun turning the D&E Platoons into a more effective forces than they had been previously.....They were his private 'Sabre' force, and were meant to carry out long-range reconnaissance patrols as the eyes and ears of the Task Force (colloquially, they were termed 'Hawk force')

- that in late May of 1969, Special Air Service (SAS) saturation reconnaissance patrols were relaying intelligence back to the Task Force, and just one of those patrols alone recorded thirty-five sightings of Viet Cong soldiers congregating in the Xuyen Moc area of the Province

- that in all, SAS counted almost 800 enemy on the move

- that some forty regular soldiers who had previously reinforced the 4th Battalion during its tour of duty, but who hadn't yet served the minimum requirement of six months 'in country', were marched into HQ Company of the Task Force– and found themselves surplus to the requirements of that Company (supernumeraries)

- that those men were then placed into an *ad hoc* platoon by Major George Pratt, the OC of HQ Company– which they believed was explicitly called the '2nd D&E Platoon' by Pratt (another D&E Platoon already existed in the Company)

- that the new platoon was then placed under the command of Armoured Corps Captain, Tom Arrowsmith as part of a combined armour/infantry force

- that the combined force was tasked with interdicting that enemy force congregating in the Xuyen Moc area as part of Operation Garry Owen

- that on May 29th 1969, the combined force successfully ambushed an enemy force numbering at *least* fifty outside the abandoned village of Thua Tich

- that the next day, May 30th 1969, certain 'contentions' occurred in the field which had serious ramifications for all

- that within days of those contentions occurring, Capt Arrowsmith's armoured troop was replaced by that of Capt Dave Lawrence's, and the infantry contingent disbanded within the week

- and that after those events, the service records of every one of those forty regular soldiers was then corrupted so as not to show any mention of the 2nd D&E Platoon, and all trace of the platoon then expunged from the record books

Of course, most of those facts weren't necessarily known to the motley crew of infantry privates who rocked up in HQ Company in May 1969 and paraded in front of Maj George Pratt. Nor was any of it of interest to us at that time.

As long as we got fed, nothing else mattered.

What we also didn't know was that there were deeper issues involved, that we were mere pawns in a greater scheme – the pursuit of gallantry medals – and the rancid nature of the Australian Defence Force revealed for what it truly is.

Nor did we know that the extraordinarily successful ambush of the Viet Cong at Thua Tich later that month would have been celebrated as a significant action and become part of Australian military folklore at any other time– except for the contentions that followed.

And it is those contentions that are at the heart of the matter.

CHAPTER 4
THE QUEST

The battle to validate the 2nd D&E Platoon was a quest that took me almost forty years to bring to fruition.

It began back in 1970, when I was still in hospital recovering from my war wounds and reflecting on my experiences in the war– as long-term patients are apt to do.

I didn't know it then, but there was no mention of any *'2nd D&E Platoon'* in any history of the Vietnam War.

Even if I had known that it didn't officially exist, I wouldn't have cared less. I had more important things to worry me back then. Corruption of military history wasn't on my list of proprieties.

In fact, on the rare times I found myself in contemplative mood, the short period I spent in the D&E Platoon was a peripheral issue. In fact, I couldn't even remember what the letters *'D'* and *'E'* stood for. All I remembered of the platoon was that it involved a completely new experience for us infantrymen– lairising around on the backs of APCs and contacting more Viet Cong than we ever had while serving with the 4th Battalion.

It was a damn sight easier than the normal infantry way of things – 'bush-bashing' – that's for sure.

What I *could* remember vividly was a proud boast by our unofficial platoon commander – an ex-English marine by the name of Cpl Jim Riddle – when the platoon was disbanded (and he was a man who had his ear to the ground when it came to these things) to the effect that we'd killed 'at least 50 Viet Cong in just over a month' without losing a man killed or wounded ourselves.

Riddle had been privy to Intel reports the rest of us weren't.

Apparently local forces reported finding many bodies in the areas around Xuyen Moc where we'd been operating. We didn't claim them all as 'kills' by the 2nd D&E Platoon (though we were condemned for suggesting it as time went by) but as a collective effort by us infantry and armour– along with a 'Possum', and 'Spooky'.

That boast of having killed 'at least fifty Viet Cong' aggravated many an infantry veteran who served in the standard battalions, as you can imagine. Everyone likes to believe they saw the worst of the war. As to its veracity, no one really knows. Actual body count was one thing; but the enemy was extraordinarily pedantic about removing bodies from the battlefield to deny the Australians (and Americans) that psychological advantage.

All I recall is being told that other units had found many fresh graves around the place afterwards– and ours had been the only unit operating in that vicinity.

Whatever the actual figure was (and make no mistake, the body count was an integral part of the war) it was due solely to the competence and professionalism of Cpl Jim Riddle (who had assumed leadership of our platoon in the absence of an officer) and Capt Tom Arrowsmith.

But back in 1970, still languishing in a hospital bed, the 2nd D&E Platoon matter and how many Viet Cong it might have killed was of no concern to me.

I was feeling mighty sick and sorry for myself. I had a hole in my hip the size of half a football and was so chock-full of infection they couldn't contain it, and was looking down the barrel of skin grafts and extensive surgery and yet another year of hospitalisation.

So it was natural that I eventually did get to reflecting on things that had gone down in Vietnam in the seven months or so I'd served there as an infantryman. Certainly the role of the 2nd D&E Platoon in that one, particularly nasty ambush that had occurred outside Thua Tich in late May of 1969.

But compared with the action in which I'd actually been wounded, six weeks later – in an assault against a Viet Cong bunker complex with the 9th Battalion – it paled by comparison.

That contact had been a nightmare, and the wound as severe as one can get and still be alive to talk about it.

So one day, there I was, sitting in the sun on a veranda at the hospital when I suddenly realised that I hadn't yet received my campaign medals from the war.

Being impulsive, and with nothing better to occupy myself, I shot off a quick letter to the Central Army Records Office (CARO) requesting same, and just happened to mention that I'd served in a 'Task Force Platoon' during my time in Vietnam.

That was actually the 2nd D&E Platoon.

It was the first time anyone had ever mentioned the platoon. This is that letter:

SS

Monday 13/7/70

Dear Sir,

I served in Vietnam from 22nd December 1968 to 23rd July 1969 when I was wounded. I served with 4 RAR (D Coy) for 4½ months, 6 weeks in a Task Force platoon and 6 weeks in 9 RAR (C Coy).

As of yet I have not received my medals. I was wondering if they could be sent to 1 MIL HOSPITAL YERONGA where I am still a patient.

I understand I qualified for them in June 1969.

Hoping this receives your attention.

Pte. Don Tate

1201907
Pte. Tate D.W.   VM VCM   s/> in PO
    Reg No 2702
        Posted 21-07-70

S

c/D

PA/PD

Back then, the actual name of the platoon wasn't a consideration. I was just a twenty-year old Private who hadn't needed to know precise military detail, nor understand the importance of it when dealing with the military.

That first mention of my involvement in a 'Task Force platoon' was the start of a quest for validation that would cause me such emotional and psychological torment through the years that at times, it was almost too much to bear.

It began with the response I received to that letter.

Central Army Records Office (CARO) had *no record* of it.

For all intents and purposes, the 2nd D&E Platoon had disappeared from the war.

Three years later, I'm renting a house on the southwest of Brisbane at a place called Goodna– which, as a boy, was the last place anyone wanted to live.

There was a prison and a mental asylum in the general area, and one of my teachers at Richlands State School often told me I'd end up in one or the other.

'See those white towers over there, Tate,' he'd say through gritted teeth, holding me off the floor of the school's veranda in a vice-like grip, 'that's where you'll end up. Just like your old man.'

It was as if he was cursing me.

So when I did end up in a rickety old wooden house in Bertha Street, Goodna, and my bride-to-be, Carole at my side, I was conscious that I hadn't yet gone too far in life.

I'd been to a war and back in an endeavour to boost the family name, been part of that noble tradition of putting one's life on the line for his country, but there I was in Goodna of all places, with nothing much to show for my war service but a steel rod through some bone grafts in my hip and a swirl of memories from Vietnam that came visiting of a night.

Then, along came two men I'd served with in the 4th Battalion– the second of the four units I ultimately served in during my time in the war.

It had been three years since I'd last seen them, and they'd rolled up unexpectedly to see how I'd got on after their battalion had sailed home in May of 1969– leaving me and every other man who'd reinforced the battalion during its tour of duty, behind.

Over a barbecue and a few beers, I told them about how I'd been wounded, about going forward with the machine-gun crew to support the first section of my platoon who'd all been killed or wounded. They were sceptical, but the scars of the wound were a graphic silencer.

Then, I told them of my escapades with the '2nd D&E Platoon' which had preceded my posting to the 9th Battalion. Told them of how the platoon had been formed, how we'd operated; and what we'd got up to while they were getting suntanned backs aboard the HMAS *Sydney* on their way home from the war.

In particular, I mentioned a major ambush we'd been involved in against the Viet Cong about a month into that platoon's operations where we'd been heavily outnumbered– yet had recorded a significant victory that night and were none the worse for it.

I still recall the gruff response from one.

'Fuckin' bullshit,' he said. 'A "second D&E Platoon"? What the fuck's a "D&E Platoon"? I've never heard of any such platoon. And if such a thing existed, there's no way you blokes would be sitting on APCs chasing Viet Cong through the jungle. Do you think we've come down in the last shower?'

His words stung. He was calling me a liar.

So it was when they left that day, I determined to prove that the 2nd D&E Platoon *had* existed.

My first port of call was the Central Army Records Office– for the second time. I wrote them seeking answers.

This time I was more specific. I told them I'd served with a platoon of infantry operating out of HQ Company during the war called the *2nd D&E Platoon* and could they provide me with details of the platoon in order that I could validate what I'd told fellow veterans?

The response was as swift as it was disappointing– there was 'no record' of any such '2nd D&E Platoon'.

I was flabbergasted, because I knew what I *knew*, and I *knew* that the platoon had existed, and *had* existed by that name, and couldn't understand why they had no record of it.

But I didn't pursue it then, because I had more pressing personal matters to deal with– the chronic infection, rehabilitation, and holding on to the woman who'd entered my life not long before and brought such joy and pleasure into it.

Pursuing the matter wasn't a priority– yet.

In 1976, another former member of the platoon – *Robert Enright* – had a bee in his bonnet. He had gotten mighty hot under the collar about repeated denials by the Liberal's

Minister for Defence, Jim Killen, that Australian soldiers had engaged in any acts of atrocity during the Vietnam War.

The political spin was more than he could take, because he'd been involved in some atrocities in Vietnam himself– in 1969.

He was to tell me, many years later, that one morning he'd woken up obsessed with memories of the 'atrocities' that had been committed by the combined infantry/armour unit under the command of Capt Tom Arrowsmith back in 1969.

Enright had developed something of a conscience by then and a deep-seated distrust of politicians and military leaders, so when he heard Killen waxing lyrical, Enright sought to unload those memories he had from that time back in Vietnam that ate away at him during the night.

He contacted a newspaper– *The Northern Territory News* on the 9th August, 1976.

The Northern Territory News is a singularly unique newspaper – serving up regular helpings of sensationalism to the residents of an essentially redneck clientele of that last frontier – from stories about crocodiles and snakes, to atrocities committed by Australian troops like those Robert Enright had just provided it with.

Naturally, Enright's revelations were welcomed with open arms by the newspaper, and before he knew it, he found himself at the centre of a media storm. Following on from the newspaper story, Enright received a call from Greg Grainger– a radio commentator on one of Australia's most popular stations, Sydney's 2UE.

Enright had initially referred to another matter that occurred when he too, was serving with the 9th Battalion after the 2nd D&E Platoon had been disbanded. His platoon had killed civilians in a sampan. But he went on to add that earlier, he'd also been involved in the destruction of bodies at a place called Thua Tich in 1969.

Highlighting those atrocities wasn't a decision that Robert Enright made lightly:

'I did what I didn't want to do because of the flack I knew I would get, so I went into the local paper, and they phoned a radio station of which I could only mumble at, as by this time I was really not liking this at all.'

I guessed he meant the attention, because after Vietnam, he had essentially become a loner like so many other veterans of that war, reclusive even, and had good reason to regret his decision to put the matter into the public domain.

The public, and veterans alike, preferred their Anzacs to be bronzed and heroic– not men likely to be involved in unsavoury acts against the spirit of the Geneva Convention.

Vietnam veteran: I shot women in ambush

— Northern Territory News

A former soldier in the Australian regular army said today he had shot women in Vietnam.

Robert Jon (Bob) Enright, 29, said he opened fire on four women in a sampan during an ambush.

The women had been sitting in the boat and were only 20 feet from him when he fired his machine gun.

A man dressed in jungle greens, had been standing on the back of the sampan using an oar. He too had been shot.

"I knew they were women. They were sittin' in the boat looking at me," Mr Enright said.

"I was the first to open up. The man went over and the sampan tipped up.

"Then there was lead spraying everywhere," Mr Enright said. "A friend of mine fired grenades from an M79."

Mr Enright cannot remember when the action took place, nor the name of the river, but it was in Phuc Tuoy Province.

He said that he could pinpoint the spot on a map.

"Everyone on the boat went into the water. One of the women was still alive, but she was shot by someone on the bank," he said.

"About two days later we found the body of one of the women washed up in a tidal creek. It had six or seven bullet holes in one side. We left it there."

He said nobody gave the order to fire.

The order had been given prior to going out on the ambush patrol — "shoot anybody who comes down the river."

Mr Enright said he was only 19 at the time and "full of glory and all that crap."

Conscience

Shooting the women had not worried him then but had been on his conscience ever since.

Mr Enright enlisted in Brisbane on May 28, 1968 and was discharged on July 13, 1973. His service number was 1202112.

According to his discharge certificate he served 333 days in Vietnam between January and December, 1969.

At the time of the ambush he was with section seven D Company, 12 Platoon of the 9th Infantry Battalion.

The platoon commander (a Lieutenant Daly was not in command.

The company sergeant major whose name he could not remember had been in charge.

Two other sections number eight and nine had also taken part in the action.

Mr Enright is a contract welder and has lived in Darwin almost four years.

He is married with two children.

The Northern Territory News, August 9, 1976

Robert Enright would pay the piper for his rashness.

So it was, that the non-existent *2nd D&E Platoon* and the word, 'atrocities', first became linked. And a clue perhaps, as to why all record of the platoon had 'disappeared' from the histories of the war.

The Australian Army is quick to close ranks when public perceptions of its traditions are threatened by unsavoury comment from any quarter– and immediately Robert Enright's comments hit the airwaves, it moved to limit the fallout.

A Major Gordon Pound was despatched to interview Enright, enquire into his allegations, and report back post haste.

He did just that.

According to Enright,

> '...a Major Pound turned up on my door step who actually said fuck all and then left, never to be seen again, and pleased at least for that. He said nothing to me about those events, just spoke to the slag I was married to, and left me out of it, then in all of three or four minutes was gone.'

And that was the entire substance of the Major Pound 'Enquiry' into allegations of atrocities having been committed in Vietnam– or at least his enquiries of the men intimately involved.

Any neutral commentator must be alarmed to learn that.

With the exception of Robert Enright, not one other man from that combined infantry/armour force had been interviewed– not Capt Tom Arrowsmith who had led it, not Cpl Jim Riddle who had led the infantry contingent, not one single trooper, not one infantryman, not one member of the engineer's mini-team that accompanied us, not one member of the mortar unit that tagged along, and none of the brass that oversaw the whole shebang.

No sir– certainly none of the brass. Not Brigadier C. Pearson, OC of the entire Task Force. Not Major George Pratt, the OC of HQ Company. Not Major Ron Rooks, the OC of the Armoured Corps. Not Major David Chinn, Pearson's Ops Officer. And not Lt Ray 'Mick' Woolan– who was actually nominated as the 'official' platoon commander of the D&E Platoon and subsequently awarded a Military Cross for his endeavours.

Such was the official Army 'enquiry'.

Although, it did result in an official, but mysterious file– the 'Major Pound Enquiry'.

Not that the world got to see it.

It was discreetly filed away from prying eyes for thirty-six years before investigative journalist Frank Walker stumbled across it in the National Archives. It was titled: 'ATROCITY ALLEGATIONS – SOUTH VIETNAM, 3 CAV. REGIMENT'

This was the same document that 'researchers' from the Australian War Memorial and the Army History Unit had been unable to find– the same document though, that a number of 'others' (most likely senior army officers and bureaucrats) had accessed over the years.

It was proof that the Australian Defence Force was guilty of duplicitous behaviour– a conclusion Walker came to in his book, *The Ghost Platoon* (Frank Walker, Hachette) – published in 2011.

But as it was, the 'Major Pound Enquiry' was always going to be a farce.

It was only done for show.

Major George Pound lives in Tasmania. I contacted him in 2006 about it during our investigations into the disappearance of the 2nd D&E Platoon, and he was just as shocked by my call as he was by my asking for information about his Enquiry.

It was a wasted effort. He 'couldn't recall conducting it', he said.

That might have been a memory lapse. But a very convenient one, I thought. From what I had ascertained, his hadn't been a traumatic life. Looked to me very much as if he'd been got at.

As for Robert Enright, all he got in the long run was some abuse from civilians, and a deeper, self-imposed alienation from the veteran community, and from the world at large.

He would re-appear more than thirty years later, oblivious to the controversy about the 2nd D&E Platoon that had raged within the veteran community for half a dozen years prior to his entrance.

And when he did, it was a far more philosophical Robert Enright who entered the fray than the young man 'interviewed' by Major Gordon Pound all those years before.

He had one particular piece of information to offer that silenced a large slice of the knockers– acknowledging that I *had* been present at the ambush at Thua Tich.

Over time, that particular point had become the focal point of much of the controversy– a 'red herring' if you like, designed to detract from the main thrust of the argument.

Enright felt no compunction to do so. He was nobody's patsy. Nor was he taking sides. He just told it as it was.

The thing about Robert Enright was– his powder was dry, he was ready for a fight.

CHAPTER 5
THE HORNET'S NEST

I discovered that I had a talent for writing. Well actually, not to sound *too* egotistical, I'd always had an innate ability to put words together coherently, but hadn't had any desire to actively pursue the art.

What's more, I'd become an English teacher in the decade since being wounded in Vietnam, and the craft of teaching English to largely disinterested students took all the gloss off the process.

But I dabbled, at times.

In 1987, I dabbled enough to put together an article about the consequences of having fought in the war as an infantryman– the reality of combat versus the romanticism portrayed in other media, if you like, and sent it off to the *Sydney Morning Herald* (SMH) on spec as a freelance piece.

In that article, I briefly described an incident where I'd witnessed a Vietnamese woman and her child shot by an APC trooper. My recall was that she was part of a group of villagers simply tending their paddy-field.

She had been fired at indiscriminately as we drove by on the APCs, at full flight, towards Xuyen Moc.

A journalist by the name of Mike Cordell contacted me and asked if I would give him permission to verify that I was a serviceman and that what I was writing in my article had any substance to it.

I told him that that was how I remembered it. And without qualification or hesitation, I gave him permission to contact Central Army Records and ascertain whatever information he wanted about my service.

That letter was sent on the 24th April, 1987.

I never heard of Mike Cordell again.

There was good reason for that.

The Army had led him astray as to my *bona fides*– they gave him false information about my service history. No doubt it was done to discredit me.

It was simple. If they could convince him that I *hadn't* served in the unit I was alluding to, nothing I said about it could be taken seriously.

Not that I was aware of this at the time.

It wasn't until many years later, suspecting that they had done so, I contacted CARO and asked for all my service records, and any correspondence contained within.

In the file was a letter written by a 'H. Seymour' on behalf of the Commanding Officer of CARO, stating that I had only served in *one* unit during my time in Vietnam– the 4th Battalion.

According to 'Seymour' I had served in that battalion from December '68 till August '69.

This was a good trick, since the battalion had returned to Australia in May, and I'd been wounded in *July*.

So the advice Cordell was given by the Defence Force was demonstrably false– as already proven, I'd actually served in four units, concluding with the 9th Battalion.

This is that letter from 'H. Seymour':

> **In reply quote:**
> CARO/Ex 1201907
>
> 12 May 1997
>
> Mr D.W. Tate
> 134 Princes Highway
> ALBION PARK RAIL   NSW
>
> Dear Mr Tate,
>
> 1.   In response to your letter of 15 April 1997, I advise that the records of this office indicate that you saw Special Service in Vietnam, with The 4th Battalion Royal Australian Regiment from 23 December 1968 to 7 August 1969. Should you have any further questions in regard to your military service, please do not hesitate to contact this office.
>
> 2.   The Department Of Veterans' Affairs have been advised of the above and should take action to ensure you are included in any future publications.
>
> 3.   This information is released pursuant to Australian Military Regulation 770.
>
> Yours sincerely,
>
> *[signature]*
> H.S. SEYMOUR
> for Commanding Officer

That advice was as false as any official document can be– the first deliberate corruption of my service records that I am aware of.

It wasn't the last.

But I can only assume now that Cordell had received exactly the same advice a decade earlier, and had concluded that I'd made up the story about the more serious matters I had written about in my article, and opted only to use the more sensational aspect– that death of the Viet Cong woman.

Didn't it hit the fan when that article came out.

I was unaware that it had even been published, at first. I'd travelled to Sydney by train that Anzac Day, and hadn't read the Sydney Morning Herald. Only when we began assembling for the march, did a few brave veterans who recognised me make their feelings clear.

And I copped the cold shoulder from others.

This was that article:

Back at home, in Shellharbour, my son received a death threat, by phone. It was the first one I received, and the fact that it was delivered to a child made it even more vicious and reprehensible.

But I was to learn that this was the way the army worked, the first time I realised that all that guff about the Anzac 'spirit' and 'mateship' was all mass-marketed guff for the masses. The reality was far different.

> # VIET VET REPRISAL THREATS
>
> By IRENE O'BRIEN
>
> **An Albion Park Rail man has received death threats to his family after a newspaper report in which he outlined alleged atrocities committed by Australians during the Vietnam War.**
>
> Mr Don Tate, who served... year-old son received a... He said a woman was...

Now, in a short space of time, the Army moved very quickly to limit the damage caused by my revelations. It trotted out Sir William Keys, President of the Returned Services League to make the ubiquitous counter-argument– that Australian troops wouldn't have done any such thing, and discouraged any investigations into the allegation.

Secondly, it trotted out its prized show-pony, former pop-star, and reluctant conscript – Normie Rowe – to defend its honour. Rowe had been the Army's pin-up boy – 'Mr Public Relations' – while he served in Vietnam, and while he was loved by the 'red-hats', was despised by the great majority of veterans. He had largely been a protected species. It irked other soldiers that while they were just fodder for the war machine, the army was keen on keeping Normie Rowe safe and intact, thank you very much.

It was a matter of politics. 'Nashos' were a political hot potato.

Anecdotal comment was that while he went about the business of being a trooper (safely ensconced inside the relatively safe, compressed aluminium hull of an APC) others from his armoured unit resented him for being subject to different rules.

There is a certain irony in that I actually made his acquaintance twice in Vietnam, which not many other infantrymen could claim, and this only added to the theatre when he intruded into the uproar over Mike Cordell's article.

In the first instance, after the successful ambush at Thua Tich and the contentions that followed, he had turned up out of the blue as part of a new Troop of APCs in Xuyen Moc.

No sooner had we been welcomed into the village by its chief and a celebratory dinner being organised, than rumours began to spread. Capt Arrowsmith was in trouble. A Major General Daly had been apoplectic when he'd heard about the manner the bodies had been treated and had given Brigadier Pearson the rounds of the kitchen.

Brigadier Pearson then went gunning for Arrowsmith. He demanded that Arrowsmith's OC – Major Ron Rooks – enquire into what had taken place. Arrowsmith had reportedly been given a boot up the backside and demoted to a desk job.

In quick succession, Arrowsmith's Troop was replaced with that of another – Capt David Lawrence's – with Normie Rowe aboard.

It came as no surprise to us that it wasn't *Rowe's* unit that was used at Thua Tich on the night of the ambush.

And Capt Lawrence was altogether a different commander to Capt Arrowsmith.

He had no time for us infantrymen, or us for him.

On return to Nui Dat, he promptly strode into Maj George Pratt's office (according to Cpl Jim Riddle) where he made his opinion of Riddle and us infantrymen quite clear.

He called Riddle a 'foul-mouthed mercenary' and us infantrymen as 'ill-disciplined animals' which seemed to be a rather generalised comment.

I certainly didn't consider myself to be an 'animal'.

In retrospect, I believe the atrocities that occurred at Thua Tich had inflamed everyone's passions within the Task Force when word got around, and Capt Lawrence erroneously thought that we infantrymen had been responsible.

At one point, Lawrence's troopers threw our backpacks out of the APCs into a running stream because they stank, which didn't ease the tension.

But that night in Xuyen Moc when we were all in a good mood after the successful contacts previous, Rowe put on an impromptu 'concert' for the boys of the 2nd D&E Platoon. He stood on a wooden plank and belted out a few of his hits, and I was all agog. He wasn't well received, and didn't stay long. But afterwards, I caught up with him and personally thanked him for making the effort. I must admit that he was the first celebrity that I had ever met, and was a bit starry-eyed.

'Piss off!' he replied. 'Fucking infantry. Bunch of deadshits!'

I was taken aback by his rudeness and abruptness, and left him to sulk.

But a day or so later, we met again. This time, I was carrying a number of claymore mines to be set up along a track we'd ambushed, and asked him to give me a hand carrying them.

'You're fucking kidding,' he said. 'I'm not allowed to do dangerous shit like that!'

Then, he promptly turned and walked away.

Years later, of course, the truth of Normie Rowe's 'service' became blurred. Time does that. The troopers who served with him knew the truth, but the Corps demanded they reconcile that 'truth' with a softer opinion; a few of us outside the Armoured Corps who had had minor dealings with him also saw that truth; thousands of other veterans who had had no contact with him during his time in Vietnam convinced themselves of a 'truth' of their own making– quick to dislike him simply because of his 'King-of-Pop' profile prior to the war; and then, there was the politics of it, that saw public relations benefits for the army in thrusting him forward as a veteran of the war who had come home unscathed, and even got him to lead the 'Welcome Home Parade' in '87 in return for a civilian 'gong'.

So, when he reappeared in my life and felt inclined to make comment about a matter he had no knowledge of, I saw red.

'It never happened,' he trumpeted in mock outrage. 'Tate is dishonouring the proud traditions of the Armoured Corps.'

Then he called for the Royal Commission.

Not that the Army was going to have a bar of that.

But if I saw red at his intrusion into the matter, it wasn't as red as I ended up being when Channel Nine rang me a day or so later and asked me if I would like to appear on the 'Today' show and talk about the atrocity matter I'd raised in Cordell's article.

I didn't hesitate.

The host of the show was my former English teacher from Inala High School, George Negus. He said he wanted to give me the opportunity to present my case. I trusted the man. What he didn't tell me was that I'd be doing it blind from the Wollongong studio looking at a blank wall, while he had Normie Rowe in his studio, almost sitting in his lap.

It was something of an ambush.

To be blunt, I had the shit shot out of me simply because I had no evidence whatsoever about the matter save for a vague recollection of the incident which had occurred a long time previous. And I hadn't had time to run around gathering that evidence.

Not that there *was* any evidence at that point.

You can't prove something happened if there are no official records of an event.

I had more than egg on my face. I looked like a damned fool.

The Defence Force issued a public statement that it would certainly take the allegation seriously, though no investigation was ever carried out (at least that I'm aware of) after the Normie Rowe intervention.

Private Peter 'Pedro' Allen learned the same lesson back in Vietnam in November 1969. Learned it the hardest of ways.

I guess he was the first real victim of the erasure of the 2nd D&E Platoon from the records of the war and the subsequent cover-up of the atrocities that were committed.

Don't get me wrong, I'm not an apologist for him.

The simple fact is, Pte Peter Allen committed murder and there's no disputing that. He tossed a grenade onto the stomach of Lt Bob Convery while Convery slept in the 9th Battalion lines and blew him to pieces.

I was back home in Australia when that happened, and didn't learn all the ins and outs of the matter for years. In fact, I was about to undergo the last major operation to do with that war wound when it happened– inserting a large pin through bone grafts in the hip, permanently rendering it immobile.

But I knew Pte Peter Allen personally. He was a member of the 2nd D&E Platoon and had been sorely affected by the ambush that went down at Thua Tich. He was at the listening post with Cpl Jim Riddle and a section of the infantry that took on that large Viet Cong force from the jungle floor a few hundred metres away from where Capt Tom Arrowsmith's lot were doing the same thing from the safety of their APCs.

Like all those involved, he was traumatised by it.

And what's more, he was already suffering the effects of PTSD from events much earlier than that, and a smarter army would have shipped him home long before he blew officer Convery up.

But they weren't too bright when it came to war neurosis, and didn't send him home. Needed every swinging dick they could get in the field. They lost an officer due solely to their ignorance and stupidity.

Some even suggest that Convery wasn't the target; that another officer being groomed for greatness was the real target, but Pte 'Pedro' Allen, drunk, and most likely high on marijuana (as he was wont to be) got the wrong officer.

Anyway, Pte Allen confessed to the murder straight off. There was conjecture that he was talked into doing so, that it would serve his best interests if he did as far as the length of jail time was concerned. But no evidence that any such arrangement had been found or presented at his trial.

They found him guilty.

And guilty he was, no doubt. But in a more enlightened time, and if he had been more savvy, more mature, he might have argued 'diminished responsibility' based on the trauma he had endured at the listening post with Cpl Jim Riddle a few months earlier.

Now that I'm sixty-four, I often reflect on that young man thrust in front of a court-martial, defending the indefensible and fighting for his freedom– all with the naiveté of an innocent. Simply, he would not have had the nous to base a defence on the psychological impact of that night at Thua Tich– an action that would have affected most men.

But there was no way he could have used that trauma in his defence even if he'd tried– because there weren't any military records to support it.

No records whatsoever of a '2nd D&E Platoon' being involved in the ambush of May 29th 1969.

And no record of *his* involvement in it either, even if it *had* received some mention somewhere, because all the service records of all of us who had served in that platoon had already been altered to show us being in other units at the time– mostly, 6RAR.

The fact that the 'after-action' report by Capt Tom Arrowsmith made mention only of a generic 'D&E Platoon' being involved wasn't necessarily his fault. He would have been unaware that there were *two* D&E Platoons operating parallel to each other, and simply recorded the infantry involvement as he understood it.

This meant that the generic D&E Platoon – made up ostensibly of failed soldiers or men found to be unfit for jungle fighting, and led by Lt Ray Woolan at the time – ended up getting the credit for the ambush.

Lt Ray Woolan who led that platoon, ended up with a Military Cross.

While Private Peter Allen got life in jail with hard labour– although he only ended up doing ten years or so.

Did I just say *only*?

CHAPTER 6
STIRRING THE POT

If there was one thing the Moratorium marches of 1970 taught me, it was the power of the media to get a point across.

I'd been caught up in one of the marches myself– a bit part, but it made the newspapers around Australia.

One minute I was standing in a pub in Brisbane's Queen Street on day leave from the Military Hospital at Yeronga, having a quiet beer and minding my own business, and the next, I was swinging punches at a mass of long-haired layabouts and unionists parading the North Vietnam flag down the street.

With fellow soldiers still spilling blood in Vietnam, I felt it was a moral imperative to defend their honour against the political white-anting going on.

There wasn't much in it. Hindered by not being able to stand on two legs, and my crutches getting knocked out from under me, I was easy meat for indiscriminate blows. I got in a few good ones for my side, but the mass was too overpowering.

The police rescued me a couple of times until I realised I was on a hiding to nothing– risking further injury, but totally ineffective in making my point.

But I followed the mass to a park at Roma Street where Labor Party speakers were preaching their propaganda to sympathetic ears and pushed my way to the podium and began to heckle the speakers.

Bemused, Senator George Georges told the assembly mockingly that I was a 'Vietnam veteran who wanted to say something'.

He handed me the microphone.

Digger had his say at rally

A WOUNDED Vietnam veteran stood on crutches at the moratorium rally in Roma Street and told the 5000 protesters: "You wouldn't know what its bloody-well all about."

The crowd heard him almost in complete silence. There was even a cheer or two.

He is Donald William Tate, 21, who was wounded in the right leg and thigh in Phuoc Tuy Province last year.

Tate had tried to grab the microphone from Labor Senator Jim Keeffe but was restrained by rally organisers.

Senator Keeffe bent and asked what he wanted and then introduced him to the crowd as a wounded Digger.

Tate told the crowd: "I've been there and you haven't. What would one per cent of you know about how it really is over there.

"The Allies are right to fight and Nixon is right to be in Cambodia. North Vietnam is the aggressor."

Tate then shouted that the rally was Communist-inspired and organised. He eventually was jeered from the platform.

All official speakers called for the immediate withdrawal of all troops from Vietnam and the repeal of the National Service Act.

They included Senators Georges and Keeffe, Queensland Trades and Labour Council president (Mr. J. Egerton), Peace Committee member (Mrs. Norma Chalmers) the Vice - Mayor (Alderman Walsh) and university and clergy representatives.

[adjacent column fragments:]

he Uni.
ot held

artments at Queens-
ay showed only one
se of the moratorium

The exception was in the Economics Department here, by request of the students, the one afternoon lecture was postponed.

Other departments said that all lectures were held or that none were scheduled.

The chemistry department said students vetoed any postponement of lectures because the only future times available for postponed lectures were before 7 a.m. and after 10 a.m.

The departments of sociology, architecture, chemistry, education, English, government, history, all held scheduled lectures.

U.S. Admiral

Guest of honour for the Coral Sea celebrations, Rear Admiral David Welch, will arrive in Brisbane on May 14 aboard a Hercules aircraft.

WOUNDED Vietnam veteran, Donald Tate, 21, battled his way on crutches to the speakers' rostrum at Roma Street gardens to tell 5000 protesters: "The allies are right to fight, and Nixon is right to be in Cambodia."

The Courier-Mail, May 1970

I had never spoken in public before and never expected to be given the opportunity on this occasion– yet, found my voice immediately.

'I've been there and you haven't,' I told them. 'You should be supporting our soldiers. The allies are right to be in Cambodia attacking Viet Cong supply lines.'

I was heckled in return, and shouted down from the podium as an 'imperialist pig' or some such, but unbeknownst to me, newspaper photographers had captured my protest within a protest, and recorded the moment for posterity, nationally.

It didn't register at the time, but speaking out publicly on that occasion was a seminal moment in my life.

Thirty years later, I was able to harness it when I needed to gather some momentum in pursuing the 2nd D&E Platoon matter.

In the early 1990's, now a lot wiser after becoming a pariah within the veteran community for raising the matter of that murder of the woman, but unable to let the corruption of history go, I decided to place all that I knew about the 2nd D&E Platoon on a new-fangled, international, encyclopaedia of knowledge– the internet.

Mastering the new technology was no easy task, despite my being a teacher of English.

But I had a son who had mastered the technology and he set up a web site for me– 'One Man's War'.

In it, I wrote down all I could recall from that time at Thua Tich and Xuyen Moc back in 1969– including my own part in it as best I could remember. I was well aware that time is the enemy of us all when it comes to pure recollection of any period in our past, and I made it clear that this was how I recalled those events, and challenged any veteran who had any knowledge of those matters and who disagreed with any aspect of it, or who could add to it in any way, to contact me.

Not once in the five years that that website existed did a single man contradict my account of what had transpired. Not one man.

I got bashed with a steel bar by a masked intruder in the winter of 1992 which, while not the most significant act of violence I experienced in my life, had repercussions in days to come in regards to the 2nd D&E Platoon matter.

I was a High School English teacher by then, and had taken a team of girls from Dapto High to a softball tournament at Blacktown, and housed them in a motel for the night. Early next morning – about 3 am – I heard a noise outside.

Like most things in my life, what happened next is one of those intriguing things that happen in a man's life that defies explanation.

The thing is, although there were three teachers in that motel room that night, it was me who got out of his bed to investigate. It was due in part to my training as an infantryman and a legacy of the war– retaining keen hearing and hyper-alertness, even in sleep.

There are a lot of veterans from that war like me still walking the earth– with the talons of Vietnam firmly embedded in their back.

I remember once standing at the door to a dental surgery and staring idly up at a tree on the property next door. I had no reason to be doing so, but there was something about the top of the tree that mesmerised me. And slowly, my eyes discerned an irregular pattern– something out of place.

Day 1, basic training Vietnam.

What it was, was a snake, coiled around the trunk of the tree just above where the first branches jutted out. I excitedly pointed it out to other patients, but no one else could make it out.

So I went next door and woke the homeowner who was bemused that I bothered– but went white when I pointed it out.

Snakes aren't that prevalent in beachside suburbs like this one.

Anyway, the National Park and Wildlife Rangers were called and were amazed that I'd spotted it as high as it was and as well-camouflaged as snakes can be, and managed to get it down– a three-metre long diamond python.

The homeowner must have brought it back with him from a jaunt through a national park– perhaps wrapped around an axle or some such thing, just like those urban 'myths'.

He was a bit shaken when he realised it.

But I digress.

As I said, I was the only one of the three teachers in that motel room that night who got out of bed and went to check on the girls in that motel room.

If anyone in that room had a predilection for poking a finger at that omnipotent force in the velvet sky and provoking it, it was me.

What I found was a man dressed all in black – black balaclava, black boots, black clothing – hard up against the brick wall of the motel. Instinctively, I charged at him and barrelled him into the wall, seeking to get a bear hug on him and use my weight to advantage.

But he came out swinging– a steel bar of some sort in his hand, and connected me around the skull a few times. I staggered; he stood over me and went to pull something from his pocket. Knife? Gun? I know not, but the lights came on, girls came running out screaming, and the assailant fled across the street and into the shadows.

In that moment, the full force of PTSD which I had hitherto ignored as pretence by pussies to secure war pensions, entered my life.

Or rather, was about to manifest itself more openly than it already had.

The physical wound was relatively minor– a cut to the forehead, bruises, etc. The greater wound was psychological.

I was discharged from hospital before daybreak and returned to the championships where my girls were warming-up for the next round.

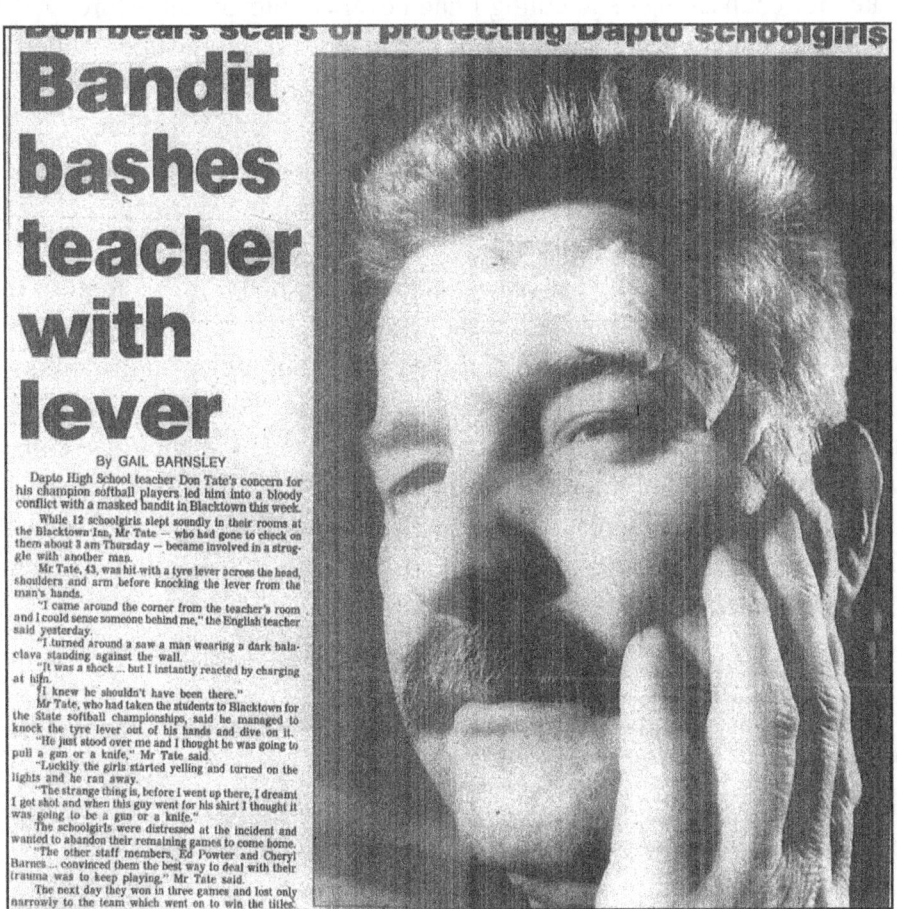

So I go back to school and received a bravery award for my actions from the principal– an act more for show than anything else because he and I had been at loggerheads for years over one thing or another.

It was a hollow gesture. Meant nothing to me whatsoever.

He had no time for me, or I for him. He saw an angry veteran of an unpopular war, and I saw a slope-shouldered excuse for a man who'd dodged it. Not having fought in Vietnam meant he knew nothing of the consequences of what the war did to a man.

So much for educators.

There are many like him.

Within days, that masked intruder changed my life. I began to be haunted by images of men in black, Viet Cong-like… ghostly, fading in and out of dreams and thoughts, in pulses.

My work was sorely effected.

I asked for counselling– something I had never countenanced before.

It was immediately denied me, and all the anger of past injustices welled up inside me in an instant.

'If I had a rifle I'd shoot the bastard,' I said idly to a fellow teacher.

By the end of the day, I wasn't only booked in for counselling, but ordered to leave the school grounds until deemed psychologically fit to resume teaching.

It wasn't just psychological, though.

I found I began to forget what I was saying at any point, lose a train of thought in mid-sentence. Bits of memory began to disappear.

I was eventually diagnosed with some sort of brain injury and offered a medical retirement from teaching which I took with open arms.

And received a large compensation payment from the victim's compensation tribunal. It was the maximum figure allowed.

But the brain injury had greater consequences for me than anyone ever envisaged. It came back to haunt me in years to come when pursuing the 2nd D&E Platoon matter turned bitter– and precise memories of detail were paramount.

In November of 1992, no longer teaching and with time on my hands, I thought I'd pursue the disappearance of the 2nd D&E Platoon a bit more forcefully.

This time I badgered the Australian War Memorial directly. The repository of all things military, I was sure they had to have had some details of the platoon.

It didn't get me too far.

One of its bureaucrats – Bronwyn Self – assured me that the Memorial had nothing on its books about the platoon, and suggested that my only recourse was to take a more aggressive approach to the Central Army Records Office.

Again.

So I did.

Proof that I was the only member of this platoon actively agitating for information pertaining to it is contained in the letter I wrote to CARO in November of 1992, although a 'Dave Edmonds' had also made an enquiry of the Australian War Memorial himself at some point.

Dave Edmonds turned out to be a former member of the 2nd D&E Platoon as well and like most of us, had been bemused at the platoon's 'disappearance' from the record books.

But he fell at the first hurdle. When his letter went unanswered, he didn't bother pursuing it.

That letter to CARO is an important element in the context of this matter.

It was written *thirteen* years before any other veteran joined me in the quest to validate the platoon, *fifteen* years before Jim Riddle bought into the fight, and *sixteen* years before my memoir, *The War Within*, was first published.

This puts paid to the argument used by my detractors that my pursuit of the 2nd D&E Platoon matter was only to promote the memoir.

The War Within wasn't even on the drawing board when I began the quest.

The only thing I was interested in was the overall integrity of my war service.

(**Note:** The administrative incompetence of army bureaucrats is obvious when you see the letter. Perhaps it's a consequence of my own previous employment as a clerk in the Queensland public service prior to going to the war, but why a bureaucrat would write *across* correspondence and not beneath it, or attach a note to it, amazes me).

This is that letter:

Gen Eng

Grote please investigate and see if we can identify personnel. You could start by talking to Dave Gibson.

134 Princes Highway
Albion Park Rail
NSW 2527
8/11/92

Dear John, 12/11/92

Names / Army no's only to go to Robinson if you are successful

Bronwyn Self, of the Australian War Memorial, suggested that I write to you.

In 1969 (about May/June) the 4th R.A.R. left Vietnam, and those of us regular soldiers from that Battalion who had not completed our 6 months, stayed on.

Some 30 or so of us were formed into a platoon called D. E Platoon, and operated from APC's for about 6 weeks.

The platoon was then disbanded, and we were then allocated to new Battalions. In my case, I went to 9 R.A.R.

Can you help me locate the names of those men who went from 4 RAR to D.E, and supply me with any information at all about the operations of D.E Platoon for those 6 weeks?

I know of only one other man (Dave Edmond). This is for a research project. Thanking you in advance, yours sincerely

Don Tate

CHAPTER 7
FULL THROTTLE

Naïve I might have been, but I was one of the very few men who was smart enough to take a small Super 8mm camera with me to the war, and took it into the jungle with me.

I recorded all aspects of my service, and of those who served.

With the exception of my time in the 2nd D&E Platoon, that is. Cpl Jim Riddle had expressly forbidden me to use it in his presence or I'd get his 'boot' up my arse.

What a mistake that turned out to be.

Those films became invaluable tools in proving my service in both the 4th and 9th Battalions, as well as being a wonderful personal record.

Anyway, in 1996, I donated the raw colour films I'd shot in Vietnam to the Australian War Memorial. I thought they were of national significance and deserved to be in the nation's premier War Memorial.

They were assessed by independent film producers acting for the Valuer-General's Department at being worth more than $90,000– and that was in 1996.

I must be honest– donating them in the national interest wasn't my only motive. I thought the donation would buy me some credit with that august institution in validating the 2nd D&E Platoon.

But I was wrong.

I hadn't counted on gatekeepers of the nation's history being more intent on protecting the reputation of their mates in the officer ranks than preserving the integrity of the nation's military history.

They were a formidable force.

And when push came to shove, and the very foundations of the Australian Defence Force shaken by revelations of the falsification of historical documents and after-action reports, the donation of my rare film footage from the war was used as a weapon *against* me by the very same men who had been entrusted with their care.

General Steve Gower, the Director, was *not* going to be on my side.

In 1997, I abandoned the web site I'd set up a couple of years earlier.

As I said, no one had contributed to it, and it hadn't advanced the 2nd D&E Platoon matter one iota.

For all intents and purposes, my pursuit of validation for the 2nd D&E Platoon had stalled. It was time to change tactics, time to bring the matter back out into the open.

So, I wrote an article about having served in the war and what it entailed, and it was subsequently published in the *Sydney Morning Herald* on August 15th 1997– just prior to Vietnam Veterans Day.

It was a comprehensive article explaining how Vietnam had affected me, and covered my service across all three units. I wrote it in stream-of-consciousness style to get as much information as possible across in the shortest space. Precise detail wasn't of importance.

There was one particular paragraph I wrote in that article though, which on reflection, stood out like the proverbial:

> 'Get blown up in an APC at dusk one day. The driver loses his leg, falls off in the arms of our section-commander, Kevin Lloyd-Thomas. Later that night, under a brilliant moon, at least 100 Viet Cong walk into our ambush position and fire off their rocket-propelled grenades. Leaves them pretty vulnerable and leaves us with a turkey shoot.'

Now, it's important to note that up to this point, not a *single* word had ever been written about the 2nd D&E Platoon, or about this particular ambush. None of us who were involved in the action had ever met, let alone discuss it, and there were no written records, either formal or informal to draw upon (or plagiarise) if one was so inclined.

Yet, that short paragraph referred to incidents only a person who had been present at the ambush at Thua Tich, could have described:

– the *100 Viet Cong*;
– the *brilliant moon*;
– and the enemy's vulnerability in the ambush

Key points– and so very vital to this record.

In days to come, my critics would seek to remove me from the scene of the ambush so that my recollections – and therefore my evidence – would be negated. But that single paragraph contained precise information of a type that precluded any reliance on it being fluke, or chance, or accident.

It would be *fifteen* years before any mention of the 2nd D&E Platoon ever surfaced again– yet there I was, including key points about its role in the ambush at Thua Tich in my article.

The incident with the APC was proven very early on after I raised it. It was accurately recorded in the Armoured Cops Narratives. The trooper's name was 'Doc' Dann– and my memory had served me well in that respect.

The other key points from that paragraph concerned the enemy count, and the brightness of the night.

To state publicly that 'at least 100 Viet Cong' had walked into an ambush was no small thing. Most contacts and ambushes involving Australian troops in Vietnam were conducted against relatively small numbers of enemy– so my statement that we had encountered such a large enemy force was outrageous, if incorrect, and open to challenge.

Similarly, clearly recording that the ambush was conducted on a *bright moonlit night* was also important in the context.

Both facts had to be relatively accurate, lest I be perceived as a liar and open to ridicule.

Yet state it I did. Fearlessly.

And as it turned out, Capt Tom Arrowsmith officially recorded the size of the enemy force as '50+' in his after-action report (he had only seen the head of the enemy column from his perspective in his APC) while much later, we learned that as many as 500 enemy soldiers could have been engaged in that ambush.

Peter Langford, a Writeways 'investigator' made light of this estimation in a letter to his boss, John Tilbrook. But a simple check of the 'Headquarters' Diaries for May 29th 1969, state: '45-50, positively definitely more'. So my '100' had been both correct, and conservative.

Despite all the contentions surrounding this matter – the atrocities that occurred the next day and the subsequent military cover-up – exactly where *I* was that night became the real crux of the matter as far as my antagonists were concerned.

While they were belting me around the ears about that, the fundamental issues about the contentions surrounding this platoon weren't being addressed.

But the question raised about my whereabouts was actually my fault.

My honesty in describing the events of that night in my memoir, *The War Within*, did me some damage. Rather than claim some grandiose involvement, I'd admitted that all I could recall of it were a series of vivid, but unconnected images.

That was the truth.

But the knives were now out for me, well and truly.

Literally.

In 1999, I got stabbed twice in the back walking down the main street of Brisbane.

Never saw the attacker. He struck from behind as cowards do– and set the tone for how the military establishment and the veteran community at large would take their own revenge against me in years to come for bringing the corruptions and contentions surrounding this matter out into the open.

The stabbing was physical and easily overcome. They missed my spinal cord and major organs.

But that it was *two* blows with a knife– *that* was harder to come to terms with. One blow was neither here nor there. But two? It spoke of malice and a preparedness of some to go to extremes. And the fact that it was likely to have been a fellow veteran who wielded that knife made it worse.

I had no idea our military would stoop to such lows. Stabbing a man in the back is so....unmanly. Like using pseudonyms on off-shore web sites to attack a man.

Unmanly– and downright cowardly.

I couldn't help but think the stabbing was somehow connected to my fight to validate the 2nd D&E Platoon, especially given the earlier death threats and the abuse coming my way from some quarters.

Frankly, I was very naïve about the nature of the 'men' who had served in the military in Vietnam. Especially those with dark deeds they wanted kept quiet.

Life can be ironic, no doubt about that.

Like when I was contacted by the editor of Australia's most prestigious news magazine, *The Bulletin*.

He rang me and said they had been aware of the 2nd D&E Platoon matter and of my fight to validate it– and were looking for a picture for their front cover that personified the fighting qualities of the Australian soldier.

They had chosen me– and could I send them any pictures I had of me in the war?

Who was I to argue?

As it turned out, I *did* have photographs, and I *could* send them.

A decade earlier, I'd received three colour photos taken of me in Vietnam. They came in the mail. No name, no pack drill. I was rapt to get them. Up to that point, I had no photographs of me in Vietnam at all.

I had hours of colour movie footage, but no photographs.

The Bulletin chose one of them– but to my horror, photo-shopped it. Gone was the mud and filth of the war. Gone were the dirty greens.

The finished product looked like it had been taken in a film studio. And there wasn't a thing I could do about it.

And that picture too, came back to bite me.

That the particular issue they chose to put me on the front cover of happened to be a celebration of the 6th Battalion's famous battle at Long Tan – and me having never set foot in the 6th Battalion, nor ever claimed to have – was a recipe for outrage.

But it was another opportunity to advance the 2nd D&E Platoon matter a tad, nevertheless.

CHAPTER 8
THE WALK

Despite my best endeavours, I made little headway in validating the 2nd D&E Platoon until a remarkable meeting one Anzac Day just before the turn of the century.

I had been invited to march with the 9th Battalion for the first time– the unit I'd been wounded with all those years ago.

In itself, this was an interesting development.

Sometime earlier, I'd tackled the flag-bearer of the 9th Battalion at a ceremony in Canberra about the fact that the 9th Battalion had left me out of its published record of its tour. His name was Greg Salmon. Turned out he was the machine-gunner who followed me into the Viet Cong bunker complex on the night when I was wounded; he, along with another rifleman– Pte John Walker. Unfortunately, both John Walker and I were wounded in the process. Walker was shot through the shoulder and lost fingers from both hands when a belt of M60 ammunition he was raising above his head was struck by a bullet.

Pte Greg Salmon was the only one of the three of us who wasn't wounded– so they gave him the Military Medal for gallantry.

It always amused me, that. Well, pissed me off, actually. Three men climb uphill and run into heavy machine-gun fire to provide covering fire for a whole section of wounded men– but only one of them gets a gallantry medal?

The fact that Walker and I had both been reinforcements to the battalion, as well as both being wounded, was probably the difference.

Anyway, he took the matter of my omission to the Executive of the 9th Battalion Association (NSW) and I received an immediate invitation to come in from the cold.

And this was the first day I was going to march with the battalion on Anzac Day. I was looking forward to it.

So I'm making my way down George Street in Sydney along with dozens of other men, all heading for the forming-up location.

I hadn't marched in Sydney before, and wasn't a regular visitor to Sydney, so I turned to a bloke walking briskly past me and asked him if he could give me directions.

'I sure can,' he replied. 'In fact, I'll take you there. I'm heading that way myself.' Then, he stopped and looked at me intently. 'I think I know you from somewhere,' he said.

I studied him myself. He was shorter than me, but impeccably dressed.

'Who'd you serve with?' he asked, but before I answered, he added, 'I did two tours myself– started with the 2nd Battalion in '67/68.'

'Too early for me,' I replied. 'I didn't get there until the end of 1968, just before Christmas. I did a few weeks in the Reinforcement Unit before joining the 4th Battalion in late January the next year.'

'4RAR?' he says, quizzically. Then he blurts out, 'You're Don Tate! We were both in "D" Company. Then you became my machine-gunner in the 2nd D&E Platoon!'

And there it was. The words were out in public. The '2nd D&E Platoon' he'd said.

He offered his hand. 'Kevin Lloyd-Thomas.'

Then, I remembered him too. Hyphenated names can do that. They stick in your mind a bit longer than most.

Kevin Lloyd-Thomas– my section-commander in that platoon!

'Kevin Lloyd-Thomas,' I echoed. 'I remember you. You know, you're the first bloke from that 2nd D&E Platoon I've ever met,' I told him. 'Never come across one other single man from it since.'

'Me either,' he said, shaking his head. 'What a small world.'

We got to talking then as we made our way up towards Hunter Street.

We talked about a lot of things from that strange time in Vietnam. About our time together in 10 Platoon of the 4th Battalion. About how I was wounded with the 9th Battalion. About those few weeks we'd spent together in that 2nd D&E Platoon. About Cpl Jim Riddle, the English marine who had stepped up to the plate and taken over the role of platoon commander of the platoon when the officer who'd been appointed to it suddenly disappeared after just a few days. About operating on APCs and a new way of doing things. And about the ambush at Thua Tich that would have repercussions for decades to come.

So many memories came flooding back. So many images.

When we got to the forming-up location, we parted company. There was a TV crew from Channel 7's 'Today/Tonight' waiting there for me.

The 9th Battalion had organised it. I would be meeting the man who had dragged me out of that Viet Cong killing field the night I was wounded, they said– Pte Noel Gibson. He, who had crawled through the mud to drag me back to safety using my leg as a rifle mount and my body as a shield before throwing me over his shoulders and dropping me in a safer place.

'This is the man who saved my life,' I said to the journalist covering the story. And I put my arm around him and we marched together for the first time.

It was great television.

Only, I learned later, that Noel Gibson *hadn't* been involved in rescuing me at all. He'd gotten the basic facts of the action from one of the others who had been heavily involved in the ambush – Major Andrew Ochiltree MM – and it allowed him to spin a story.

The 9th Battalion had set me up.

Truth was, I'd had no idea who *had* rescued me. Time and trauma takes its toll on memory, so I was always open to any information that assisted me in clarifying the details of my service.

I have learned since that the men who actually got me to safety that night were the platoon's medic, Cpl Peter Bunn and another rifleman, Pte Mick Davidson.

If Noel Gibson was up there helping to drag men out of that killing field, he must have gotten me confused with someone else. Some say he never went forward to assist anyone at all. I don't know the truth of it. Not that it's relevant here.

But while all that was happening at the march that Anzac Day, Kevin Lloyd-Thomas quietly moved off to march with the 2nd Battalion, promising to keep in touch with me afterwards and that we'd pursue the 2nd D&E Platoon matter together.

He kept his word. He was the sort of man who would.

More importantly, I finally had an ally.

In 2006, I focussed media attention – and the eyes of the veteran community – back on the 2nd D&E Platoon by constructing a 'Vietnam Veterans Commemorative Walk' around a local sporting field in Albion Park Rail. It was a project financed by the Department of Veteran Affairs.

In all, the project involved the construction of spectator surrounds requiring thousands of tonnes of soil, extensive grass-planting, and the planting out of more than 230 trees around it.

I designed it as a living, breathing monument to those who had fought the Vietnam War in whatever capacity– an investment in the community of substance that would have benefits for decades to come.

I saw no point in lifeless stone monoliths scattered around the place.

This project though, was fraught with controversy from start to finish.

It had come about after a Vietnam Veterans Lifestyle Program my wife and I had attended in 1999– an initiative of the Vietnam Veterans Counselling Service.

The idea was that by involving ourselves in a community project, we could raise the profile of Vietnam veterans in general. Sounded like a plan.

So, in 2000, as the President of the local cricket club at the time, I suggested turning the ground into a place where veterans could go and contemplate their navels if they so desired– and a 'walk' seemed appropriate.

But the local Council – Shellharbour – wasn't all that keen about any of it.

Its General Manager, Brian Weir, wasn't a veteran of the war and couldn't care less about anything to do with it or those who had. He had a bigger agenda for the community and his own ideas about what veterans could and should have– and in this case, it was a cold, lifeless space overlooking the local Bunnings store!

So he knocked the project on the head– and I came out swinging.

Not surprisingly, there was no support from the bureaucracy within the VVCS. It was one thing to suggest projects, but altogether another to support the veterans when they found themselves at the mercy of an insensitive bureaucracy.

I took the matter to the veteran community instead. All hell broke loose.

I encountered two formidable opponents at opposite ends of the veteran community. One was Bob Buick– the revered 'hero' of the battle of Long Tan. And the other was Frank Grady, an average soldier who served in the Company Q-store in the 3rd Battalion, but had somehow managed to become President of the Vietnam Veterans Association of Australia by exaggerating his service.

Neither assisted me; both became enemies in this minor local skirmish– and both played significant roles in attempting to discredit me years later as I fought to prove that the 2nd D&E Platoon had existed. If nothing else, they spoiled the atmosphere in which the 2nd D&E Platoon matter could be debated intelligently.

Buick operated a computer network attached to off-shore web sites where anonymous contributors could dump on any target at will– hiding behind pseudonyms. And Grady had a massive internet email base and commanded considerable veteran support as an advocate, and as an officer of the ex-service organisation.

As it turned out, they were formidable men to make enemies of.

Both would eventually be exposed as men of straw, and both came unstuck.

But they did me some considerable damage in the process– personally, and in attempting to derail our fight for recognition of the platoon.

I'd actually contacted Buick in the first place.

The only reason I involved him was because I thought he was a real hero– a genuine man of integrity. Somehow, I thought the words 'hero' and 'integrity' were intertwined.

I was dead wrong. I had never involved myself much in veterans' affairs or ex-service organisations, and I hadn't been aware at the time that Buick was an 'establishment' man through and through, but that his 'hero' crown was slipping. Veterans across Australia were questioning his 'heroics' at Long Tan, especially in the light of anecdotal comment that was surfacing.

In particular, the issue of his murdering a wounded, unarmed enemy soldier threatened to taint both his battalion, and the ethos of the Australian soldier. It had also come to the attention of a barrister from the A.C.T. – James Fergusson Thomson.

Thomson had been an army staff legal officer in Vietnam a year after the murder had occurred, and made his opinions about Buick's actions quite clear in a letter to the editor of *The Weekend Australian* in August 2000.

(Incidentally, James Fergus Thomson's claim that he was a staff legal officer 'just after' the battle of Long Tan is a long stretch of the bow. He actually arrived in Vietnam *ten months* after the battle! Some men do like to bask in the reflected 'glory' of that battle....)

But they hadn't court-martialled Buick. They'd 'disappeared' some of the contentious Signals that recorded those particular matters out of the War Memorial's records and given him a gallantry medal instead.

> **Viet killing**
>
> ACCORDING to the 7.30 Report (18/8), former Australian army sergeant Bob Buick claims to have executed a wounded enemy soldier on the day after the battle of Long Tan in Vietnam.
>
> Buick says this was a "mercy killing". It was not. It was murder, pure and simple. If it happened, it is a disgraceful stain on Buick's battalion, on the soldiers who fought so valiantly at Long Tan and on the Australian army.
>
> I was legal staff officer on Taskforce HQ at Nui Dat just after the battle at Long Tan. If I had known of Buick's claimed action he would have been prosecuted for murder and tried by court martial.
>
> **FERGUS THOMSON**
> Weetangera, ACT

There was a price to pay though. Buick then became the lapdog of the military in return– fiercely defending the establishment against any critic.

He wasn't a go-to man.

He was a run-away-from man.

'We don't shit in our own nests,' was all he said, dismissing my request for help, and no doubt in relation to my earlier assertions about the atrocities at Thua Tich.

Buick then entered the debate about the 2nd D&E Platoon in no uncertain terms, boasting of his knowledge of the military as a former Warrant Officer. He had firm opinions about the legality of the platoon's status, and wasn't backwards in coming forward about them.

He wrote (sic):

> *'Tate, Colmer and others do not understand the during my service Warrant Officers 2 in Infantry had to complete a 12 weeks promotion course and examination to qualify, we were taught and tested on all matter pertaining to an Infantry company, administration, Q, discipline, law etc some dozen or more element to run and administer a rifle company because 80% of Inf WOII were posted to CMF with half alone in country regions. This training was so intensive that WOII were relied on by all CMF Officers for guidance in all aspects of military requirements a point unknown by Tate, Colmer and their supporters, even Officers, like McGurgan, Corse etc never did the WO's course. WOI course was at battalion level and covered additional procedures and at a higher level.*
>
> *I know from experience that without supporting documents directly associated with an event history will not be changed. It was only because of such a document that Harry Smith was successful in upgrading the awards for his platoon commanders at Long Tan. Colmer and Tate do not have supporting documents as there never was any, the smokescreen about roll books by Colmer will not support the 2nd D&E Pl claim, roll books are not evidence of the formation of a platoon, it is an administrative tool to support other administrative needs such as rationing, attachment/detachment, hospitalisation etc of individuals...'*

This from a man who, years later and despite his claims to have a thorough knowledge of all things military, accepted and falsely wore the LS&GC Medal he had no right to!

The problem was, the more he attacked us, the more vocal other veterans became in attacking *him* about contentious things that had occurred at Long Tan and afterwards– matters that had been buried for years: the manner in which his platoon commander,

Lt Gordon Sharp was killed; about his actions in running from the battle, and leaving wounded men behind in the process; about not stopping to assist other men wounded alongside him as he ran for his life; and about his confession to having murdered that enemy soldier with a couple of bullets through the heart the next day; and having illegally worn that LS&GC Medal for years– a federal offence.

Faced with attacks by other veterans who despised him, Buick made an astonishing revelation before he retreated in embarrassment. He wrote (sic):

'I would never entered this 2nd DE Pl fiasco has Tate and others had no behave is such an arrogant and mischievous manner. My support is very strong and at the highest levels of government and military.'

And there it was, as poorly expressed as it was– *'support at the highest levels of the government and military'*.

It was a sensational outburst. It confirmed what we had believed all along– that politicians and generals alike were party to a conspiracy about the 2nd D&E Platoon. It was also proof that the dogs had been loosed by the 'establishment', and that Buick was at the end of the leash.

Only, he hadn't left the battle. He'd simply gone underground– and in years to follow, would maintain his attack via off-shore web sites like ANZMI and the Australian Veterans Matters website (AVM) and encourage other cowards to join him in condemning me and any other who dared utter a criticism of the military or ex-officers.

In fact, Buick's internet network and operations were so sophisticated, one couldn't help but ponder if he had received government assistance in conducting them– even the Department of Veterans Affairs perhaps? And if so, which politicians were behind it, or facilitating it?

A 'hero', he most certainly wasn't. Not by a long shot.

A coward, he most certainly was.

Frank Grady, on the other hand, intervened in the matter out of ego.

As the top dog in the Vietnam Veterans Association, he was irked that I was pursuing a project that cut across his stage. Not only hadn't he sanctioned it, he wouldn't be involved in it, have no control of the finances, or get any credit from it.

So even though we were both fellow veterans and there were other veterans involved in the project with me, he sided with the General Manager against us, agreeing that a memorial at the new Shellharbour village was more appropriate than the tree-planting project I was pursuing.

Undeterred by the Council's refusal to allow the Walk, I went ahead with the tree-planting part of the walk regardless– ironically, with Council actually supplying many of the trees.

But having done so, I considered it would have been a pointless exercise if there wasn't some recognition of who had planted the trees, and why.

I demanded that Council allow a plaque to acknowledge the effort. After all, it had taken me three years and a great deal of physical effort to complete it with a body already breaking down– and I saw no reason why the community shouldn't be aware that it had been a project completed by veterans of the most unpopular war the servicemen of this country had ever fought.

But the Council wouldn't have a bar of any reference to *Vietnam veterans* having been involved in the project.

The absurdity of the situation was that only a couple of years earlier, a troop of Chilean Boy Scouts had planted two trees in the same complex– and *they'd* been allowed a plaque acknowledging it.

I saw the hypocrisy through the prism of rejection all veterans had suffered at the hands of an insensitive society for decades.

So I sought the intervention of fellow veterans, and put the matter through the hands of various 'postmen' within the community.

In return, Grady used his position within the Association to prevent my communications being read, but at the same time, used his internet network to attack me any which way he could.

The Council got caught in the middle.

Two senior ex-army officers, 'Alby' Morrison – former CO of the 9th Battalion, and David Thompson, former CO of the 4th Battalion – made individual submissions to Shellharbour City Council on my behalf, and a well-respected South Australian veteran, Anthony Pahl, placed a petition on the internet urging veterans to have an opinion.

Support was overwhelming.

Frank Grady's opposition to the project became irrelevant.

I pushed the envelope then (as well as the 2nd D&E Platoon matter) by applying to the Department of Veteran Affairs for a grant of $2000 for the rock and plaque, and advised the veteran community that I would be recognising the *de facto* platoon commander of the 2nd D&E Platoon – Cpl Jim Riddle – on that plaque when it went up.

It was a provocative, in-your-face action.

This was the advice I sent to veterans:

'After a seven-year battle, Shellharbour City Council has given me permission to erect a plaque at Neville Hilton Oval to acknowledge the fact that six local Vietnam veterans planted more than 200 trees at this site as part of a "commemorative walk".

You might recall that after we planted the trees, the same Council refused to allow us a plaque at the ground which contained any mention of the Vietnam War.

This became a very contentious issue within the veteran community for a short time- until a Frank Grady, President of the VVAA used his position (and the internet) to undermine the integrity of the project- even though he was never part of it, and knew nothing about it. He sided with the General Manager, Brian Weir- an act of sheer bastardry. On the other hand, the project was supported by the previous president of the local VVAA- Peter Ellis.

Subsequently, the VVAA supported Grady and withdrew their support for our fight. I continued it, mostly alone. My only support came from two old leaders- 'Alby' Morrison, the CO of 9RAR; and the Hon. Gen. David Thompson, ex-CO of 4RAR. The only organisation who got behind me was the 9th Battalion, NSW branch, for which I was very grateful.

I also took the issue of the 2nd D&E Platoon fiasco to Bob Buick., thinking he might assist a fellow veteran. But Buick laid low, and did nothing to assist. I guess there was nothing in it for him.

The veterans (and our wives) who planted those trees were: Kevin and Judith Skippen (artillery); Tony and Pat May (infantry); Phillip and Robyn Lamond (104 Flight Recce); Allan and Maureen Kelly (infantry); Don and Lynn Wooster (infantry); my wife, Carole, and myself.

The DVA supported the project and donated $2000 towards the cost of the trees. This year, they have donated a further $1500 towards the cost of establishing the commemorative sandstone rock, and plaque. This should let every veteran know that the project always was a valid one- with all the right intentions behind it.

It is my intention to ask Jim B. Riddle, platoon commander of the 'discrete infantry force' HQ 1ATF to unveil the plaque which "acknowledges that the trees were planted by local Vietnam War veterans as a community project to honour the sacrifices of all veterans of the War. Lest we forget." Jim Riddle's name will be on the plaque- and NOT any Australian army officer's. After what was done to the 35 men of the 2nd D&E Platoon, it would not be right to ask any officer to complete this task.

It is my intention to formally invite the members of the 2nd D&E Platoon, and any other vets who are interested, to an official unveiling- hopefully this spring.

I have taken this step to highlight Jim Riddle's service to this country- almost 900 days in Vietnam across 5 different units; promised two bravery awards, but received none; and particularly, his leadership of the 'discrete infantry force' (the 2nd D&E Platoon) against a vastly superior enemy force, numerically, on the 29th and 30th May- exploits which were deleted or erased from official records of the Vietnam War (but now, at least, recognised by the Australian War Memorial)

If there be any man who has an objection to my use of Jim's name on this plaque (Jim has proudly accepted the honour) please feel free to advise me why. I believe this country has done a great disservice to Jim (and indeed, all the 35 members of the 2ⁿ D&E Platoon) and this is one small way to re-dress the matter.

Regards

Don Tate, 1201907: - ex-4RAR; ex-2nd D&E Platoon; ex-9RAR'

There were no dissenting voices.

And with the support of the MacArthur Branch of the Vietnam Veterans Association, the 'Vietnam Veterans Commemorative Walk' at Albion Park Rail was formally opened, and the plaque unveiled.

Unfortunately, Jim Riddle was unable to attend on the day. He had become mightily sick up in Queensland.

I offered to drive up and pick him up and bring him down and return him at my own expense– a 4000 kilometre trip. I thought he was worth the effort.

But he declined. He didn't think his body could handle it.

In his absence, the plaque was unveiled by me and my former section-commander from the 2nd D&E Platoon days– Kevin Lloyd-Thomas.

I made sure that the local Member of Parliament was present – the Hon Jennie George MP – along with the media to record the event, maintaining the pressure on politicians about the 2nd D&E Platoon matter.

It was also recorded on film, and uploaded to Youtube. The reference is:

http://www.youtube.com/watch?v=TJalzuZ0JnA

I couldn't help myself. I made sure that I gave both Bob Buick an uppercut (and Frank Grady a good left jab at the same time) when I advised fellow veterans about what had transpired.

Both Buick and Grady would come back at me, hard.

CHAPTER 9
THE CRUX OF THE MATTER

It's true, if you went to any historical record of the war, whether it be held by the Australian War Memorial, or even within Army Narratives or unit histories, you will not find a single mention of the *2nd D&E Platoon*.

Yet, two senior Australian Army officers were prepared to state publicly that despite there being no *official* record, such a platoon *had* existed, and had existed by *that* name.

The first public acknowledgement came from Major George Pratt– the OC of HQ Company of the Australian Task Force. In a private email to documentary-maker– Adam Rainford, dated 27th February 2007, Pratt stated that he had *'formed the 2nd D&E Platoon'*. There was enough validation in that.

> *Dear Adam,*
>
> *I am George Pratt and I was OC HQ Coy 1 ATF at Nui Dat in 1969-70. One of my tasks when I arrived at the Task Force HQ was to reinvigorate the D and E platoon for the protection of Brigadier Sandy Pearson's HQ when he was in the field.*
>
> *This was successful and later on we grew in numbers and formed the 2nd D and E platoon. I came home in Feb 1970.*

Major George Pratt hadn't made it to any of the battalions. He found his niche in the HQ Company.

The platoons under his command – including the generic D&E Platoon, commanded by Lt Ray Woolan – were his private army. Pratt was loathe to actually leave the Nui Dat compound and fight the enemy himself. He preferred to fight the war from a desk.

Trouble was, he wasn't much of an administrator.

He might've *formed* the 2nd D&E Platoon– but hadn't bothered with the paperwork that validated it.

Nor was he bothered to ensure that the Roll Book of HQ Company was accurate, despite clear instructions inside the front cover that it needed to be.

When I finally received copies of the HQ Company Roll-Books for May/June 1969 from the Australian War Memorial, I was astonished to see the paucity of clerical information inside them.

The fact that he did not officially record the creation of the 2nd D&E Platoon on any document (or if he did, such documents having been subsequently destroyed) was the singular fact on which the entire 2nd D&E Platoon matter revolved.

If he *had,* there would have been an historical record of it– and no need for us to be pursuing the matter forty years later.

And if he did, and those records subsequently destroyed after the atrocities were committed in May of 1969, then it says more about the integrity of the army than anything else.

Whatever the reason was– Maj George Pratt compensated for any incompetence on his part when he sent that email to my son-in-law.

Because there it was– the fundamental piece of evidence we needed to validate the existence of the platoon. Right from the horse's mouth.

Is that enough proof?

What price the word of an Australian Army officer– that's the real question?

If a former senior officer publicly declares that he *formed the 2nd D&E Platoon*, why didn't that seal the matter straight away? Who would dare to differ? What possible motive could he have had in flying in the face of veteran opinion in acknowledging something so contentious when he had nothing to gain by it, and a damn sight more to lose?

Yet– it made little impact on those on the sidelines who simply refused to accept that the military they had served so proudly was possible of such maladministration.

Nor on the politicians.

Nor on the Australian War Memorial.

Nor on the military 'establishment' as a whole, I suggest, because it was the last peep we heard out of Maj George Pratt. Not another word.

Just like they'd put the muzzle on Major Gordon Pound about his earlier 'Enquiry'. The fix was in.

But Major George Pratt had taken the finger out of the dyke.

His revelation that he had 'formed the 2nd D&E Platoon' was followed by a second email from another officer– and corroborated that of Major Pratt.

It came from Major Barry Parkin– a former platoon commander in Vietnam with the 4th Battalion, and the 2nd D&E Platoon's first (and only) platoon commander with pips on his shoulder.

Not that he was ever recorded as such.

Parkin's email set out the circumstances of the platoon's creation (sic):

> *Don, my recollections are as follows:*
>
> *During middle May 69 whilst assisting the rear party of 4RAR and the in country familiarization training of 6 RAR I was told to report to Maj G Pratt at HQ 1 ATF. On reporting to Maj Pratt I was briefed that a second D&E Platoon was to be raised from the soldiers of 4RAR who had remained in country as they had not served the minimum period of service before being able to RTA. I was further told the platoon would be carrying out independent duties with the APC Sqn and also to act as a ready reaction force. As part of these duties could be along the rivers in the Baria area we were to undertake assault boat training ASAP. This was carried out in the Baria area. However no water patrol action was ever carried out. This unit of soldiers was always referred to as the 2nd D&E Pl.*
>
> *Shortly after this I proceeded on R&R. On returning I remember being briefed on other significant actions carried out by the Pl. Soon after this (about 19 Jun 69) the Pl was disbanded (to be used as reinforcements I guess) and I was posted to 1 ARU until late Feb 70. I am not aware of any role played by Maj Chinn in the activities of the 2 D&E Pl but as the Ops Officer of 1 ATF he would have fully known if not ordered the raising of the Platoon.*

Barry Parkin's letter was clear enough; one might have thought. But challenged as to why he hadn't entered the debate earlier, Parkin added to his earlier advice:

> *Don, I know it has been a matter of concern to many (including myself) as to why the existence of the 2nd D&E Pl was never acknowledged and our service with that unit never recorded. I believe the reason was that when the fighting 4th Battalion went home we were sent (attached) to HQ Coy 1 ATF until we could be absorbed as reinforcements to some other unit. The OC HQ Coy (Maj George Pratt) had asked HQ 1 ATF what he should do with all these spare soldiers he had. It was then decided to raise a 2nd D&E Pl to work with the APC sqn as a ready reaction force.*
>
> *I was with the Pl more than a few days as you inferred in your original email calling for information, I remember doing watermanship training down near Baria in assault boats and during that time we decided to go fishing using hand grenades. These underwater explosions caused us to have a visit from a US Navy swift boat stationed nearby.*
>
> *I recall two operations with the D&E Pl. The first in and around Xuyen Moc with Arrowsmith and another with Dave Lawrence but cannot remember the AO. I recall the incident when the PL and the APCs came across the VC wheeling a 500lb bomb done the road and the following firefight. This is the incident when the pictures of the soldier (whose name I cannot remember) firing his M60 while standing on top of an APC. I was on R&R at the time and I think the Pl Sgt (who was a WO) was in charge)......'*
>
> Barry

Trouble was, Parkin's recollections threw a spanner in the works because it contained facts that were not consistent with the evidence we had already located.

A breathless, former member of the platoon– Dennis Manski, emailed me immediately (sic):

> 'Don,
> Some things in this story aren't right. The bloke firing the gun atop the APC was Len Ellcombe and it happened during the ambush on the way out back to Xuyen Moc. We did NOT have a Pl Sgt who was a WO. The only Sgt that was with the platoon was during the training and He was Sgt John Chainey who then went home with 4RAR. There was an old WO who was with us at Thua Tich but he was an observer only and he was with Jim and me and the rest down the road from the APCs during the ambush. I don't think anyone went to 5 RAR either so this person's recollections are not credible.'

Parkin's entry into the matter became quite divisive. The mixed messages contained in his comments were baffling. Given that he was a former officer who had reached a substantial rank, one had to wonder if this was a question of memory impairment or deliberate sabotage.

The one clear memory a number of us had was that on one of our first outings with the APCs with Parkin in charge, we got lost and had to find our way back by having flares sent up from the base at Nui Dat.

I said as much to him direct.

Parkin cleared that matter up to some extent, but knowing we were seeking as much detail as possible, added to the confusion with his last message (sic):

> 'Hi,
> I may be able to help with info you may require. I do take exception to the statement that I got the platoon lost and had to be brought in by flares as I have no recollection of this. I do recall find a pile of bodies east of Xuyen Moc and having a heated argument with Arrowsmith as to the exact location of these bodies. Our locstat was later verified by use of Arty ranging shots. These bodies were later blown up by engineers using a large amount of C4. Our the years I have been contacted by various advocates and others looking into repat cases for DVA and have always verified the existence of the 2nd D&E Pl. Email me if you require further info. Regards,
> Barry Parkin'

It was our understanding that after those initial first couple of days, Lt Parkin had gone on R&R, and thereafter had gone on to some dealings with the U.S. forces. But it was hearsay. According to our research, Parkin didn't go on R&R until July!

More intrigue.

As it was, a Warrant Officer – Ernie Hayden – actually took over the role of platoon commander when Parkin left. But he never exercised any authority over the platoon in any respect, content with allowing Cpl Jim Riddle to run the show.

No one remembers Hayden. We believe he died in the 1970's.

It was the same for Parkin. No one has any recall of him out with us on any operation with Capt Arrowsmith's Troop whatsoever. Nor did his comment about finding a pile of bodies make any sense. If true, it was news to us.

However, if nothing else, his verification of the manner in which bodies were disposed of, added weight to our argument that bodies had been destroyed.

Those irritations aside, Barry Parkin had at least given our quest some substance– reinforcing Major George Pratt's contention that he had formed the 2nd D&E Platoon.

In a normal world where common-sense prevailed, one might have thought the word of *two* former senior officers validating the existence and operations of a platoon of Australian infantrymen in a war might have counted for something.

It didn't.

Especially not in the disbelieving Vietnam-veteran community.

Generally speaking, it wanted to believe only what it *wanted* to believe– and the very last thing it wanted to believe was that an ex-Private soldier could rock their little worlds and prove that the military 'establishment' could be so corrupt as to discreetly corrupt official records to protect the reputations of a few senior officers.

So no– they weren't going to accept the word of those former officers however credible they were, or what rank they achieved, or how high they had climbed within the military, or the value of their word.

There was an unspoken but clearly perceptible sentiment that existed– no matter what proof he provided, Don Tate would *not* win this fight.

But, two pieces of evidence were uncovered in quick succession– and like every scrap of evidence that came my way, I sent it out into the veteran community with comment, slowly establishing the case that the 2nd D&E Platoon had been erased for reasons I only hinted at.

There were other aces up my sleeve I didn't want to waste.

The first real breakthrough (other than the admissions by George Pratt and Barry Parkin) was full of irony, in that while we ex-military types were vainly sifting through infantry records for any mention of the 2nd D&E Platoon for some proof of its existence, Adam Rainford – a young man without any military experience whatsoever – stumbled upon a document in a source far removed from the records of the infantry.

He found a single entry in the *Engineer's Narratives*.

Dated the 14th May 1969, a Major R. Rowe records a seemingly innocuous activity. A section of engineers had been tasked with training a *'new D&E Platoon'* in the use of water craft at the Song Cao May bridge area near Baria.

That activity was absurdly titled 'watermanship'.

It was an extraordinary piece of evidence, pivoting on the use of the adjective *new*– a 'new' D&E Platoon.

I'm not sure if Adam Rainford really appreciated the significance of that entry when he found it, but *I* certainly did. Because it meant that an officer in the Engineers Corps – unaware of the intrigue surrounding the creation of the 2nd D&E Platoon within the Infantry – had made it as clear as day that there were *two* D&E Platoons in existence.

And if there were *two*– there had to be a way of differentiating between them. Being the military and all, calling one of them the *2nd D&E Platoon* made a lot of sense.

As it was, *'watermanship training'* involved placing pairs of infantrymen on flat-bottomed, metal boats where they could float around on mosquito-infested mangrove swamps to take the war to the Viet Cong who, apparently, controlled the swamp areas. That we were extremely vulnerable was offset by the provision of flak jackets and steel helmets for which we were very grateful.

Luckily, we were never called upon to put the new tactic to work. I assume that the fool who thought it up was quickly put back behind a desk.

The second piece of evidence was located in the 'Headquarters 1ATF' Diary–held within the Australian War Memorial's Collections. The 'Headquarters 1ATF' Diary contains the general outline of how the war was conducted by the brains trust of the Task Force. These records can be verified at:

https://www.awm.gov.au/collection/records/awm95/1/4/awm95-1-4-151.pdf

In those documents there is a document titled 'MESSAGE FORM'. It was sent from 1ATF to HQ Company with the references 'R 852/1/11' and 'Ops 729'. There is a hand-written notation on the top right-hand corner– 'C32'.

That document advises that the 'D&E Platoon' had permission to conduct *'live firing with small arms'* during the watermanship training taking place at Baria on the 12th and 13th May 1969, and was signed by a Captain whose signature is illegible.

This photograph shows the stupidity of the enterprise:

Nothing untoward about that except that it could only have applied to the 'new' D&E Platoon because the official D&E Platoon was out and about on various operations with cavalry units at the time on Operation *Mailed Fist!*

The official D&E Platoon couldn't have been in two places at once.

Similarly, an analysis of all the logs for May 1969 showed that a 'D&E Platoon' was involved in a number of contacts with the enemy and other events– but that a simple analysis of the LOCSTATS of each action and the dates on which they occurred, made it abundantly clear to any discerning investigator that there had to be *two* platoons in action at the same time, but in vastly different locations.

(That list of contacts is provided later in this narrative).

But unaware of this arrangement, unsuspecting officers lodging after-action reports like Capt Tom Arrowsmith had no reason to record the infantry elements as anything other than 'D&E Platoon'.

They can be forgiven that administrative error.

On the other hand, somehow, the 'researchers' at the Australian War Memorial had been unable to put two and two together in analysing that data, which says much about their research skills.

Or, more likely, they had been instructed *not* to make the connection by interested parties keen to maintain a corrupt history. And I'll come back to that too.

In the hands of our small investigative team, a door to validating the 2nd D&E Platoon had been opened.

This was how the 2nd D&E Platoon operated

CHAPTER 10
MANIPULATING MANPOWER

In examining all facets of the 2nd D&E Platoon matter, the military's propensity to deceive is of paramount concern– as is its capacity to disguise it.

If the 2nd D&E Platoon actually existed as two officers have verified, yet there be no proof of it, is the reason because the platoon was created illegally?

That suggestion emanated from a letter we had received from the Minister for Veterans Affairs – Bruce Billson MP – early in the piece. He wrote that there was 'no authority' to create a second D&E Platoon. So it followed that if it did exist, it must have been done illegally.

We came across one particular letter that seems to infer that deception was par for the course in the conduct of the Vietnam War.

On the 17th November 1968, Major R. Joshua (GSO2 DSD) sent a letter from AHQ Canberra, to Major A.W. Campbell MC, in Vietnam. It is a rather innocuous letter– mostly dealing with administrative matters (and an interesting aside about him 'not missing downtown Saigon').

The first paragraph of that letter deals with 'Manpower'.

Or in other words, playing tunes with men's lives.

This is the letter:

The first paragraph dealt with 'Manpower' in Vietnam, thus:

From: Maj R. Jo. UA

SECRET
AUSTRALIAN MILITARY FORCES

F26

MILITARY BOARD
(CHIEF OF THE GENERAL STAFF)

Quote in Reply

ARMY HEADQUARTERS
CANBERRA, ACT

17 Nov 68

Maj A.W. Campbell MC

Dear Mal,

Thank you for the NZ Staff Table which has solved a number of problems for us.

This letter is practically my swan song as GSO2 DSD (Plans, Policy and Mounting), as next week I shall go to GSO2 (Ops) DMO and P. In the new job I shall of course read your sitreps etc with great interest and no doubt, we shall correspond in that field. My replacement here will be Ken Hutchison who will have fairly firm guidance from Mal Lander the GSO1.

In the fields which DSD act we now have fairly clear procedures, although from time to time we have a flurry of signals to clear up obvious points of misunderstanding.

1.   a. <u>Manpower</u>. The current ceiling for AFV (Army Component) is 6,886. This is most unlikely to change as it requires Cabinet and Defence approval to do so. The Prime Minister's public statements would support this view. However, within the ceiling we can play a number of tunes which generally enable us to provide what you require. From the staff table which we produce each month, you can see what part of the manpower ceiling has been expended and where it is located. Of the balance, AHQ reserves 50 positions against unforeseen contingencies. What is left is for you to use as you see fit. It is good practise to look ahead each quarter and let us know the lines on which you are thinking. At present, we are mentally reserving 26 positions of your slice against the AFV band requirement. There is also the thought that about 22 positions may be required for a commercial type radio station. The main point here is to keep us both on net in regard to major expenditures of say, more than five or six new positions.

As one of my fellow 2nd D&E Platoon members put it, 'It's all about cooking the books and fudging the figures.'

That is to say, done without the knowledge of the Australian Cabinet.

I was interested in a letter I received from a fellow veteran (from the 6th Battalion) that put a new slant on why the 2nd D&E Platoon had disappeared.

> 'Don.
>
> *Something just crossed my mind.*
>
> *Do you think it was possible that the 2nd D&E platoon was created in order to act as a "sacrificial unit"?*
>
> *By that I mean that perhaps the government at home was starting to realise that the war was becoming unpopular and was looking for an excuse to get out of Vietnam.*
>
> *If by some chance a few dozen volunteers were wiped out then they may be able to use that as an excuse to pack up and call it a day.*
>
> *Against all expectations, the fact that the Second D&E Platoon was so effective, merely aborted their conspiracy somewhat so they then did their level best to "cash in" on that particular "success" and await another day for another opportunity.*
>
> *Just a thought.*
>
> *L. Bodey* '

To which I replied:

> *'Mate- what I've learned since the days I was a young, naive 18 year-old regular who just wanted to fight for his country because I thought there was nothing more honourable a man could do, is that this Australian Army stinks to high heaven. Its leaders were deceitful bastards who gave, and took medals they had no right to, denied them to men who should have got them, were prepared to let men die to further their own ambitions, and who have been prepared to stay silent, hide, and leave us floundering, trying to sort it out. The Australian Army prides itself on its proud traditions- what a load of bullshit.'*

The erasure of the 2nd D&E Platoon matter had embittered me well and truly.

There was a storm brewing in Phuoc Tuy Province in May 1969.

A young SAS officer – Lt T.J. Nolan – didn't know it at the time, but he was going to be front and centre of it, though it would be about forty years before his role in the 2nd D&E Platoon issue became a matter of interest, and of historical significance.

He was just doing his job at the time, which, during that month of May, was being part of saturation reconnaissance patrols aimed at gathering intelligence on enemy movements along their major logistics supply routes.

The particular supply route of interest for these patrols ran from the Xuyen Moc and Tam Bo/ Ho Tram Cape area through to the Nui May Tao mountain complex north of Phuoc Tuy Province.

In a two-week period, SAS patrols like that of Lt Nolan's unit, performing covert reconnaissance under the most perilous conditions, spotted and recorded some thirty-five groups of enemy soldiers on the move, numbering almost 800– at one point coming within metres of his patrol.

And this was just five kilometres or so from Thua Tich.

While it wasn't immediately apparent what the enemy's motive was, there seemed to only be two possibilities the enemy had in mind– an assault against the Australian Task Force base at Nui Dat which would have had significant psychological consequences on the Australian effort and the politicians back home; or a full-on attack against the more vulnerable, but strategically important provincial village of Baria, situated half way between the major Australian base at Nui Dat and the important sea port of Vung Tau which the Australians needed for re-supplies.

Back in Nui Dat, the Commanding Officer of the Australian Task Force – Brigadier C.M. Pearson MC – faced with this Intel from SAS, had a dilemma.

On the one hand, he had just placed his three battalions into position in other areas of Phuoc Tuy, along with the support elements, and on the other, was suddenly faced with a developing strategic crisis– a large enemy force on his doorstep.

To compound the matter, the other major unit he might have used in such a situation – the SAS – was on the nose as far as he was concerned. According to Major David Chinn, (Brigadier Pearson's Operations Officer) Pearson had become disenchanted with the SAS because of its predilection for demanding extraction whenever it got hairy.

I am informed that Pearson had previously clashed with SAS back in Australia, and is likely to have held a grudge since then. Most likely, Pearson knew little or nothing about the true role and capabilities of SAS, and more importantly, their limitations.

'No sooner do we put them in, they scream to be taken out!' Pearson is reported to have said– a costly exercise.

We did not necessarily accept this as fact when we were told it (at a meeting with General Steve Gower at the AWM) but an examination of the Narratives seemed to confirm some truth in it.

It may just have been coincidental, but the fact is that the actual number of SAS patrols declined in the same period that the 2nd D&E Platoon operated.

But, while military types were rushing to analyse the Narratives to verify that fact and put their own spin on it (a storm within a storm) and while that debate raged within the veteran community, I received a letter that stood the veteran community on its head.

The significance of the letter is that it not only confirms Pearson's opinion of SAS, but at the same time, provides a feasible explanation for the sudden creation of the 2nd D&E Platoon– a platoon of infantrymen that was prepared to tackle the enemy and not just watch them walk by.

If Pearson *did* consider that infantrymen weren't too far removed from the expertise of SAS, it explains why his eyes lit up when there was a sudden surge of infantrymen at his disposal in the HQ Company when the forty reinforcement from the 4th Battalion suddenly rocked up, waiting to be re-posted to other battalions.

Pearson had a large enemy force congregating on his turf, and a platoon of experienced riflemen at his disposal. And he was the Commanding Officer of the Task Force with the power to do whatever needed to be done to get the job done.

He did exactly what any real leader would have done– illegal or not.

Right from the start of the debate, the argument that Brigadier Pearson could do whatever he wanted with soldiers at his disposal– including creating sub-units at will, was put forward by his apologists.

It is an argument hard to argue against.

It made sense to utilise his resources however he wanted, for any contingency.

And since AHQ had made it clear that the brass in Vietnam could manipulate the manpower however it saw fit – *'playing a tune'* as they put it – creating a new platoon to take on that large enemy force congregating in the Xuyen Moc area seemed a right and proper thing to do.

But time was a critical factor. An opportunity to strike at a large enemy force had presented itself. He had no time for bothering with strict military and political protocol.

So, it was done on the sly. No formal paperwork was done to accompany it.

No problem with that of course– paperwork could always be taken care of later.

Unless the sub-unit happened to get itself involved in a series of atrocities.

That could certainly complicate the issue.

Here, Pearson's defenders would argue so what?

So he created a platoon for a specific task, for a short period of time, and got the job done. Where was the harm?

Well the harm lay in the manner in which the platoon was created, the way it operated, and the total disregard for the welfare of the soldiers involved.

Like I said, when the 4th Battalion was returned to Australia, it left behind the forty men who had reinforced it during its tour– all Regular soldiers. But an equal number of national servicemen had *also* joined the battalion during its tour and they, too, had served less than the minimum six months. But in their case, they went home with the battalion.

Three of those men were from my very platoon in "D" Company – Privates Margetts, Foley, and Dooley.

So why did Brigadier Pearson only retain the Regular soldiers for the risky enterprise, and not the 'nashos'?

The only conclusion one can make is that he had one eye on the strategic dilemma that was developing, and another on the politics of the matter with a view to the war's unpopularity back home. But to discriminate between regular soldiers and 'nashos' as Pearson did in this instance, could only lead to ill-feeling between the soldiers involved– that one group received preferential treatment by going home in one piece, while the other became bait.

The second aspect concerns the manner in which the 2nd D&E Platoon was expected to operate– compromising the safety of the men even more than regular infantry activities did.

I refer to the fact that the 2nd D&E Platoon had no officer to command it (which would have occurred should Cabinet have ratified its creation); had no platoon sergeant to organise it (a significant role in any infantry platoon); had no medic or medical supplies (standard in all other infantry platoons); and operated outside the range of artillery (not a regular occurrence).

One cannot make light of those things.

If protocols existed for the operation of an infantry platoon within its normal environment – a battalion – why would such protocols not apply to any *ad hoc* platoon like the 2nd D&E Platoon?

To suggest, as many have, that an officer was not required for the operation of the platoon, is nonsense. Why have officers in charge of infantry platoons at all then?

(Interestingly, for the first few days of the 2nd D&E Platoon's existence, it had both an officer *and* a sergeant– Lt Barry Parkin, and a 'Sgt John Chainey'. Neither remained with the platoon for more than a few days. The only conclusion one can make about that, is that it was initially done for appearance's sake).

Oh yes– there was more to this matter than meets the eye.

This is the letter about Pearson's opinion of SAS that shocked the veteran community, sent to me *and* the Australian War Memorial. It was signed, and contained the author's address:

IN STRICT CONFIDENCE

It is most crucial that the confidential nature of this letter is understood. I have no wish to either distress or embarrass any person. It, I think, corroborates certain claims on the establishment of a "Sabre" Platoon during the tenure of Maj Gen Sandy Pearson whilst he was Commander, 1st Australian Task Force at Nui Dat, South Vietnam.

In the late Nineties, I had lunch with Maj Gen Pearson, at the Union Club, Sydney, of which we are both members. The purpose was to discuss matters relating to the Association of First Infantry Battalions.

After this, discussion broadened and I suggested that, given some extra training, the average Rifleman or Infantry Company could perform as well as the Special Air Service Troopers and Squadrons, or at least to an acceptable level of capability that any shortcomings would be indiscernible. Gen Pearson agreed and then, quite unprompted, said, "Do you know, I suspended the SAS Squadron from operations when I was Task Force Commander".

Gen Pearson went on to reveal:
- He was dissatisfied with the increasing tendency of SAS patrols to call for extraction at the slightest hint they had been observed or would contact the enemy. This was diminishing the flow of good Intelligence and restricting his options as Commander.
- A fairly 'forthright' discussion was held with the Officer Commanding the SAS Sqn, indicating that, if his SAS soldiers were not willing to do their job, he would find alternatives.
- The SAS Sqn was immediately to be withdrawn from operations – the distinct implication was that they were not fit for such and were hindering, if not endangering, TF ops.
- This suspension was indefinite until "retraining" was completed and the SAS Sqn commander could assure him that his soldiers were fit for ops and would not repeat previous behaviour.
- The period of this suspension was, at least, a month.
- Maj Gen Pearson did not further elaborate on this, not did I press him.

However, it was a stunning revelation, given the commonly held view of SAS and, I am sure, Maj Gen Pearson told me to underline his faith in the Australian Infantryman. It is hard to imagine, then, that a Commander of Maj Gen Pearson's skill would leave the gap in his force's capability created by suspension of the SAS Sqn.

Beyond this, I would not further conjecture. I trust that this is useful.

Of course, whether or not the Commander of the SAS would accept that it happened this way is a moot point. He was probably outraged by it. Like I said, it's all about perspective.

Then, there is the question of Intelligence-gathering. I have reason to suspect ASIO had to have played no small part in the formation (and closing down) of the 2nd D&E Platoon.

If ASIO could ever be forced to come clean, I'm convinced that it would have to admit that the Australian Task Force Commanders in Vietnam had access to Intelligence-gathering devices and communication systems far more sophisticated than the enemy ever had. But to admit to having such equipment, would have been to compromise the advantage it provided.

Like what happened back in 1966. The 547 Signals Troop had tracked an army of Viet Cong advancing on Nui Dat carrying a large radio transmitter across the Province for a fortnight (clear evidence of an impending large-scale offensive) but the Commanding Officer – Brigadier David Jackson – had to look the other way and pretend he was unaware of it. Better 6RAR be 'ambushed' and good men die.

So, three years later, when Brigadier Pearson was made aware that another large enemy force was marching down Highway 328 with Baria squarely in its sights, he too, had to play dumb. If he had suddenly stuck one of his battalions in its path, the communications advantage the Australians enjoyed would surely have been negated. So placing an expendable force of left-over, regular infantrymen in the path of that force instead of a regular battalion maintained the status quo.

Mission accomplished. No harm done.

The more we delved into the matter, the more we learned about the army.

For instance, we learned that there had been many *ad hoc* D&E Platoons created as sub-units in Vietnam during the ten years of the war, and done so for various contingencies. Like ours was, they too, were eventually disbanded and the members dispersed after completing whatever they had been tasked with. So if there *were* others, what was the big deal then, about the '2nd D&E Platoon'?

Well, there were two key points– the first relates to the question of leadership; and the second relates to the magnitude of the task set before them.

All the other *ad hoc* platoons were fully functional. They had a legitimate platoon commander and a subordinate chain of command. Therefore, it could go about its task confident that it was operating as Australian infantry platoons were meant to, and with the welfare of the ordinary infantrymen taken into account.

But the 2nd D&E Platoon had no officer commanding it after Lt Barry Parkin was surreptitiously removed. And while Cpl Jim Riddle assumed the role of platoon commander (which he had no right to do) and Major Pratt and Capt Tom Arrowsmith both appeared to be happy with the arrangement, it didn't make it legitimate, or competent.

Indeed, until Riddle assumed control of the infantry contingent, it seemed to escape any officer's attention that having forty infantrymen scattered across APCs without direct leadership was a disaster waiting to happen. The only chain of command that ever existed was that which Cpl Riddle put in place. He 'created' a chain of command as best he could, by selecting men as section-commanders and gave them 'corporal' status, yet had no legal right to do that either. Then to top it off, Riddle was dispensing potent drugs in the field – Dapsone and Paludrine – which he wasn't legally entitled to do either. It was the job of an officer.

On their own, these were significant things that set the 2nd D&E Platoon apart from other *ad hoc* platoons. But as well, it has been generally accepted that no other *ad hoc* D&E Platoon (or any platoon for that matter) was ever tasked with tackling an enemy force as large and as potentially dangerous as the one congregating in the Xuyen Moc area of Phuoc Tuy Province in May of 1969.

It was the *2nd D&E Platoon* that was tasked with interdicting, and engaging that enemy force.

As the debate became more vitriolic, and me bearing the brunt of the enmity, the notion that command of the platoon had been devolved to the Armoured Corps Captain took the argument to a new level.

Could Capt Tom Arrowsmith exercise command of not only his troop of armoured personnel carriers and the men of his Corps, but also a platoon of forty infantrymen scattered throughout that troop of APCs?

Our critics were clutching at straws with that one if they thought he could. Simply, it wasn't feasible that command could be carried out effectively, especially when the combined force was splintered at various times– especially on night ambushes.

How could Arrowsmith possibly exercise effective command from inside an APC at one location, with his force of APCs split into three or four other locations at the very same time– and at each of those positions, a section of infantrymen lying out in the jungle also needing command and direction?

Senior officers might disagree, but it defies belief that any military man could consider such an arrangement satisfactory. The infantry private laying out in the jungle had a completely different perspective.

What it was doing, was playing with men's lives– especially when the full ramifications of what Brigadier Pearson had set the combined force to do, became apparent.

It was negligence. Or dereliction of duty. Or both.

All covered up by deleting any trace of the '2nd D&E Platoon' from the histories of the war.

CHAPTER 11
IN ACTION

In essence, the 2nd D&E Platoon only existed for about a month– from the 12th May to the second week of June or so, at which point it was quickly disbanded.

There were very good reasons for the speed of its disappearance.

But before it was disbanded, the 2nd D&E Platoon certainly made its presence felt. During that month of May, it was involved in a number of engagements with the enemy, especially three significant clashes on the 25th, 29th, and 30th May.

All references to the 'D&E Platoon' (and the emerging threat to the Task Force) are listed below. These include movement, administration, and actual contacts with the enemy. They are taken from the official *'Southeast Asian Conflict diaries'* held by the Australian War Memorial– specifically the 'Headquarters' diary.

Unfortunately, a lot of the army jargon (like SITREPS and LOCSTATS) will mean little to the man in the street, but are included here for military men who care to do a little research of their own should they wish to validate them.

SPECIFIC REFERENCES CONCERNING THE *2nd D&E Platoon* **IN OFFICIAL DOCUMENTS:**

- *11 May '69: (Watermanship Trg -D&E Pl 12-13 May' 69) Annex: C32*
- *12 May '69: (Watermanship Trg - New D&E Pl) 1 Fd Sqn RAE, Item: 4/2/47 Narrative*
- *13 May '69: (D445 LF Bn (Ba Long) East of Dat Do/ South of Xuyen Moc- May ' 69) Annex: C37C*

- *14 May '69: (D&E Pl lifted out by Cav, resupply 2 Tp Cav, AO-SCORPION) Annex: E14*
- *14 May '69: (D&E Pl resupply 2 Tp SCORPION) Maj Rook's Cav Narrative Item: 2/5/1*
- *16 May '69: (D&E Pl -Xuyen Moc, with 2 Tp Cav & 3 Pl W-Coy 4RAR) Sheet: 108, Serial: 1380*
- *16 May '69: (Dustoff - Xuyen Moc, malaria) Sheet: 110, Serial: 1407*
- *16 May '69: (D&E Pl- Xuyen Moc, 2 Tp Cav & 3 Pl W Coy 4RAR) Sheet: 111, Serial 1412*
- *18 May '69: (INTSUM NO: 138-69-PART:12- Comments: expected Baria assaults, Long Green Dat Do, 18-20 May) Annex: G18 See Annex: COMD D G2 Para: 4, re: D445 Bn LF Bn movements between Long Green & Xuyen Moc*
- *18 May '69: (SITREP: 18-21 May '69- Xuyen Moc: refs to D445 Bn here, using beaches, Formosan fishing vessels to re-supply, or Taiwanese poaching?) Annex:G32*
- *18-27 May '69: (3 SAS Sqn patrol reports: 780+ (black & khaki) not green, 10 kms from Thua Tich OPS 69/69*
- *19 May '69: (D&E Pl patrolling -Xuyen Moc & D&E Pl with 2 Tp Cav) Sheet: 128, Serial: 1644*
- *19 May '69: (D&E Pl, Xuyen Moc) Sheet: 132, Serial: 1695*
- *20 May '69: (D&E Pl - Xuyen Moc, with 2 Tp Cav) Sheet: 137, Serial: 1769*
- *22 May '69: (Dustoff - Xuyen Moc, Urgent shrapnel wounds, Dann) Sheet: 150, Serial: 1939*
- *22 May '69: (Mine Incident Report - Xuyen Moc, 30 lbs explosive, 2 WIA (Sappers Targett and Baird) Sheet: 151, Serial: 1956*
- *23 May '69: (SITREP: D&E Pl sweeping area, Xuyen Moc) Sheet: 156, Serial: 2026*
- *23 May '69: (Contact Report: 7 -8 VC, Elms 63 deployed for search) Sheet: 156, Serial 2035.H.*
- *23 May '69: (D&E Pl, with 2 Tp Cav, Xuyen Moc) Sheet: 159, Serial: 2070, HQ Narrative*
- *24 May '69: (I-63 - Xuyen Moc) Sheet: 168, Serial: 2194. HQ Narrative*
- *25 May '69: (D&E Pl - Xuyen Moc,) Sheet: 174, Serial: 2269. HQ Narrative*
- *25 May '69: (2 Tp & D&E Pl-Contact 20 VC, entered D & E ambush, 7 VC Killing Ground) Annex: E25*
- *25 May '69: (D&E Pl ambushed squad size VC) Annex: G 25, Item: 1/ 4 / 152 HQ Narrative*
- *25 May '69: (I - 63, D&E Pl - Xuyen Moc) Sheet: 175, Serial: 2289*
- *25 May '69: (I-63 Contact, 20 VC, Xuyen Moc, hot extraction 2 Tp) Sheet: 175, Serial: 2294*
- *25 May '69: (I-63 D&E Pl, Xuyen Moc in Contact. Sheet: 175, Serial: 2295*

- *26 May '69: (D&E Pl) I-63-2 Tp Cav, Xuyen Moc, 7 Plus KIA, not confirm. Sheet: 176, Serial: 2297.*
- *26 May '69: (Contact sweep no BC VC) Sheet: 177, Serial: 3012*
- *26 May '69: (SCORPION elements to Xuyen Moc for resupply) Sheet: 178, Serial: 3030*
- *27 May '69: (TA elements hit mine Xuyen Moc, standby Dustoff) Sheet: 185, Serial: 3136*
- *27 May' 69: (Dustoff - Urgent unconscious , Xuyen Moc) Sheet: 185, Serial: 3137*
- *27 May '69: (Mine Incident Report - TA21A, Xuyen Moc, 60 lbs explosive) Sheet: 187, Serial: 3157*
- *28 May '69: (D&E Pl & 2 Tp Cav, Xuyen Moc) Sheet: 191, Serial: 2314*
- *28 May '69: (2 Tp 3 Cav Gp, D&E Pl - Xuyen Moc) Sheet: 191, Serial: 2318*
- *28 May '69: (D&E Pl - Xuyen Moc) Sheet: 193, Serial: 3249*
- *29 May '69: (TA2 & D&E Pl- 50VC Ambush) B Sqn 1 Armd Rgt Narrative Item: 2/2/4 (page 2)*
- *29 May '69: (Spooky under op con TA2 -AO - FROG, withdrawal area) Sheet: 199, Serial: 3344*
- *29 May '69: (TA2 has Contact - 50 VC - 10 VC KIA (BC) VC Scattered. Sheet: 199, Serial: 3346*
- *29 May '69: (TA2 & I-63, Thua Tich, 50 VC more. 8 VC (BC) Sheet: 199, Serial: 3347*
- *29 May '69: (I-63 D&E Pl, Thua Tich) Sheet: 199, Serial: 3350*
- *29 May '69: (D&E Pl & 2 Tp ambush Thua Tich, 50 +VC) Maj Rooks Narrative, B Sqn 3 Cav Item: 2/5/1*
- *29 & 30 May '69: (Annex: M- Rook's Ambush Report Thua Tich, D&E Pl call sign 63- 7 mentioned)*
- *29 & 30 May '69:(Annex: M, No: 2 Ambush Map with D&E Pl initialled at listening post) Rooks*
- *29 May '69: (Ambush Thua Tich- INTSUM NO: 150-69- Enemy were composite group Para: 12 (a) (b) Annex: G30*
- *29 May '69: (RE: HQ 1 ALSG INTSUM: Expanded Report: Extract 1 ATF INTSUM 150-69 of 30 May '69) 1 ALSG ANN:34*
- *29 May '69: (D&E Pl engaged 50 enemy Thua Tich) PART: 1 Annex: 34 - 1 ALSG*
- *30 May '69: (Amended Loc Thua Tich, D&E Pl (I-63)Sheet: 200, Serial: 3360*
- *30 May '69: (Bellis- Photos: BEL/69/0351/VN -55 & 0364 -0378, with D&E Pl - 6 mentions)*
- *30 May '69: (0445H Thua Tich claymores fired TA2 - VC in vicinity) Sheet: 200, Serial: 3363*

- *30 May '69: (2 Tp contact, 2 more bodies in front of I-63 loc by sweep) Sheet: 200, Serial: 3364*
- *30 May '69: (1020H - District Chief wants 11 VC KIA village) Seagull Affirm. Sheet: 202, Serial: 3393*
- *30 May '69: (2 Tp Contact, 50 VC more, 11 KIA (BC) 3 (BT) etc. Sheet: 202, Serial: 3399.*
- *30 May '69: (TA2 in Contact receiving RPG, small arms fire, 1410H) Sheet: 203, Serial: 3412.*
- *30 May '69: (SITREP: Contact TA2 hit by RPG) Sheet: 204, Serial: 3421.*
- *30 May '69: (Bushranger 71. TA2 contact: 3 KBA (BC) 8 KBA (Poss), 2 KIA (BC) Sheet: 204, Serial: 3430.*
- *30 May '69: (Bushranger 71. spotted 2-3 VC trees, smoke -fired at) Sheet: 205, Serial: 3431.*
- *30 May '69: (2 Tp at Xuyen Moc 1920H) Sheet: 206, Serial: 3445.*
- *30 May '69: (Contact Report: 9 dressed in khaki & black etc & body count: 18 KIA) Sheet: 206, Serial: 3450*
- *30 May '69: (Serial numbers: AK47s) Sheet: 206, Serial: 3451.*
- *30 May '69: (Bushranger 71. claims: 4 VC KBA, 8 VC KBA (Poss) Sheet: 206, Serial: 3453.*
- *31 May '69: (Bushranger 71. reports 3 bodies removed, 6 pits (grave site) empty. Sheet: 208, Serial: 3480.*
- *31 May '69: (Bushranger 71. 7 KIA total route: 328) Sheet: 208, Serial: 3481.*
- *31 May '69: (SHQ & supporting elements back to Nui Dat) Sheet: 209, Serial: 3492.*
- *31 May '69: (2 Tp group return to Nui Dat from AO - SCORPION) with Woolan's Pl from FSPB: Virginia.*
- *2 June '69: (D&E Pl & 1 Tp (Lawrence) Xuyen Moc "Garry Owen") Sheet: 11, Serial: 160 HQ Narrative Item: 1 / 4 / 153*
- *2 June '69: (1 Tp plus HQ 1 ATF def Pl AO- Scorpion) Maj Rooks RAAC, Item: 2 / 5 / 2, 1 - 30 June 1969*
- *2 June '69: (SITREP: Pearson, has 1 Tp plus HQ 1 ATF def Pl AO-SCORPION) Annex: E2 Item: 1 / 4 / 156 Page: 2, (d) (2) has 1 Tp plus HQ 1 ATF def Pl & one sect Mor Pl, 5 RAR, Scorpion. Pearson CMI Brig*
- *Comd Orders. Annex: E 2, Item: 1 / 4 / 156, Annexes E - N, 1 -30 June 1969. These Sitrep orders signed on behalf of CMI Pearson Brig Comd, by Officer Maj Chinn, S3. These are orders signed recognising HQ 1ATF Def Pl, in AO-Scorpion.*
- *3 June '69: (1 Tp AO - SCORPION-ambushing) Sheet: 20, Serial: 291*
- *4 June '69: (Mine Incident - 45 lbs explosive) Sheet: 25, Serial: 349.*
- *4 June '69: (1 Tp Contact Scorpion- receiving AK47 fire) Sheet: 25, Serial: 354 & 355.*
- *4 June '69: (1 Tp with HQ 1ATF Def Pl, in AO-Scorpion) Maj Rooks, Item: 2 / 5 / 2 RAAC*

- *5 June '69: (1 Tp & D&E Pl at Xuyen Moc) Sheet: 34, Serial: 474,*
- *6 June '69: (Dustoff, 1 Tp) Sheet: 43, Serial: 600.*
- *6 June '69: (1 Tp in Contact: 8 VC 2310H -returning fire RPG) This is D&E Pl (though not mentioned) Sheet: 47 Serial: 659*
- *6 June '69: (SITREP: has this contact above- 6 June, 84 Rear Services Group NVA) Annex: G32, page 2, part: 4 (b)(d)with Conclusions: Part: 5,. The bulk of D445 LF Bn remains unlocated but may have moved into Long Hais*
- *6 June '69: (HQ 1 ALSG INTSUM 1 June '69 -PART I, (d) refers to D&E Pl, 29/5/69, (h) 6 June contact Intell reports)*
- *7 June '69: (SITREP: 1 Tp Elem HQ & D&E Pl, continued AIF Scorpion) Sheet: 49, Serial: 691*
- *7 June '69: (Contact Amend TA 12 - Xuyen Moc - 2 VC KIA) Sheet: 52, Serial: 742*
- *7 June '69: (D and E PL - Xuyen Moc with 1 Tp) Sheet: 57., Serial: 821*
- *8 June '69: (1 Tp left Xuyen Moc now at YS623650) Sheet: 63, Serial 902*
- *8 June '69: (1 Tp and D and E Pl back in NUI DAT) Sheet: 63, Serial: 913*
- *8 June '69: (SITREP has 1 Tp returning to 1 ATF base from AO-FROG) Annex: E8*
- *8 June '69: (1 Tp returned from AO-FROG and remained in 1 ATF Base) Maj Rooks, Item: 2 /5 / 2 RAAC Narrative June '69*
- *9 June: (1 Tp returned from ambushing in AO FROG) Sheet; 65, Serial: 941.*
- *9 June '69: (1 Tp TA elms, & elms D&E Pl back to Xuyen Moc , Scorpion & Frog - Woolan's Platoon Elms) Sheet: 72, Serial 1032*
- *9 June '69: 1 Tp continued with phase: 2 OPS "Garry Owen" AO- Scorpion after a short period in 1 ATF) Maj Rooks (as above)*
- *12-13 June '69: (most of 2nd D&E Pl attend R&C Vung Tau, with others posted to Woolan's Pl Saigon Guard)*
- *18 June '69 (most members of 2nd D&E Pl posted to 9RAR)*

As far as infantry actions are concerned, at least until the events of May 29th and 30th, they were unremarkable. Small contacts; small, section-sized ambushes. What was certainly different, was the method of deployment (on APCs); a new awareness of the danger of mines; the manner in which the infantry were used (section-sized ambushes); and the method of laying down ambushes involving other sub-units.

And when it is all boiled down, it is the 2nd D&E Platoon's involvement in the ambush that occurred at the gates to that ruined, abandoned village called Thua Tich on the evening of May 29th 1969 that matters most– an ambush that exemplified all the very best in the noble traditions of the Australian fighting man.

And at the same time, tarnished the reputation of the Australian Defence Force in ways that would always haunt every man involved for the rest of our lives.

To elaborate on the detailed list provided above, I now include references from the Armoured Corps Narratives (also found in the *Southeast Asian diaries*) and especially to the following entries:

https://www.awm.gov.au/collection/records/awm95/2/5/awm95-2-5-1.pdf

In which the following hand-written notes appear:

- (entry of the 29th May): "2 Tp supported by the D&E Pl ambushed and (sic) estimated 50+ enemy moving along the road from South to North resulting in 8 en KIA (BC)…….Spooky assisted 2 TP in denying the enemy an FUP (forming up place) and infiltrating the killing area…."

- (entry also of the 29th May, on the next page): "Further to the 2 Tp contact at 292030h. Sweeps at first light locate 11 enemy KIA (BC); 3 WIA (blood trails)…"

- (entry of the 30th May): "2 Tp was engaged by three to four enemy with RPG 7 whilst returning to Xuyen Moc. 2 Tp swept through the contact area containing a further seven to ten enemy resulting in five enemy KIA (BC)……."

And in Annexe M of that document, type-written notes provide a fuller overview of Arrowsmith's organisation of the ambush location.

2 Troop was divided into four units, spread around the general area of Thua Tich, as follows:

- Arrowsmith's HQ plus a Mortar Carrier and an APC Recovery vehicle were hidden among trees at the gates to Thua Tich (supported by a section of the infantry led by Cpl Kevin Lloyd-Thomas)
- a section of the 2nd D&E Platoon (led by Cpl James Riddle) was located approximately 500 metres south of Arrowsmith's position in a 'listening post' position, without APC support;
- while the remaining sections of APCs– each with a group of infantrymen from the 2nd D&E Platoon attached, were located in cut-off positions a couple of clicks from Arrowsmith's position

That the combined force at Thua Tich that night included the Mortar Carrier and an APC Recovery vehicle (both located at Arrowsmith's position) along with the specific placement of sub-units by Brig Pearson *and* Arrowsmith is a clear indication that the brass expected something major to occur that night.

As did the presence of a powerful gunship – a Douglas AC-47, colloquially called 'Spooky' – sitting idly by in Xuyen Moc.

More proof that this was no accidental, or incidental, ambush we were about to be involved in.

This was a direct response to the Intelligence gathered by SAS and other means, suggesting that the congregating force spied by those SAS reconnaissance patrols was on its way down Highway 328 towards Thua Tich– and there we were, the 2nd D&E Platoon, without an officer or a platoon sergeant, divided into four sections and scattered across four sets of APCs sitting there like lambs to the slaughter.

And experts will still argue that Arrowsmith could 'lead' effectively from where he was located?

No– any objective analysis of the prevailing situation that night makes it obvious that this was a clear case of deliberate endangerment of the infantry contingent regardless of whichever direction the enemy came.

And the men endangered the most were those at the listening post with Cpl Jim Riddle. They were on their own– not only without APC support, but almost in the cross-hairs of Arrowsmith's machine-guns.

That the entire force was also outside the range of artillery, as Arrowsmith attests to in *Fighting to the Finish* (Ekins, Allan & Unwin) renders Brigadier Pearson's decision to employ the force as he did, reckless at best.

Luckily, 'Spooky' saved the day.

That– and the heroics by Cpl Jim Riddle's section.

For there to be such an arrangement meant that there had to have been gallantry medals at stake.

There were.

CHAPTER 12
THE CORRUPTIONS

It was what happened afterwards though, upon which this narrative hinges.

One successful ambush is hardly worth writing home about– let alone a book. And the thing that underpins it all is the series of contentions that occurred the very next day, which resulted in the corruption of the service records of every man in that platoon.

The 2nd D&E Platoon was disbanded less than a week later.

There are no documents explaining why the platoon was disbanded, simply because there are no documents even recording its creation. Therefore, the explanations can only be subjective.

There can only be one explanation for the swift disbandment of that platoon and the scattering of its members cross other units– to obviate the potential for those contentions that occurred to be discussed widely by the men involved.

Thrust into new units like we were gave us little opportunity to reflect on, or gossip about what had transpired. Just fitting in took enough effort.

At best, the service records of all of us showed only that we had served in 'HQ Company'. The trouble with *that*, is that HQ Company was considered to be something of an infantry graveyard.

No man wanted that on their service records.

But what it was, was a master-stroke of the military. Erase all the evidence of an illegally created platoon by officially lumping us all in together into the one, legitimate D&E Platoon on paper, and it would also serve to disguise any contentions.

Except for the thirty-nine infantry Privates caught up in it– men whose service records needed to be accurate in decades to come when what they actually *did* in the war was a necessary component for claiming a war pension.

Or when other veterans refuted their stories of exploits with the '2nd D&E Platoon'.

Not that it was a consideration for the senior officers involved in these corruptions. After all, their salaries, their superannuation and their pensions were always guaranteed.

No, not only would the men of the 2nd D&E Platoon always have to point to a blank spot in their service records, and still try to prove they had been involved in matters of substance, they would also have to contend with a disbelieving veteran community howling them down.

It would be a difficult task– a task made even more difficult when official documents had been doctored.

But given the gravity of what unfolded at Thua Tich, the individual service records of the lowly infantry Private soldier was a minor concern of those officers involved.

What *they* had to contend with was the fact that there is no statute of limitations applying to war crimes.

Two photographers – army sergeant Chris Bellis and civilian photographer Dennis Gibbons – had joined the combined armour/infantry force under Capt Tom Arrowsmith's command.

Not one– but *two* photographers.

There were hundreds of units and sub-units at work in Vietnam at that time, yet *two* photographers were embedded just in this one particular platoon?

Most veterans would agree that having a single photographer embedded in an infantry platoon at any time was unusual. Having *two* photographers embedded in a makeshift, combined force was extraordinary.

I never saw a photographer at any other time, in any other unit I served in– just on those few days in May of 1969 with that improvised armour/infantry force.

There had to be a good reason to have *two* of them embedded with us. I could only conclude that something big was in the air, and the 'brass' needed to record it for resumes, and medals.

And they didn't hold back either. They photographed everything.

Everything.

Including the atrocities that were committed.

Strangely, what they didn't record that night were any images of 'Spooky' in action– the fixed-wing aircraft that was capable of massive firepower, and which, by any measure, probably saved the combined force from annihilation during that ambush, despite the great bravery shown by the soldiers on the ground.

Given that Dennis Gibbons would eventually tell one of our sleuths, Ted Colmer, that he'd been rushed from Saigon to join the combined force the night before, but didn't manage to take any pictures prior to the ambush, or of the actual ambush, adds to the intrigue.

As Ted Colmer reported (sic):

> *'...I have also spoken to Gibbons [about forty minutes] via phone, and he insists he was transported from Saigon for the night ambush with Arrowsmith, and they, Pearson et al, expected a major battle [Thua Tich] on the afternoon or evening of the 28 May 69?? Said Sandy (Pearson) was one of his closest friends and wouldn't release any Thua Tich pics, albeit, the AWM will release any other Denis Gibbons' collection pics readily. Yes, Dennis Gibbons [and please call me Dr Gibbons?] wanker!! 79 years old, was, and I repeat; maintains he was at the ambush site for the duration with Arrowsmith?? Why then not take night pics of Spooky etc.. Utter bullshit, and well scripted.'*

I will come back to the actual ambush later in this narrative.

It is the atrocities that occurred that need to be outlined here because all else is secondary. What might have been celebrated as a great victory, was sidelined by the urgent attempts to cover-up those atrocities.

They were the headline act.

Not that they were recorded at the time, either. No sir– there isn't any mention of *them* in any record either. Not in the after-action reports submitted by Capt Tom Arrowsmith. And not in any of the Narratives which serve as the historical record.

Just in the photographs taken by those two photographers– and in the memory banks of the men concerned.

And over time, both sources were becoming diminished too. Photographs were destroyed; memories faded.

But there was just enough carelessness, just enough evidence not hidden, and just enough guts by those of us willing to stand apart and tell the whole story, for the truth to be revealed.

The facts of the matter were simple and clear cut.

In the morning after the ambush at Thua Tich, infantrymen were ordered to drag a number of bodies into a bomb crater where the Engineer's mini-team that was present wired them up with C4 and claymore mines– and blew them up.

This is alleged war crime number *one*– the mutilation of corpses.

Other bodies were strung upside down to the backs of APCs – including that of the troop commander's vehicle, Capt Tom Arrowsmith's – to be taken into the village of Xuyen Moc as trophies in what was nothing more than a propaganda exercise.

This is alleged war crime number *two*– the degrading of enemy dead.

Jim Riddle – the former English Marine who took over the reins of the 2nd D&E Platoon when Lt Barry Parkin disappeared – placed that matter firmly on the public record in 2005 when he said (sic):

> *'...The day after the Thua Tich ambush, we all gathered to dispose of the dead, except for those we tied to the tailgates of the APCs. The Brigadier came out and shook hands and then we started off in column to Xuyen Moc……..'*

As had happened to me in 1987, this comment resulted in swift condemnation by former members of the Armoured Corps.

Their outrage was but a smokescreen; treating bodies that way wasn't exactly a new phenomenon.

Only a couple of months earlier in 1969, Lt Col J. Fitzgerald (Field Liaison Division) records comments by Brigadier Pearson and others in a Memorandum from a CORDS Conference held in Nui Dat, suggesting that 'displaying bodies in some 'inoffensive manner' might be an effective propaganda tool in assisting locals with their own defence against Viet Cong influence.

Of course, exactly how that would be put into action, wasn't spelled out.

But over time, various stories had begun to emerge about how the bodies of enemy dead were dealt with in other situations.

It was a subject I had never pondered to any degree. I had always just gone with the flow, doing what was asked of me in any situation. Never questioning, never needing to.

When I was first posted to the 4th Battalion – one of the nation's most respected battalions – it was impressed on me very quickly that enemy bodies were to be treated with dignity, to be neatly buried where they died if possible, or taken into the nearest village for burial, and *not* degraded or displayed in any offensive manner.

I guess in war men have to deal with decisions like that and the officers of the 4th Battalion sleep well, I think.

Not like some.

The fact was, the events that happened at Thua Tich that morning – blowing them up in bomb craters and strapping them upside down to the backs of APCs – was tantamount to *degrading* bodies, and such treatment was covered by the Geneva Conventions which we were signatories to.

Brigadier C. Pearson's overt support for such treatment of dead bodies may have left him open to a charge of war crimes– except that he was the nation's foremost military leader in the war zone, and the hierarchy back in Australia weren't necessarily always aware of what was happening on the ground.

The mistake that Brigadier Pearson made, with the prospect of a major clash with the enemy getting him very excited (as long as he wasn't personally involved) was ensuring that *two* photographers were embedded in the combined force to record what he expected would be a major action, and let them snap, snap, snap away.

As it was, eventually, those photographs duly landed on the desk of Major General Stuart Graham, Deputy Chief of the General Staff at Army Headquarters, Canberra, as well as the Australian Army Public Relations Service.

Major General Graham was horrified by the images.

In turn, the matter went up the chain to Major General A. MacDonald– the Adjutant General, who was just as horrified. As a consequence, he was compelled to instruct the brass back in Vietnam that humane treatment of the dead was *mandatory* under the Conventions.

Accordingly, Brigadier Pearson was forced to amend his philosophy that dropping shattered, headless bodies in village squares was an effective propaganda exercise. Two months after the events at Thua Tich, he issued instructions to all commanders under his command to *'ensure that every effort is made to comply with the Conventions'* – and that, from then on, enemy dead were to be *'treated with the respect due to a human being'*.

Someone had been given a swift kick up the backside.

This was all well and good– except that what happened at Thua Tich had happened under the *old* rules.

And did not take into account a third matter that occurred later on the afternoon of May 30th 1969– as the combined armoured/ infantry force moved at speed towards the village of Xuyen Moc where those bodies were finally cut loose and deposited in the town square.

Like I said in *The War Within*, some sleeping dogs should be left sleeping– except that Ted Colmer poked a stick at this one in an email which set tongues wagging.

He mentioned the villagers of Xuyen Moc hating us,

'……*for brassing them up en route to the village.*'

"…*brassing them up*," did he say?

He had. The genie was out.

Alleged war crime number *three*. Indiscriminate shooting at civilians.

Three illegal acts, all on the one day. It had to be a record for Australian soldiers in the war.

This was the incident I wrote about in the article published in the SMH almost twenty years earlier– where troopers opened fire on a group of villagers tending their fields and where, in my recall, a woman and child were killed.

In an interview with Frank Waker, Jim Riddle echoed my version. He said that he recalled 'bullets ripping into a youth leading a water buffalo' first of all, and then a woman and child 'knocked flat as bullets slammed into her' and 'the infant sent flying through the air.'

As well as me, both Ted Colmer and Jim Riddle had now confirmed that third serious matter.

And they weren't to be the last to validate it.

No wonder all trace of the 2nd D&E Platoon had 'disappeared'.

Proving that atrocities had been committed was one thing; proving that the 2nd D&E Platoon was erased from all records of the war to cover those atrocities up, was altogether another.

Luckily, there were those photographs.

What had been designed as a record of a great victory and the means to secure gallantry awards for more officers became the link.

CHAPTER 13
THE COLLECTIVE

If one could have taken a step back, one might have observed an interesting phenomenon.

Six of us, in particular – all striving for one common purpose – went about a collective task via routes as distinctly different as our personalities and skills levels.

Ted 'the Fed' Colmer had been an ASIS-trained undercover cop (so he told us) before becoming a whistle-blower and finding himself out of a career. By his own admission, he had become a cocaine-addict, a recluse and a drunk, and needed to get his teeth into a project to break the cycle. He jumped at the opportunity to utilise his policing experience in the gathering of evidence, and the close analysis of documentation and military detail. But probably more than anyone else, he suffered from PTSD and had to be kept at arm's length.

Kevin Lloyd-Thomas had done two tours of Vietnam as an infantryman, and had been my section-commander in the 2nd D&E Platoon during one tour. In recent years, he had become more a man of the sea, sailing yachts from one place to another. He generally moved in a higher social scene than the rest of us– a people person, polite and restrained, more a negotiator than a confrontationist.

Richard Bigwood was a communicator at the everyman level– a friend and good man to all, not prone to excitability, and moved easily within veteran circles without ruffling feathers. He connected, and gathered like a squirrel.

Dennis Manski was a reluctant conscript to the matter. He'd contacted me in 1995 requesting a copy of the movie films I'd shot in the war. Other than Lloyd-Thomas, he was the only other man from the 2nd D&E Platoon I had ever stumbled across, and since I was searching for my own truths about the matter, I'd asked him what he remembered about the Platoon. He said he had 'no recollections' of the 2nd D&E Platoon, other than that he 'had served in it', had 'some memories' of what had gone down, but that they were 'all jumbled up', or something similar. He urged me to let the matter go, to be at peace with the world (which was his own wish) and we never spoke again. He did enter the battle about 2006, but remained a distant collaborator, only contributing if his memory was jogged or when directly asked, or if he spotted something being written that he disagreed with, or that didn't gel.

Allan Roach was a quiet achiever, drawing the line at his efforts being made public. He preferred anonymity– and made it clear he wasn't interested in provoking controversy or being drawn into any. He recoiled from the shit fight that had broken out across the veteran community in relation to the matter, and chose to focus on the make-up of the platoon membership as his contribution, and together with his wife Kay, worked assiduously at it.

Other former members of the platoon just wanted no angst in their lives. Richard Appleby wrote:

> *'Don, Thank You Don! For fighting for recognition for us, even if it meant for everyone, yes you are right, wardrobe experts will come out of the woodwork and be critical,* (their opinion is irrelevant) *and your continued support for Jimmy Riddle is a credit to you. I do not have anything to do with any RSL or veterans groups or associations, just an old bloke fading away with the Grandkids and Family. Anyway Don Thanks and God Bless'*

Bob Secrett had a bigger battle to contend with at the time– severe infection of a knee replacement. So, he advised that he wouldn't be directly involved in the fight, but wanted to be kept abreast of every development.

And Des Blazely wrote out his recollections in a seven-page letter and sent it to me to use however necessary. Included in his recollections were the following points (sic):

> *'……I remember Don Tate as a tall, blonde, fit, conscientious soldier……*(after the ambush at Thua Tich) *…….we secured the area, and the bodies, weapons, ammo, etc. were given an Engineers burial in a bomb crater in the vicinity of the Thua Tich gates. We moved to a safe distance but did still receive remnants of human bodies fall out of the sky…*(after the VC ambush on the way to Xuyen Moc)*…at least two of*

these dead VC were ordered to be attached to the rear of an APC and towed back to Xuyen Moc. I recall that one of these bodies was a woman. On arrival back in Xuyen Moc, these bodies were put 'on show' in the village square behind a barbed wire barrier...in Xuyen Moc I remember Normie Rowe playing a guitar and singing ...I was in the CP at FSB Dampier when the initial contact involving Don Tate (now in 9RAR) was in action. I recall some of the advice/instructions offered at that time...I find it very hard to believe that there could be any reason to deny existence of that 2nd D&E Platoon... I would be only too happy to be interviewed in relation to the facts presented...

While I saw *my* role as the driver– moving the matter forward, keeping it before the veteran community, using any opportunity, any tactic, to advance the investigation. Words were my weapon – best used to effect in emails to men of significance – chasing down shadows, forcing the debate, challenging officers to speak out, and the like. It was throwing word grenades as it were, much like we did when we threw hand grenades into the swamps at Baria all those years ago.

Although both were murky environments, the difference between 'fishing' at Baria and 'fishing' within the veteran community was that at Baria absolutely nothing floated to the surface.

On the other hand, you never knew what might float to the top in Australia.

For example, as my memoir – *The War Within* – was in the final pre-publishing stage, Murdoch Books became anxious about using Capt Tom Arrowsmith's name in it. Like in all memoirs, using real names can be a tricky exercise. At times, names or individual characteristics of a real person must be altered to hide a person's identity.

But I saw no point in writing an historical account and not including historical figures, wherever possible.

It was an opportune time. Ted Colmer had just located an interview conducted between an ABC reporter and Capt Tom Arrowsmith just after the ambush at Thua Tich. He found it under the noses of the Memorial's so-called 'researchers'.

So I sent out an abrupt email into the veteran community.

'If anyone else has any doubt that Captain Tom Arrowsmith was the troop commander of the force that included the 2nd D&E Platoon, here is film evidence, and proof. My publishers have requested I delete Arrowsmith from my work because I cannot prove who ordered the destruction of bodies at Thua Tich. I am open to suggestions- WHO DID ORDER THE INFANTRYMEN TO ATTACH BODIES TO

THE BACKS OF APCs AND BLOW OTHER BODIES UP ON MAY 30th? Why has the 'official' version changed three times over 38 years, and why is it that in the two enquiries carried out, why is it that not one infantryman from that platoon, nor George Pratt, nor Lt Parkin, nor Brigadier Pearson ever been asked to an enquiry, let alone give evidence? Who is being protected?

Of course, 'grenades' like that didn't necessarily win friends and influence people. But it brought the contentions into focus, and sent a clear message.

Right from the outset, we were beset with two difficulties.

In the first place, we had all only been infantry Privates and therefore had a very limited knowledge of military terms, organisation, and its record-keeping. Thus, our ability to interpret and understand the ramifications of much of the military information we examined, could be flawed.

And secondly, we didn't approach the task in an intelligent or orderly way– each one of us pursued the matter privately, proudly announcing every 'find' as if it was a contest, and disseminating it widely with our own interpretation and opinions attached. It was a fragmented, scattergun approach.

Yet strangely, it kept the veteran community interested (even if was only to throw stones at us) and bit by bit, the evidence accumulated.

And from that, just like a jigsaw puzzle, the pieces began to fit and the bigger picture emerged to an incredulous audience.

Allan Roach and Edward (Ted) Colmer were two of the first to make solid contributions.

Roach focussed on determining the list of members who formed the 2nd D&E Platoon.

It was a difficult task– given that the 4th Battalion Roll Books weren't available to draw from. According to the Australian War Memorial, they'd been 'destroyed', despite their historical significance.

Curiously, documents recording the contribution of men in war, like Roll Books, had been destroyed.

If indeed they had been.

We'd learned not to trust anything the Australian War Memorial said.

It was just the sort of battle that Ted Colmer liked to pursue– putting the sword to bureaucrats. He took the battle to the Administrative Appeals Tribunal.

It didn't get him too far though. The 'establishment' had shut up shop.

He kept us informed of his progress, thus:

> '...I have been pursuing these matters with the AAT [tribunal privilege] because the disappearance of Rollbooks identifies the source of the documentary Disposal Schedules: 371 & 374 - ARMY FORMATIONS VIETNAM, with absolute evidence of clandestine AWM entrustment [Robert O'Neill AWM, Bruce White 'Secretary to Army 1971' and Thea Exley 'Chief Archivist 1971'] proposed and consented to the disposal schedule's Vietnam 1971 & 1973, concerning all historical and evidentiary Vietnam war records, and especially those records compromising Defence. More importantly, these disposal schedules provide an entry point of investigation to understanding and identifying the primary motives of their most maliciously contrived cover-ups, with exposure of an "evidentiary trail" that directly and exclusively involves the AWM's repository ability to conceal damning records! The Registrar AAT has now finally directed the NAA Solicitor to conduct a search of the AWM [conference 23 October 2008] so I am still waiting for the expected and up-dated T-Documents - with the AWM denying the Rollbooks are in their custody. What they don't realise, is that I already have reference to the CERTIFICATES OF DISPOSAL DOCUMENTS HQ 1ATF IN MY POSSESSION, so I am anxiously waiting for this Solicitor to provide written evidence of the AWM's denial!...'

Colmer had unlocked one of the military's best-kept secrets– the sanitisation of documents which may have compromised or embarrassed the army and its senior officers. What he was getting at was what we all feared– alleging that the Australian War Memorial was party to the deliberate fudging of history, to obfuscation, and used various methods to withhold information or deny it to inquisitive eyes.

What's more, forcing them to produce anything via government administrative tribunals was virtually impossible.

Wheels within wheels were turning.

Colmer's frustration at the bureaucratic roadblocks began to bubble over. He wrote (sic):

> 'The AAT is a toothless tiger run by "dikes" with no inherent power, except the statutes brought before it. The Federal Court is the place to exact the truth about

this AWM autonomous endemically corrupt entity. I questioned the overwhelming preponderance of real feministic overbearing "women" working within the AAT, via an Attorney General complaint. That wouldn't have gone over very well....'

I agreed– it wouldn't have gone over too well at all. Especially that first comment.

Eventually, Colmer abandoned the Tribunal option. Too much bureaucracy; too much time between hearing dates; too many excuses.

We had to be content with the knowledge that if nothing else, we had learned how 'history' could be manipulated to maintain the desired image of the Anzac 'legend'.

Allan Roach came up with a full list of names of the men who had formed the 2nd D&E Platoon– with a little help from others:

NOMINAL ROLL OF THE 2nd DEFENCE & EMPLOYMENT PLATOON:

Pte Peter Denzil ALLEN, 61905
Pte Richard Henry APPLEBY, 111814
Pte John Louis ARNOLD, 157064
Pte Melville Leonard BANN, 12021065
Pte Robert Stanley BELGROVE, 218472
Pte Richard Alan BIGWOOD, 218582
Pte Hugh Gray BROWNING, 1202046
Pte Desmond John BLAZELY, 61841
Pte Robert Joseph CAIRNS, 218602
Pte Raymond James CLARK, 312589
Pte Edward William COLMER, 218512
Pte Cecil Roley EBSWORTH, 218536
Pte Ray Charles ELLIS, 154459
Pte Leonard ELLCOMBE, 312601
Pte Robert Jon ENRIGHT, 1202112
Pte Colin James FAHY, 1201633
Pte Richard Brian HOWIE, 4402
Pte Graham John HYDE, 312567
Pte Kevin Godfrey LLOYD-THOMAS, 216853
Pte Dennis Noel MANSKI, 175509

Pte Michael Paul MCAULAY, 1202043
Pte Dennis James MCGREGOR, 312644
Pte Athol Evan MILLAR, 61925
Pte Peter Stuart MORGAN, 218084
Pte Donald Richmond MOSS, 218523
Pte Steven Francis PATERSON, 5411720
Pte Ian Raymond RAMADGE, 39871
Pte Brian RENNIE, 312641 (Deceased DOW 9RAR)
Pte James Bertram RIDDLE, 311858,
Pte Allan James ROACH, 218488
Pte Stuart Alban ROSS, 123326
Pte Owen William SCHULER, 1201677
Pte Robert Stanley SECRET, 7121
Pte Anthony SEYCHELL, 39483
Pte David Halliday SIMPSON, 1202045
Pte Terry John SLATTERY, 44826
Pte Donald William TATE, 1201907
Pte William Harold WHITNEY, 54802
Pte Geoffrey Clynton WILLIAMS, 44795

Thirty-nine men in all— all but discarded from this part of the histories of the war. In a nutshell then, the facts were simple.

- Thirty-nine riflemen— all regular army, and all from the 4th Battalion, were gathered on the 11th May 1969 to form a 'new' D&E Platoon in HQ Company the next day;

- 2nd Lt Barry Parkin was detached from 4RAR and attached to this Platoon, for the purpose of raising, and training it;

- Some reacall a 'Sgt John Henry Chainey/ Cheney' who was supposedly, temporarily seconded from 4RAR's Pioneer Section to assist in such training (but his name doesn't appear in the 4RAR Roll-Call). But after the 'watermanship training' stint at Baria, that sergeant returned to Australia with the rest of the 4th Battalion, and Lt Barry Parkin disappeared;

- Two days later, we embarked on Phase 2 of Operation Garry Owen as 'assault troopers' under the command of Captain Tom Arrowsmith of B Sqn 3 Cavalry Regiment.

The rest didn't quite make the history books.

CHAPTER 14
ASSAULT TROOPERS

During this time, I received two interesting sets of documents from the Australian War Memorial– the Roll Books of HQ Company; and a comprehensive pile of records relating specifically to the 'D&E Platoon'.

The HQ Company Roll Books made interesting reading. Especially since those from the battalions had supposedly been destroyed.

They confirmed our arrival in the Company– but for some reason, they record the date of our arrival as the 19th May 1969.

Yet there we'd been, throwing grenades into the swamps at the Song Cao Bridge at Baria on the 12th and 13th May.

Somewhere along the way, if you are stupid enough to believe Army documentation, we had all 'disappeared' for five days during the war!

The actual Roll Books pages are included at the end of this narrative.

There are four pages of them that record our attendance in HQ Company– as well as leave, sick parades, and so on.

Most importantly, they show who was where, and when, on any given day. And they clearly show me as being present on every day of this platoon's operations.

And damned if the men of the 2nd D&E Platoon weren't *'assault troopers'*. It was quite a revelation when we heard about it.

There we were thinking we were just a rag-bag assortment of leftover infantrymen carrying rifles– and there was the Commander of the Task Force apparently seriously considering us as his personal *assault troopers*.

Brigadier Pearson was kind enough to send me a personal letter informing me of it.

How that even came about was an interesting aside, yet in the greater scheme of things, Brigadier Pearson's involvement in the battle to validate the platoon raised more questions than answers. What's more, rather than enhancing our profile among other infantry veterans, being regarded as 'assault troopers' became another source of ridicule.

Especially since there'd been some considerable banter among veterans about the performance of the elite SAS Regiment during the same period that the 2nd D&E Platoon was out and about.

How Brigadier Pearson became another cog in the process of validating the platoon he had actually created (and disbanded very quickly) arose out of another 'ambush'– albeit it of a different kind.

By August 2007, Adam Rainford's documentary was coming along nicely, but it was essentially personality-driven, light on concrete evidence. My personal battle had been the focus from the start, and I had done a few set pieces. Kevin Lloyd-Thomas and Jim Riddle had given him interviews.

But Ted Colmer and Richard Bigwood were both reluctant to do so.

Colmer – who also had a hand on the steering wheel – had a phobia about being seen in public on account of his previous employment, and was reluctant to do interviews of any sort. Actually, he'd been sacked as an undercover cop we learned, and the revelation gave our opponents another angle to attack us from.

Any chink in the personal armour was fair game.

But Colmer did have a flair for the dramatic. He liked to maintain a low profile, slide in from the shadows, and resisted the limelight. But he harboured recognition, and was keen on a documentary of his own. Not that he broadcast that fact to all and sundry.

With the exception of Major George Pratt, the other officers who played significant roles in the matter maintained a strict public silence. They knew what side their bread was buttered on– and assisting us in any way to prove that they had been complicit in military corruption, in any respect, wasn't a wise move.

Major George Pratt had obviously learned that.

Following his interview with Adam Rainford, he was set upon by his peers. He never uttered another word. Even moved house.

Major David Chinn– Pearson's Ops Officer in Vietnam, and the man most likely to have done the administrative work in creating the 2nd D&E Platoon, had died without clarifying any aspect of the matter. That was most unfortunate.

Major Ron Rooks– former CO of the Armoured Corps, and the 'Seagull' who ordered compliance with the request for bodies to be taken into Xuyen Moc for 'propaganda purposes' wouldn't say a word.

Captain Tom Arrowsmith had been an inveterate traveller ever since the furore had started and couldn't be located, though he *did* ring me once. It was Christmas, 2006. He wasn't happy with the way our investigation was going, but did give me some insights into various aspects of the matter– specifically that Pearson had been 'shitting himself' all night knowing what he'd done and being aware of the possible consequences of pitting a vastly-outnumbered force against an army of Viet Cong.

Lt Ray Woolan– the officer who'd led the other D&E Platoon, had spoken with officials from the Australian War Memorial and had had a private conversation with Kevin Lloyd-Thomas, but made it obvious he wasn't about to comment publicly either.

So, there was only one possibility left to engage – the ageing, revered former Commanding officer of the Australian Task Force in Vietnam, 1968-1969 – Brigadier C.M.I. Pearson himself.

And the only way we were going to actually get *him* to speak was to catch him off guard.

That opportunity arose at the Vietnam Veterans March held in the Blue Mountains in August 2007.

I'd gone there as a flag-bearer for the 9th Battalion. I'd be sharing the honour with Richard Bigwood. In my case, this would be the last time I'd ever march in such a parade before my hip and knee gave away completely. That I'd be carrying the flag for the 9th Battalion was a nice touch– especially since I hadn't been officially recorded as serving with them in Vietnam.

Not till 1998, anyway.

Adam Rainford had brought a film crew up to record the march.

And who just happened to be at the march that day? Brigadier Pearson.

What a coincidence.

The opportunity had presented itself. The only question was– how were we going to convince him to speak on the subject when everyone else was keeping their mouths shut?

He was cornered coming out of a veteran's luncheon– rain-coated from the rain, brittle, fragile, showing his age. I guess he was well into his nineties then.

He walked right into an ambush– though it *was* accidental. We couldn't have known his plans for the day, where he was likely to be, what direction he'd be coming from, whether he'd even be walking.

Don Tate meeting Major General C.M. Pearson, August 2007

But there he was, suddenly, coming straight for us.

And there *we* were, Ted Colmer and me– and a documentary-maker, a cameraman, and a boom operator, all slap bang in front of him.

I extended my hand and introduced myself.

'Mr Pearson,' I said, 'my name is Don Tate. I served under you in Vietnam. I was wondering if I could ask you a couple of questions about the 2nd D&E Platoon?'

And there it was. The top and the bottom of the military pile– confronting each other on a wind-swept, fog-shrouded street in Katoomba about a matter that no doubt Pearson thought had long ago been put aside and out of sight.

He never said much, and tried to shrug me off. But that wasn't about to happen. We'd come too far with the matter, taken too much crap, been vilified and harassed, called *liars* and *frauds* and *wannabees* and the like– so this was no time to go soft on the man who had once held our lives in the palm of his hands or the stroke of a pen.

As our former Commanding Officer, he had an obligation still, to be concerned for the welfare of men he had once led in war.

'Mr Pearson, this interview is being recorded for a documentary we'll be looking to have produced for television– perhaps SBS,' I told him. I hoped it would have some sense of gravitas, let him know he were serious.

'The *2nd D&E Platoon*,' Adam Rainford added. 'What can you tell us about it?'

Pearson looked at all of us intently. He knew he'd been cornered. And at stake, was his reputation. A life's work. Highs and highs– World War 2, New Guinea, Korea. And then, to command a 7000-strong Australian force in a war being fought on Asian soil against an enemy that held all the advantages. And yet, here he was in his dotage, reduced to commenting about some minor platoon he'd created for a very short time, for a specific task, all those years ago and which had the potential to derail his legacy.

But at the same time, one could almost see that mind clicking into gear. There would not be idle words said on that street. He was way too wise to the ways of the world than to speak about a matter on camera which he knew had a twist in the tail.

'Don,' he said, 'I have no recollection of that platoon. Contact me at my private address and I'll look into the records and get you whatever information I can.'

And with that, he gave me his address, before being hurried away.

I felt the opportunity had been lost.

Claiming he had 'no recollection' of the platoon was curious, given that the ambush had received widespread acclaim back in Australia almost immediately (see 'The Historical Perspective', earlier). And even more curious given that at first light the morning after the ambush, Pearson had arrived at Thua Tich by chopper along with a select group of tagalongs (including an American officer) – all of whom had to have been collected the day before and made ready for that flight at first light.

I'm sure they would have scattered to the four corners quick smart if we'd been shot to bits that night.

And there Pearson was in the photographs, strolling around the enemy dead sprawled on the road, congratulating this one and that one on a successful enterprise.

He couldn't help but know what platoon I was referring to.

But I wrote to him on spec anyway a day or so later, just as he had asked.

And then we met with him on a couple more occasions— me and Barney Bigwood, and Kevin Lloyd-Thomas, and Ted Colmer. Adam Rainford and his crew was there as well to capture the moments. But while Pearson allowed himself to be filmed, he was adamant that nothing he actually *said* was to be recorded.

Against my better judgement, we honoured that.

And so to the SAS contention…….

Its role in Vietnam was essentially as intelligence-gatherers— but they weren't men to be taken lightly when the occasion warranted it. Their record is second to none in that regard, as you'd expect it to be.

The trouble was, in Brigadier Pearson's opinion, SAS was over-rated, as I've said.

In our meeting with Major General Steve Gower of the War Memorial in 2007, he told us as much. He said that Major David Chinn had made Pearson's feelings about SAS very clear in various discussions with him, just before Chinn died.

When I made it public about how Brigadier Pearson had regarded the SAS, and that he regarded the leftover infantrymen from the 4th Battalion as 'assault troopers', the shock waves were seismic. And then, when I ensured that the veteran community understood the connection between SAS's 'quiet period' in Vietnam, and the corresponding creation and activities of the 2nd D&E Platoon, didn't the flak fly.

Such comments were anathema to SAS— and to many other veterans as well.

But the assertions were credible.

Not that Ted Colmer necessarily agreed. He was conscious that we were making more enemies than friends, alienating most by even raising the point.

He emailed me in muck lather, believing that the AWM had misread the tactical situation (sic):

> '……*Ekins* (and I'm going to get that bastard)* said we were 30 clicks away from the action in Xuyen Moc, when they had the evidence before, and during, the whole time of our operational deployment and predicament. Gower and Ekins' understood the situation and caused me misery! This is gigantic, and SAS certainly did their job from April to May. They just couldn't and shouldn't have engaged; and

were instructed by Major Chinn GS02 (OPS) not to engage, and how could they with such huge odds against them; so don't give anything to the media about SAS! It is Pearson who purposely put us in harm's way!'

(*Ekins is the national historian)

On a roll, Colmer was hard to stop (sic):

'Pearson, Chinn, Arrowsmith etc. realised that we were encircled by HUNDREDS TO OUR IMMEDIATE EAST, SOUTH AND NORTH (within a few clicks, and not exaggerating) with the 2nd D&E Platoon, the only infantry force with Cavalry and Sappers protecting this huge part of the Province from the possibility of this onslaught (with the exception of 3 Pl W Coy 4RAR/NZ); and what really shits me, is that they understood the strength of the D445 LF Battalion and others, but used us anyway in small, section-sized ambushes; first on the 25th May 69 knowing there was 199 enemy sighted in that immediate area by SAS. I cannot begin to explain the perceived enemy nature of things until you see this MAP (that now provides substantive evidence that Pearson was fully aware) and the extra 3 SQN SAS Patrol Reports 17- 22 April 69, which qualifies the purpose in commencing Operation Garry Owen on the 2nd May 69.

If you say anything against SAS you will be making a huge mistake, because they did their job well, and were told by Chinn NOT TO ENGAGE, except on the last day of patrol, which would have been impossible (suicidal) given the strength of these particular sightings. I can't find any evidence where SAS actually were stood down for this period [all patrols seemed to be operating normally], and certainly can't back up that accusation, because I think it is something CMI Pearson has said to cover his arse, or whatever?

Pearson understood the perilous nature of the situation from the middle of April to 27 May 69 in Xuyen Moc and Thua Tich, yet allowed a small ARA section size ambushes "scouts" to be made, with potential lethal "cannon fodder" consequences!

SAS WERE NOT STOOD DOWN DURING THIS PERIOD, AND PERFORMED THEIR DUTY WITH HONOUR'

Hmmmm!

Actually, I didn't have any opinion whatsoever about SAS or what role they played. Others did.

Historian – Ashley Ekins – was one of those. In 'Fighting to the Finish', he writes:

> '...(Pearson) felt SAS troops 'were misemployed completely in Vietnam'. Their primary role, in his view, was to carry out reconnaissance and gather intelligence on enemy forces to assist in planning task force operations. Although SAS patrols were undoubtedly effective in ambush operations, he considered this a secondary role and an uneconomical use of SAS skills and task force resources. Too frequently, on contact with the enemy, SAS patrols called for rapid extraction, diverting helicopters and manpower from other tasks: for one period Pearson said, 'I had to ban them making contact.' As a more 'cost effective' approach, he turned to the infantry of the task force Defence and Employment (D&E Platoon)...an influx of 4RAR troops to task force Headquarters Company, where they were 'held over', expanded the numbers available to Pearson...'

But here we had a situation where, on the one hand, a senior officer recorded the details of a private conversation with Brigadier Pearson about the role of SAS long *after* the war; and on the other, a former federal police investigator poring over official, all-but-obscure military records long ignored– and which were either apparently deliberately misinterpreted by the historian, Ashley Ekins and his researchers, or at best, misunderstood.

At least, in Colmer's eyes.

The fact was though– the strategic situation developing in the Xuyen Moc area demanded an immediate response.

And if Pearson's attitude to SAS was correct, it *does* explain the rapid formation of the 2nd D&E Platoon and its attachment to Capt Arrowsmith's troop of APCs as a combined force. It also explains its hasty deployment to the abandoned village of Thua Tich, complete with a team of Engineers, a contingent of Mortars, and a couple of photographers embedded in the force to capture the moment, with 'Spooky' sitting idly by in the village of Xuyen Moc, just for good measure.

Too many coincidences. And there we were, sitting ducks– all but surrounded.

True to his word, Brigadier Pearson wrote me about his recollections of the 2nd D&E Platoon:

338 Sailors Bay Rd
Northbridge 2063
13 November 07

Dear Don,

I am writing to set out the results of my enquiries of the employment of the D&E Platoon during the period you and your colleagues served in that organisation.

The D&E Platoon as you are aware was part of the establishment of HQ 1ATF and had a role to protect the Task Force HQ and undertake duties as directed.

From time to time the Platoon was used to carry soldiers who, for whatever reason had not completed a tour of duty with their parent unit and were awaiting reposting. Such soldiers were supernumeraries to the Platoon's establishment all were experienced and trained soldiers.

This was normal practice. As the Platoon would have been overstrength because of this practice at the time you were in the Platoon, I understand the additional men came to be referred to informally as the "2nd D&E Platoon". I have no recollection of this nor does my then Operations Major. Whatever, I do not believe there was any such official designation at that time.

Notwithstanding, the additional D&E elements were used in operations against the enemy as you would expect and know.

I would have to say that such operations were routine and in no way special.

The group who were unofficially termed the "2nd D&E Platoon" did

> 3
>
> conduct themselves with distinction when used with a Cavalry Troop (the modern term woucd be "assault troopers) in the Xuyen Moc area in late May 1969. This was, to their credit a most successful operation under the Cavalry Commander, Captain Crouchsmith. I understand he was recognised for his command in this action.
>
> Both Veteran Affairs and Australian War Memorial are aware of this letter.
>
> Yours Sincerely,
>
> *[signature]*
>
> (Major General C.M.I. PEARSON
> AO, DSO, OBE, MC (Ret))

SAS and the infantrymen who had served in all the other battalions were not impressed.

No sir. Not one bit.

CHAPTER 15
THE MONEY SHOTS

The closer we came to proving that the 2nd D&E Platoon *had* existed in Vietnam and had been erased to cover-up the actions of senior army officers– the greater the opposition against us, and the harsher the attacks on our characters and integrity.

Three particular photographs taken by army photographer Sgt Chris Bellis didn't help. They created a furore when we released them.

Curiously, the reaction was both hysterical and comical.

The commentary surrounding the 'manipulation' of these photographs (posted on the ANZMI and AVM websites) was designed to shoot the messenger well and truly. This was always the plan, of course– throw enough mud and the target would eventually leave the matter alone, and walk away.

Talk about sheer gutlessness.

And sadly, too many good men within the veteran community were prone to being swayed by the personal vendetta being waged. When hysterical reaction is accepted as fact– it colours all else.

But I shrugged it off. It was all I could do. They picked the wrong man to attack.

That's not to say it didn't have an adverse effect on me and my family. I just learned to live with it– and became even more determined to see the fight to the end.

As it was, the photographs (as we first saw them, overleaf) were dynamite.

Children of Xuyen Moc look on as the bodies of Viet Cong are dragged into the village by Australian armoured personnel carriers. This was intended as a warning to Viet Cong sympathisers. (Photograph courtesy of Australian War Memorial.)

Australian soldiers collect the bodies of Viet Cong they have killed in a contact near the village of Thua Thi. (Photograph courtesy of Australian War Memorial.)

That graphic is of poor quality, but is precisely how we received them– photocopied from a book.

I include it here, in the same state, for good reason.

First, because they arrived at an opportune time in the debate and added fuel to the fire; and secondly because I was later accused of 'manipulating' them to advance our cause.

I had actually seen those photographs many years previous. They were published in a Time-Life Magazine, *Vietnam: The Australian Perspective*.

I had long forgotten about them.

But one day, Richard Bigwood sent them to me as a PDF file.

(I should point out that at a later date we located all the originals of these photographs within the Australian War Memorial's Photographic Collection, and they can be accessed by anyone).

They also demonstrate what we were working with as we tried to put names to faces in the photographs. It was very difficult. Many years had passed since the days of our prime. And even then, the short time we had spent in that platoon precluded remembering each other, in most instances.

That aside– what do those three photographs show?

I should start with the third photograph first– the one showing villagers recoiling in horror.

This photograph shows the reactions of villagers in Xuyen Moc to the sight of the bodies being dragged into their village by Capt Arrowsmith for 'propaganda' purposes. Sgt Bellis, riding atop Arrowsmith's APC, photographed the reaction of the villagers from that height, clearly showing their horror and disgust at what they were witnessing. Not only had the bodies been quite mutilated by bullet and shrapnel, but were rendered headless as a result of being dragged by the APCs travelling at speed.

Today, one can only wonder at the psychological damage done to those children by that act.

Perhaps Robert Enright sums it up best when he wrote (sic):

'……I know you realise this……those kids staring aghast at a young girl their own age hanging from that APC……can you imagine the trauma those kids are forevermore suppressing??... kids that age, subject to death by horror by us anzacs of intrigue….some things shouldn't be……kids that age…fighting for their country they were….'

Yes– a horror that was obvious to us young Private soldiers, but seemingly beneath the comprehension or sensitivities of generals more concerned with 'propaganda'.

Before I forwarded that photograph into the veteran community at large, I trimmed off the rough edges and the text. It says much about the sensitivity of veteran's, that I was then howled down for 'falsifying photographs' or 'manipulating' them to help make my case.

Like I said– blokes who had once stood proud and tall were now reduced to acting like hysterical schoolgirls. They'd attack from any angle, over anything.

That the *original* photograph was still intact, stored away in the Australian War Memorial's Photographic Collections, and available for anyone to locate and compare, was irrelevant. Such stupidity.

All I'd done was use it to facilitate our argument, and make it more presentable and accessible to those too lazy to look for it.

The original photograph may be viewed on the internet for comparison at:

http://www.awm.gov.au/collection/BEL/69/0376/VN/

It includes the Summary by the photographer, as follows (sic):

> '*Xuyen Moc, South Vietnam. 1969-06. Villagers in eastern Phuoc Tuy Province recoil at the sight of the bodies (not in view) of dead Viet Cong (VC) killed when they attempted to ambush armoured personnel carriers (APCs) of 2 Troop, B Squadron, 3rd Cavalry Regiment, in an area north of the village.*'

That summary is important.

Nevertheless, despite the summary being written by the eye-witness, there were those 'experts' who dismissed the photograph as 'evidence', claiming that it proved nothing whatsoever.

One former veteran of the 4th Battalion– a 'Garry Moseley', had boasted of having become a policeman of some note in later life, and in his lofty, considered opinion, maintained that the picture could 'just as easily have depicted the villagers looking at a field mouse or a tank.'

Moseley had had limited infantry experience in Vietnam – just seven minor contacts with the enemy during his whole twelve months – so I could forgive his ignorance. Except for the fact that he had become a police officer. Trouble was, he also boasted of having an extensive network of 'contacts' and was keen to humiliate me if he could.

Sure it was a field mouse that caused them to hold their nose and pull faces!

Even though the photographer clearly indicated that they were looking *'at bodies (not in view)'* as the photographer noted, Moseley wouldn't accept it.

This was indicative of the recalcitrance of other soldiers to believe anything that contrasted with their own set of personal experiences, *their* notion of honour, or affected their sense of *espirit de corps* no matter how valid the evidence.

I didn't bother telling Moseley that the same photograph is held in another place with a slightly different summary. It includes the phrase *'bodies being dragged along* behind an armoured personnel carrier'. It was deleted from the AWMs version as part of the general sanitisation of photographs in 1969 and 1971.

I figured if Moseley was any sort of expert investigator, he'd find it for himself.

But other eyebrows began to rise. Veterans were moved to comment.

One such comment came from an ex-officer – Barry Corse – a man with enough experience as a soldier and courage enough to say what he thought without worrying about what others thought of him.

He wrote (sic):

'If I was correctly advised, the 2nd D&E Lads who were ordered by the APC Command to string the 3 Enemy KIA up by the feet attached to the APC ramp door, completed stat decs to this effect? The reason for the external body carriage was understandably the APC crew did not want the blood and guts sloshing around inside their mobile home. (very difficult to clean and the stench would last for weeks)

The feet-strung-up enemy bodies, including the female doctor, travelling cross country, purportedly caused the heads to smash against the external exterior of the armoured ramp door. Purportedly, by the time the APCs arrived at the village, they were either headless and or pulped.

Purportedly, approval to "take and show" the bodies was at the request of the ARVN commander and approved by 1 ATF operations command HQ, evidenced by the primary source evidence radio log discovered by Ted Colmer.

Understandably the APC commander asserts that the enemy KIA were carriaged nicely, wrapped in groundsheets inside the APCs. Purportedly, the then Chief of the General Staff (Maj-General McDonald) was disgusted when briefed on this alleged recorded, deliberate, perceived atrocity, and that this may have had some impact on a recommended decoration being downgraded, and then many years later, being upgraded.

The understandable anger of some of the 2nd D&E platoon ANZACs re this "mysteriously misplaced Major Pound inquiry" is the essence of this photographic primary source, at law, evidence. Consistent with the high command mushroom farm mentality of then, it was probably assumed fair and responsible to NOT ask any actual witnesses about this matter, after all, "we who do really know better must act in the best interests of the service and our culture".

For a platoon that an elitist, small minority, select few, still assert did not exist, the photographic evidence of the 2nd D&E Platoon of that brief time proves that the 2nd D&E Platoon did exist and compliments the at-law validation of the *official "misplaced" evidence presented to the executive government by the ADF high command which caused the public endorsement vide Mike Kelly that the 2nd D&E Platoon with or without formal formation approval, did at-law exist. The photographs were official, and officially annotated by SGT Christopher John BELLIS. Denial of the pictorial evidence at law by others, becomes an accusation of perjury and misrepresentation by Bellis. The photographs below need to be viewed inclusive of all Bellis' photographs of that day.*

Barry Corse'

He made some very astute, and pertinent points.

The second photograph from that sequence was also a source of contention. It was taken on the raised dirt road that led into Thua Tich. The imposing 'gates' are in the background. It shows a group of soldiers staring at dead Viet Cong bodies lying on the road.

At the time we received that set of photographs, we were attempting to put together a list of the men who actually formed the 2nd D&E Platoon– a difficult enough task given that we had come together from different Companies of the 4th Battalion, most of us having never crossed paths while we were in it, and had only served together in the 2nd D&E Platoon for a month or so before it was disbanded.

And even during that short period in the 2nd D&E Platoon, we hadn't been a close, cohesive unit. Mostly, we'd operated in small sections where the membership was in a state of flux, and spread out across a troop of armoured personnel carriers. I don't recall *any* time when we paraded together, or even sat together at any one location other than when we first rolled up in Pratt's Company.

So putting names to faces was no easy task, and when I dared suggest that one of the tall, blonde soldiers, mid-frame (one is partially obscured) could have been me, I was accused again of 'manipulating' the photograph for my own ends.

Now– take another look at that photo and let me ask, why wouldn't I suggest it was me?

By what measure is that 'manipulation'?

To this day, even with the original photograph blown up, the identity of that soldier isn't clear.

But the fact was, *any* opportunity to discredit me was eagerly taken up by the jackasses protecting the 'establishment' or who had rolled over– like my former collaborator, Ted

Colmer did. His jealousy at the success of my memoir, *The War Within*, had incensed him, even as we worked together, and had spilled over.

He wanted *his* share of the spoils, such as they were– but had nothing original to offer.

Like greed got to Gollum, jealousy ate away at Colmer.

Colmer's shift of allegiance from the collaborative effort to vociferous opponent was spectacular, and quite peculiar– but some gave him the benefit of the doubt and thought it symptomatic of the manner PTSD had gripped him.

Whatever, he had lost all credibility. No one took much notice of anything he had to say from that point on.

To his credit, Richard Bigwood *did* attempt to clarify the issue of my 'manipulation' of those photographs. I had never actually had any discussions with the AWM about the photographs whatsoever, but was accused of having done so. Bigwood clarified the matter (sic):

> '*Don the AVM website has given you a real slanderous spray in its recent update, claiming you doctored photographs and had the Australian War Memorial change the names in the captions. It's a load of crap. The photo with the caption relating to dead bodies being dragged by the APC (which "Mogwli" claims you fixed) was changed after I started discussions in May last year and again in September 2008 in discussion with Ian Jackson curator of the Collection, Photographs, so there was no witch-hunt by the AWM to discredit Don Tate as alleged.*'

The Australian War Memorial knew that to be the truth, as well. I requested of the Memorial a statement acknowledging that I had never 'manipulated' any photographs held by the Memorial.

Karen Ely, the Executive Officer of Corporate Services of the Memorial wrote, in reply, on the 5th August 2013: '*No photographs held in the Memorial's collection have been manipulated by external sources. Any manipulation done by the Memorial would be for preservation reasons only and would in no way impact on the historical content or accuracy of the image.*'

Enough said.

But it was the first photograph from that set of three that furthered the notion that a conspiracy was afoot– the evidence of a very successful ambush.

Early on in our discussions about the manner in which the combined force was created and the purpose set for it, the question of gallantry medals had come up.

It was a well-known fact that gallantry medals weren't necessarily awarded on merit, that a quota system was operating, and that 'used-by' dates applied. If they weren't awarded, they were lost– so officers, in particular, were getting in for their chop.

There seemed to be one criteria though, generally abided by. They had to be shared fairly equitably between the Corps.

But by May 1969, the Armoured Corps had fallen behind and were due to score one or two.

That Capt Tom Arrowsmith of the Armoured Corps was in line for one became patently obvious. Especially given Brigadier Pearson's favouritism towards the Armoured Corps from earlier in his career, as some pointed out.

So there an Armoured Corps Captain just happened to be, early in May 1969, commanding a combined armoured/infantry force against a significant enemy concentration where he was outnumbered by about 15:1.

A gallantry medal was his for the taking– as long as all went well.

Some casualties wouldn't have gone astray, either. It was a rule of thumb– there was more likely to be gallantry medals awarded if a battle resulted in casualties for the home side. Gallantry medals added gravitas to the occasion– somehow compensating for the losses, and appeasing both the military and the public.

The military had taken it to extremes after Long Tan.

And although we suffered no casualties on our side at Thua Tich (or during that whole month, for that matter) a gallantry medal or two *did* eventuate.

We know now that Capt Tom Arrowsmith received a Mention-in-Dispatches (should have been a Military Cross) while Lt Ray Woolan (from the *other* D&E Platoon) somehow managed to score a Military Cross.

Cpl Jim Riddle's actions at the listening post didn't rate a mention.

Ted Colmer was of the opinion though, that a 'citation switch' had occurred – that the gallantry medal set aside for the Armoured Corps went instead to Lt Ray Woolan of the Infantry – even though Woolan hadn't been involved in the ambush at Thua Tich – and Arrowsmith had to settle for something minor.

When I asked Colmer to explain what he meant, he wrote (sic):

> '.......I didn't mean to suggest Bellis was actually involved in collective conspiracy collaboration with "High Brass" officers! They would never have allowed such deceit to be known by a Sergeant. Nevertheless, Bellis (Public Relations Army)

will qualify, was kept with this consorted deceit (as official photographer) and must have realised everything, from the body disposal, and corpse propaganda at Xuyen Moc to the 'switch of Citations' from Arrowsmith to Woolan! Very interesting if you were in a position to interview Chris Bellis, and he was co-operative?

……The reality is that this is a "factual conspiracy" situation about "Gongs!' and "Cover-ups".

Please refer to PDF photo's with Bellis involved in everything? See BEL/69/0488/VN of Xuyen Moc, dated: 1969- 7, with Village Chief, General Daly, and Pearson, discussing pacification, and reopening of route: 23.

Now see PDF photo BEL/69/0500/VN of Bellis taking photo of Woolan with M16 Nui Dat 1969 - 7? Just 2 photo frames later [above] knowing Woolan was going to be cited for MC, and invited to 4th July gathering Xuyen Moc "High Brass"

Now please see photo of Bellis photo, Thua Tich, of David Simpson and I, but not released for publication to Manly Daily Newspaper until July 3rd, 1969 a day before "High Brass" gathering 4th July 1969 at Xuyen Moc, with Woolan present representing D&E Pl?

Now read Woolan's concocted Citation, and go to all the war diary references and note the incongruous embellishment of the Citation (with reference to Courtenay Rubber).

Given that I still think Woolan was a great bloke and good "Skipper" Don, and made reference to a group of us in the HQ Coy 1 ATF Bar about why he couldn't understand being awarded an MC, I believe he knew exactly what transpired, between commissioned officers, and just told us what we wanted to hear! Why has he kept so quiet about this matter, refusing to even remember the 2nd D & E Platoon, which is absolute bullshit?

As a matter of interest see the Australian Infantry Magazine, and I wonder if we could acquire a 1969 copy which I'm sure has the Thua Tich engagement in it. The beach scene is Xuyen Moc with APC (I was there) 1969- 6 (late June about 26-30). Phase: 2 Op Garry Owen, with D&E Pl, and Woolan (still trying to roll over the whole Thua Tich thing into June 69) and fuck the 2nd D&E Platoon, because they didn't exist?'

The photograph I'm referring to in that sequence shows a close-up of a dead Viet Cong body killed on May 29th 1969.

But strangely, the date on the Summary of that same photograph was changed to *June*, by persons unknown, at a later date– and used as part of the travelling *Impressions*

Exhibition. As such, it added weight to the citation for Lt Woolan in that it 'bulks up' the kills by *his* D&E Platoon after our platoon had been disbanded.

Colmer's theory wasn't all that fanciful.

But it wasn't one that the veteran community was going to embrace, because it called into question the whole matter of how gallantry awards were awarded during the war– especially the inordinate number of bravery awards awarded to officers who weren't actually at the coalface.

The 'establishment' *would* look after its own.

One only needs to read Lt Ray Woolan's citation to raise the eyebrows.

Ostensibly, he received it for an action in 'driving off' a large enemy force one night early in May 1969. There are differing opinions as to how many of the enemy were actually involved, and the distance between the enemy and Woolan's unit. Whatever, there didn't seem to be any conspicuous gallantry involved– his 'actions' involving nothing more than directing firepower, calling in mortars, and calling in APCs to assist.

The other odd thing was that the citation refers to his having 'raised' the D&E Platoon into a *'most efficient fighting force that was recognised and admired throughout the Task Force'*.

(This contrasts significantly with Maj George Pratt's opinion that these men were 'inferior' soldiers– an opinion, incidentally, that was shared by other senior officers in theatre at the time).

And of course, that comment also raises a very interesting question– if Woolan's D&E Platoon was so 'efficient' and 'admired', why wasn't *his* platoon chosen to be part of Capt Tom Arrowsmith's combined force instead of the 'leaderless', rag-tag, *ad hoc* group of soldiers parading as the 2nd D&E Platoon?

But as these things go, it's more than interesting to note that Capt Tom Arrowsmith *did* end up with a higher award than the MID he'd been awarded at first.

In 1998 (almost thirty years after these events) a select panel awarded him the Medal of Gallantry (MG) in the End-of-War List.

One of those panel-members responsible for Arrowsmith's upgrade was a fellow officer, Arthur Clive Mitchell-Taylor. And wouldn't you know it, Arthur Clive Mitchell-Taylor just happened to score a civilian gong himself not long after– the Order of Australia Medal, no less, for 'services to the ex-service community.'

What the panel that made that award didn't know, was that Mitchell-Taylor had admitted to being one of the cowards who contributed to the AVM web site using the pseudonym, ACTION.

There was a collective groan from veterans when *that* fact was revealed.

(from left): Major Lee Van Que; Brigadier Pearson; and General Daly

CHAPTER 16
THE RIDDLE

In July 2005, I received an email from Jim Riddle– the corporal who had stepped up to the plate in May of 1969 and led the 2nd D&E Platoon in place of an officer. It was completely unexpected. I thought he was long dead, and he thought the same about me.

His son had found my web site and a comment I'd made about Jim, and brought it to his attention. I'd called him a 'big, pommy bastard.'

Riddle had ripped off an email to me into cyberspace, not expecting a response.

When it arrived in my mailbox I couldn't believe it, but I answered straight off. I told him that I was most certainly alive and kicking. But I wanted to be sure that he was who he said he was. You know…some proof.

In his reply, he verified himself. And it didn't take too long before some of Jim Riddle's personal demons began to surface.

He said that he was the 'ex-marine' who had served in '4RAR, D&E, 9RAR, 8RAR, D&E again, and then 4RAR again'. He said he had left Vietnam for a break between his first stint in 4RAR (where I'd first served with him) and a short stint back in England, burying his mother. He had then returned to Vietnam 'doing the war thing for some time', and eventually to 9RAR where he 'got repatriated to Australia with gut and leg wounds.' (These were concussion-based injuries, not open wounds). After his final stint with 4RAR he had then returned to England once more– this time to bury his father. At this point he 'was then refused an Australian passport.' Further, he had also been advised that although he had served Australia in the war for some 982 days as an infantryman, he wasn't entitled to an Australian war pension because he wasn't an Australian citizen (sic):

A mellow James Bertram Riddle in his 60's

> 'Weird" he wrote, "but while I was doing the Vietnam thing, I thought I was Australian. Seems they only remember the ones who get killed. Where would you have buried me if I'd been killed... somewhere where you didn't have to put flowers eh? I saved more Australians diggers by being a grouchy professional soldier. I had already been through four wars. They called me 'Shell Shock' cos I was .. and I did my bit... We Shall Remember Them! Yerr right!!"
> Jim Riddle Sgt RM 17253 and Aust Infantry 311589.

I told him I wasn't a veteran's advocate, but I was sure he'd been misinformed about his pension entitlements. I promised him I would contact the Department of Veteran Affairs immediately, and begin the process of rectifying the situation.

I also told him I would see what I could do about getting him repatriated to Australia– but he was sceptical that I could do either. I guess he thought I was still the naive youth he'd known back in the war.

I set out to surprise him, and accomplished both.

On that very first day, I arranged for the application forms for his pension to be sent to his address in England; and then I began a campaign to repatriate him to Australia, via the media. A number of those letters were published in NSW newspapers during July of 2005, and garnered considerable support.

With contact now established, Jim Riddle rushed to correspond. Emails flashed back and forth, and the 2nd D&E Platoon became centre-stage.

This was the exchange (sic):

> *'Don.. I went into shock when I got your email response. I thought it was a sort of distant web page that was unattached. I didn't expect a response. ...Bloody hell mate, I am so sorry you went thru all that unnecessary negligence and suffering. I so well recall the most cheerful bloke in Vietnam.. mate you were a life-saving diamond. I had started a long and amazing friendship with one of the world's most complex survivors. We shipped out and joined 4RAR, then D&E, then they found we were too embarrassingly good, so they disbanded us and we went to 9RAR and destruction. I have so many recalls of you my old pal that I could and would love to write a book about them. I thought you were absolutely indispensable to any outfit I served in. As a matter of fact you were well loved by everyone, wherever you went. You actually WERE a legend in the Australian forces....No word of exaggeration, but I had people coming from other units into the lines at 4RAR, asking to see you. ....'*

But then, in that initial response, some venom– aimed squarely at a country that had used him, then abandoned him (sic):

> *'The Australian Embassy still says there's no proof I was in Australia, although the Military at Melbourne agree I'm entitled to a war pension as of 2000.. but only if I live in Australia. They are a bunch of lying cheating cowardly bastards. The last denial was from a Ms Chang!! Blimey, refused citizenship to Australia by a boat person!!! Enough of my whinging mate..I recall most of the details of our service, and with honesty I say that knowing you was the best part of a very bad job. Thank Christ you survived mate...Let's get chatting if you want to.'*

And so we did.

I must say, reading those words from a man of Jim Riddle's ilk was a salve to the soul. My own opinion of my soldiering experiences was largely negative. In fact, in my memoir, *The War Within*, I was unhesitatingly self-deprecating. Saw no point in pretending otherwise.

And yet, I *was* a fully-trained infantryman, and had completed the harsh jungle training stint at Canungra prior to going to the war, and had served as a rifleman throughout my tour of duty.

But Jim Riddle's opinion of me was in stark contrast. And his opinion mattered. After all, the man had soldiered far and wide– and he'd seen the best and worst of men.

So what a soldier like Jim Riddle thought of me would stand me in good stead in the conflict we were engaging in– especially the personal vitriol that was coming my way from those who had never served alongside me.

More importantly though, was his statement that he recalled 'most of the details of our service'. If that boast was true, and given that the collective recollections of our little group was so poor, it meant that we could start filling in the blanks. I wrote (sic):

> 'Mate, how could I ever forget the most professional soldier I ever met? Wherever I have gone, I tell people about this bloody big English marine who was more of a soldier than any of us Aussies would ever be. I always hoped I'd run into you again somewhere, but I always heard you were either dead, in jail, or had become a tramp etc. etc. I should've known better. I'm not the same bloke you knew in Vietnam. Grew up a bit. I spent two years in hospital after 9RAR. Did you know that there is no record in military history of the D&E Platoon we served with, and I've always battled to tell that part of the story, even if it was only for about six weeks or so. Real glad you made contact. Remember you very fondly. <u>Remember that night with D&E when they split the platoon up and we ended up in a huge contact and had to call in that chopper and one of us had to stand there with a flare to let them know where NOT to hit? And the ambush on the APCs?</u>'

Now, significantly, the final two sentences (underlined) of that particular letter I wrote that day in 2005 weren't half as important *then*, as they were much later in the battle to validate this platoon– especially when contradictions about my involvement in it began to arise.

That I had recalled *two* of the ambushes we had been involved in with the 2nd D&E Platoon– when there was no evidence that the platoon had even existed, no documentation of any sort to verify that it was our platoon that had been involved in those actions, and where, in the thirty-five years that had elapsed, none of the men from the platoon had ever met, let alone discussed the incidents and make some effort to collude (if they were so inclined) was singularly important.

It raised the question that no critic was able to answer or counter then, or since– how was it that I was able to recall and comment on those two significant clashes with the enemy if I hadn't been directly involved in them?

Not that that question was important in the initial exchange of correspondence.

But over time as we corresponded, bits and pieces like that just popped out, unexpectedly– each piece adding to the unfolding narrative, and which I intentionally forwarded into the mainstream veteran network as usual, to maintain their interest in the saga.

It was becoming quite a drama. Battle lines had been drawn. There were the disbelievers who thought we lived in a fantasy world and were simply concocting a story for self-aggrandisement; there were those who felt that we were attacking the whole Anzac ethos and that no good could come of dragging all veterans down with allegations of corrupt behaviour; and then there were those who had been victims themselves of army maladministration or deceit at other times, who realised they could piggy-back our efforts to pursue their own vested interest.

So every piece of information was important, one way or another.

The boys *did* like being stimulated regularly. It was a legacy of the war. Men who had once been positively charged with testosterone and adrenalin now found themselves at the end of their life with a cause to stir their emotions– either to argue against us, or assist us in the quest.

Jim Riddle was unaware of all this when he first contacted me. And his emergence into the fray was a game-changer.

But the battle-hardened Jim Riddle I had left behind in Vietnam now revealed a softer side. It had never been obvious in the time I'd known him, either during our infantry training at Ingleburn or in the war, but Jim Riddle had changed (sic):

> *'Don me old Pal.. I'm still having difficulty accepting that I'm taking to you.. Bloody amazing is what it is. Don, I've read most of your website, and seen the photos of you, and I can read a whole mountain of pain in your eyes mate. You are certainly changed. No-one should go through the bloody stuff you've suffered, and certainly not one I recall was a decent and laid- back youth. Someone owes you a*

> huge apology. I can't claim the same, cos I was a different sort of animal……I'll be proud to keep in touch, and maybe we'll meet someday this side of death! ……'

And (sic):

> 'I had no mates. You may recall this. I considered all the soldiers anywhere near me to be my responsibility. I just was a very dangerous mother hen, and you were one of the chicks.. but I have to admit, you were more interesting than, say, ten others. Cos you could, I don't know, like bring sunlight when we were slumped. NO-ONE ever stayed slumped when you were there. I know you didn't see things through other folk's eyes… I am witness, and what I say is only questionable to my face.. there are none who qualify in this respect….'

So I was buoyed, because they weren't idle words, either. Not from a man like Jim Riddle. And in the context of what was transpiring as the war of words went from brush fire to firestorm in a very short time, they were comforting.

I wrote back (sic):

> 'I hope you didn't take offence at my calling you 'mate'. (You said you didn't have 'mates'.) Even though you were so much older and more experienced, I regarded you as a mate, simply because we spent time together in a rough place, at a rough time, and I looked up to you. You wouldn't believe how many people I've told about this 'big pommie bastard, ex-marine, who'd seen action in Crete and Cyprus' who I'd have followed into any battle. Over the years, I've analysed leadership a lot, and concluded that there are various types of leaders: those who you follow because you trust them implicitly, but who may be aloof; those who are one of the 'boys' who you'd follow because you know they'd not let you down; and those who assume leadership, or find it thrust upon them, who have not earned it, nor have an inclination for it, and who you wouldn't trust in any situation. You filled those first two criteria. Not once, in 4RAR did I ever think there was a situation we'd get into that you (above all others) wouldn't be able to extricate us from it. If you ever come back to Oz, I trust you'd meet up with me and mine. I'd make you very welcome….'

Meant it too. And when he did come back two years later, I honoured the promise.

But in a very short time in that flurry of emails, the matter of the existence of the 2nd D&E Platoon came up.

There were so many questions that needed answering. And Jim wanted to talk. He had already begun writing an account of his own exploits across the four wars he'd fought (sic):

> *'OK, now about my writin'.... I've already started and I'll ask your permission before mentioning you, but remember that I would never down you. The guy I knew was a young dreamy kid with a shy smile who kept us all laughing in the worst of times. I also have to explain that my memories of how things happened may differ from yours in details. A lot of what I did is imprinted in my memory, and I can run it through like a live movie, speech and all. So when you read my account, remember that I wasn't young or shocked.. I knew what was happening and often knew what, why, and how, even before things happened. Anyway, read it when it's ready, and give me your honest feedback ....'*

At first, because we were corresponding roughly, and taking no care with formal titles and so on, we only referred to our platoon as the 'D&E'. Only later, when it was important that a distinction be made between the generic 'D&E Platoon' (led by Lt Ray Woolan) and our *ad hoc* platoon, did we give it the title bestowed on us by Major Pratt back in HQ Company– '2ⁿᵈ D&E Platoon.'

But it was Jim Riddle's various responses to questions I asked, and in his own reflections (both in our email exchanges and a longer narrative he provided soon after) that fuelled those fires, and the controversy.

I asked him about that matter I'd first raised in 1987– the murder of the young woman and child. I asked him if he recalled it (he could have had no knowledge of the controversy that raged after that article had been published) yet his response was immediate, and telling (sic):

> *'I recall the girl who was killed at the ambush.. and there was another on the way back, after the ambush, when the tracks were in a panic and heading at speed while firing at people in the fields.. on the way to Xuyen Moc the following morning. That was while we dragged the bodies behind us.. yes. the lads came and asked me what I thought about that, and I told them I was pissed off.. but it was the thing soldiers do who are in their first combat and are 'out of their lids'. I'd seen it before, and felt bad, but war is not for humans.. so for a while we were not human. ....'*

Again, in another letter, Riddle elaborated (sic):

> *'...Shortly after that, the lead tracks ran into a space with villagers doing dry paddy work, and that's where you saw the woman and kid killed by the tracks. It wasn't a deliberate killing, it was pure and simple panic by trackies who had just been ambushed and were shit scared. We tried to stop them shooting, but we were all standing up in the back of the tracks and couldn't get at the gunners in time. These gunners were the untried ones.. they joined us after the night ambush....'*

Thus, in an instant, this veteran of four wars had validated two of the three atrocities that occurred that day– the indiscriminate shooting at civilians, and the dragging of bodies behind APCs. He had also validated my allegation about the murder of that woman.

For me, the sad part was that all those others who had witnessed this matter, infantrymen, engineers, and troopers alike, had chosen to stay mute rather than back me up. Yet here was a man– divorced from the veteran community by virtue of geography, unhesitating in validating it.

He was immune to the cowardice that stifled honest comment in our armed forces.

As it turned out though, the atrocities which Riddle and I, and others (at a later date) all verified, would become a new front in the war of words– even more divisive, and this time, the growing divisions within our small group would become more obvious, and eventually tear it apart.

Riddle recalled some of the men from the 2nd D&E Platoon as if they were in the room with him, and the memories were flooding back, (sic):

> *'...I don't recall Allen (The Fragger) from our D&E exploits but, I actually met him when I got sent to Vung Tau detention for 14 days for slapping a sergeant cook. It was during my boob time that I again met 'Snow' Manski (Dennis). I was on chain gang duty and loading supplies into containers. He talked to me, but seemed withdrawn. I recall taking him out into the killing ground at Thua Thich (where we'd killed a bout a dozen Viet Cong) to see his first dead, and he threw up. I figured I was doing him a favour, letting him see the real war. Maybe I was insensitive... I well remember Kevin Lloyd-Thomas. He was a shortish feller, with pointy face, sandy or brown hair and he was pretty cluey... Regarding those who deny the little excitement of 2 D&E: I found that as men left the war-zone for home, they always seemed to assume that the war was over... like for everyone! Idiots like myself, who seemed to stay there forever, felt that the war lasted a lifetime. It got so bad that eventually I*

didn't know or care where I was, who I was with, what I was doing or where I would be tomorrow. It was like being a ghost in a long running nightmare movie, where they kept changing the rest of the cast. The odd thing about it was that I didn't ever want to leave! That should have been a dead give away for a basket case! With 20/20 perfect hindsight vision, I now realise that I had been on active service since 1962. Borneo for two years, then another two in Aden then shifting to Vietnam for three years. I think it's possible that I drank too often from the well of courage and it didn't refill!'

All this in a short time, and a flurry of correspondence, and as yet, Jim Riddle was not even aware of the greater controversy flaring– that all trace of the 2nd D&E Platoon had 'disappeared' from the history books, that our identity had been stolen. And that our service histories had been corrupted as a consequence.

When it was time, I let him know that the platoon he'd led for that short time did not exist in the official records.

I wrote (sic):

'You know, I told some vets about us hitting that large VC force when we were with D&E and they just said bullshit! I went to War Records, to verify it, but there's no record of the unit existing. There is a D&E Platoon (with a web site in Australia) but I think their primary function was to ride shotgun for vehicles travelling between Vungers and the Dat.'

I had to admit that I knew nothing about the 'D&E' Platoons. Didn't know anything about them in Vietnam, and didn't care to know anything more about them in my civilian life. It simply wasn't important to me. In Vietnam, everything I learned was at the lowest level. I got only what I needed to know. Nor was I a student of military organisation, administration, or protocol. I didn't hang around with veterans, or ex-service organisations. Rarely went to a reunion; rarely marched on Anzac days.

But once the battle to validate this platoon began, my ignorance of such things became a hindrance.

Not Jim Riddle. As a career soldier – a mercenary even – Riddle knew the army inside out. It was important to him that he knew how the systems worked. After all, he was involved in life and death stuff. He made it his business to know.

And when the question arose as to exactly what a 'D&E Platoon' was, he didn't hesitate. But at the same time, his commentary contained criticism and comment about other aspects of the Australian military role in the war which was enlightening.

He wrote (sic):

> '...Their official title was 'D&E Platoon, HQ Company, 1st Australian Task Force', and they MUST have that on record. In 1969 there was a cleaning outfit of steady staff, who did odd jobs around the ATF HQ Coy area. Then as you recall, they put us to use to be a true Cav unit, based on the US style. As you know, it was an experiment to exploit some intelligence being brought in from local ARVN Units. We were very lucky in our big hits and nil casualties, but I heard it on the grapevine that the Brigade were asked why this small unit was being so successful, particularly in the Nil Friendly KIA/WIA quota? The answer seemed to highlight incompetence and even gross ignorance of basic military knowledge.. The Battalion Commanders were sitting behind the lines like 1st World War Generals, totally out of touch. So the answer was to disband us. Made sense....!'

This was all interesting stuff to me. It was the first time I got an inkling of what 'D&E Platoons' actually did; it was the first time anyone other than our little group had actually used the term '2nd D&E'; the first time I'd heard that we ever had a call sign; and the first time I really got a glimpse of how the army worked.

So we were on a roll.

But it was his response about the ambushes that got me excited because my own memories of it were very vague.

He wrote (sic):

> 'Regarding that big ambush.. It was the biggest successful hit by Australian troops before or since, and mainly because we had nil casualties. Of course having nil casualties also works against the records' cos they only give medals to cover disasters. We also went on from that ambush to being ambushed on the way back, and Bluey Pearson was choppering overhead when I warned all Indians (infantry) to be prepared for an ambush soon. He went ahead in his Sioux chopper and spotted it and we killed a few more. Shortly after that the lead tracks ran into a space with villagers doing dry paddy work, and that's where you saw the woman and kid killed

by the tracks. It wasn't a deliberate killing, it was pure and simple panic by trackies who had just been ambushed and were shit scared. We tried to stop them shooting, but we were all standing up in the back of the tracks and couldn't get at the gunners in time. These gunners were the untried ones.. they joined us after the night ambush. Our kills were totalled, from both days, at about 50. This was a figure brought back from local intelligence a few days later. We had smashed the recruiting drive of a NVA and hardcore brigade who were moving North to link with a newly formed army. Like I say.. No friendly KIAs = No Drama.. but it all happened mate. Later I was told I was in for a medal from Australia and another from the Vietnamese, but I screwed that up that evening in Xuyen Moc when I told the debriefing officer to f. off when he told me to stop calling a Yank major MATE!.. Assholes. D&E was famous for the time. We were IT.. That's why they disbanded us.. the other full Battalions were getting shit kicked out of them 'cos they were led by wankers. Don't forget 9RAR was 'Fookin Death battalion', my own words to you blokes when we found where we were going..'

(**Note:** Riddle was in error by stating that a 'Bluey Pearson' had spotted the enemy waiting in ambush– but don't hold that against him. It was four decades ago, and he would only have been going on whatever info he had at the time as to who was flying around above us).

But there it all was. The guts of the matter. A successful ambush all right– but because we'd not lost any men killed or wounded, the army tended not to get too excited.

Had to have casualties, you see to get the generals excited.

Another day, Jim Riddle added more detail that wouldn't have made the Armoured Corps smile (sic):

'We were attached to a new and totally green bunch of trackies under Capt Laurence (I believe). The group included Normie Rowe. The claymores were fired off at night when someone on sentry heard some faint noise and triggered it. The next morning I stood the infantry to, including you as I well recall, and then I went out front and collected 4 AK47's from the dead. I came back into the ambush position and handed the weapons to Laurence. He had no idea we had killed anyone, assuming it had been a misfire, and that we no longer had any claymores to defend our location, he panicked and tried to rush his whole outfit, including us grunts, out of the trees and over the clearing to a large open grass area. I hopped into his APC and told him to warn his

trackies to avoid the areas directly to our front where the 4 bodies were, and he got all tough and 'theatrical callous' and told them, over the radio, to just drive straight out over the dead cong. I grabbed him and told him that if they did that, then his fuckwits could search the bodies, not us! As you know, when a body gets run over by tanks or tracks it becomes a mixture of blood, bones and clothing wrapped around cats meat. Not easy to search at all. So he immediately stopped being 'theatrical hardman' and told them to alter their directions of charge according to my directions. We then broke out of the ambush, across the path and out across the fire trail, out into a wide open grassy plain, and I said I had to go back with some 'Indians' to sort out the bodies. This was his first action and he was in some panic at being undefended and in jungle. He was a total tosser. Later that afternoon, he left us grunts out in the grassland and drove into a village. There, his tosspot tankies emptied all our packs out of each APC and of course it pissed down torrents. When we caught up with their defensive circle, our kit was swimming down gullies. They hadn't even bothered to bring it in out of the storm. I was well f... mad at him, and that's how I came to Normie and to give Laurence a good snarling at. He reported me and the whole D&E Infantry as "a bunch of ill-disciplined animals controlled by a disgusting foul-mouthed mercenary." Blimey Don, calling me disgusting was a bit of a blow to my pride. When we got back to BHQ at the Dat, I was fronted up to OC HQ Coy (Major G.Pratt, if I recall) a real idiot pom, who told us we would get more kills if we aimed carefully and held our breath and squeezed the trigger when triggering ambushes!! No shit. Anyway Don, this was the ambush when I called you to get off the back of an APC where you were manning our M60 as sentry, and you came running to the back of the carrier and ran straight off the back, as though there was no 7ft drop! The M60 nose-dived into the earth and had to be cleared while we were out in the grassland. I believe you came back to search and 'bury' the VC. This was the time I discreetly collected many thousands of Dong from one of the couriers. These guys were going into Dat Do to buy supplies. The Yanks played it that the VC used to just plunder what they wanted, but that's another yank bullshit story. Later I put the whole cash collection behind a bar at Vung Tau and we all had lots of free beer. That was the last I saw of Jock Rennie, 'cos he was killed in 9RAR some weeks later. Well mate, that's my solid recall as it happened. I hope this all helps to place some missing bits of your jigsaw. There's quite a lot more...'

That singular comment, *'You must have been there...',* made me sit up and really take notice, because he was placing me a the listening post with him– and this had become a real bone of contention.

Even though I was able to recall some specific images (the *'100 enemy'* and the *'moonlit night'* etc. as recorded earlier) Ted Colmer had maintained that I *wasn't* at the listening post.

He reckoned he should know– because *he* was there.

And I couldn't honestly say I was because I had no memory of it.

But if Jim Riddle put me there in his narrative, then I'd accept it.

Except that, sometime later, Kevin Lloyd-Thomas complicated the issue when he declared that I was with him at Capt Arrowsmith's ambush position instead, manning the M60. If *that* was true, from that vantage point, my recall of the enemy mass and the moonlight was equally feasible.

Excellent soldier that I was though, I couldn't have been in two positions at once.

'Ready for action- Jim Riddle at left, and Pte Bob Secrett beside him......'

Jim Riddle's importance to this narrative is two-fold: he was the platoon's *de facto* leader during the entire period we operated with Captain Tom Arrowsmith's Armoured Corps Troop; and his recall of events and detail is second to none.

It is the way of the world though, that there were those who were quick to dismiss Riddle's account, just as they did his soldiering ability. Jealousy does that, as did Riddle's disdain for officers and authority earn him no friends in high places.

But his actions that night at the listening post most likely saved all our hides from being lost, from both positions being over-run.

His section of infantry at the listening post had been very vulnerable. It was thickish scrub, but cover was scarce. All he had going for him in that position was the element of surprise which has made the difference in so many other battles over time.

And as the main body of the enemy force made its way past his position, that vulnerability was made more manifest. Riddle estimated that 'about 250' enemy were involved.

His was a conservative estimate.

And when Arrowsmith initiated the ambush, five hundred metres away, Riddle could do nothing at first, but watch.

Eventually, he could see that the enemy were re-forming along a ridge (a 'forming-up place or FUP in military-speak) preparing an offensive against Arrowsmith's position.

And despite his APC fire-power, Arrowsmith too, was heavily outnumbered.

So, in the best traditions of the Anzac spirit, Riddle opened up on the enemy column as well from the listening post– effectively creating a second front.

It was a bold move.

The enemy had no idea how big his force was, or how far along the track it was emplaced.

That was the scenario that unfolded on that moonlit evening of May 29th 1969, and despite the bravery of the men at that listening post, the simple fact is, the enemy should have won the day.

Except that 'Spooky', or 'Puff the Magic Dragon' as it was also called – capable of enormous firepower – just happened to be sitting nearby in Xuyen Moc.

It came from nowhere and made two passes around both Australian positions, a couple of hours apart, no doubt inflicting a heavy toll.

Jim Riddle describes that scene (sic):

'The ground in front of me seemed to suddenly grow into a forest of brown trees. As the torrent of bullets struck the dry earth, they threw up explosions of soil, each bullet kicked up a

'bush' of earth, and in the orange light of the hanging flares it looked to me, from very close to the ground, that the world was exploding. The leaping ground seemed to run towards us in a wave of loud farting sounds.'

What annoyed me most about Riddle's recall was the realisation at how badly my own memory was shot. Such frustration.

Then, with a flourish, and snarl, Riddle concluded our email exchanges by declaring that he'd be joining in the battle to validate the 2nd D&E Platoon if he ever got back to Australia (sic):

'I was very moved when you got posted to 9RAR and came to say goodbye, and said, "Thanks for looking after me Jim". That was a REAL medal I won't forget. Take care, and I sincerely hope yer still alive mate! You never could be trusted to watch a tin of spaghetti and meatballs being inflated on a hexi cooker.. bastard!! I still have the scars..It's all going to come out. and you were a hero mate, like the rest of us, we were all reluctant heroes. Take Care.. and Fuck em all. I will embarrass the f.. lot if I can.'

They were fighting words.

When he *did* arrive back in Australia, he didn't hesitate to join in the fight. After all, he had been the star of the show in Vietnam– not that he had anything to show for it.

No– *that* medal he'd been promised had gone elsewhere.

As it was, the Department of Veteran Affairs made a right royal show of welcoming Jim Riddle back to Australia. Politicians shook his hand and pinned his medals to his chest. Media men like Perth's Howard Sattler (6PR) interviewed him. Newspapers ran stories.

But when the hoo-ha died down, and with no real ties to anyone, no job, and no direction– Jim Riddle resorted to the bottle to get by.

'Shell-shock' or PTSD had well and truly set in.

The Daily Telegraph (NSW) records Jim Riddle's return to Australia in 2006

Then– with the 2nd D&E Platoon battle gaining momentum, and Jim Riddle front and centre, fellow veterans turned on him with a vengeance, as well. His service to this country was belittled by men who had done a great, great deal less; old enemies came out of the woodwork to attack him; his heroics at the listening post with the 2nd D&E Platoon – and later, with the 4th and 8th Battalions – were scoffed at.

And those closest to him, began to drift away. He did fight the good fight for about eighteen months, but was disappointed at the enmity that came his way. His health deteriorated.

The final indignity for Jim Riddle was an incident that occurred between he and another veteran at Angus House in Brisbane. It was a halfway house for veterans, run by the Returned Services League. Ostensibly a 'dry' house, Jim and his attacker were both drunk when the assault occurred.

Jim Riddle had spoken once too often, and too loudly, of days past, and about the 2nd D&E Platoon in particular, and was bashed into unconsciousness. Soon after, he suffered a stroke, and suffered irreversible damage to his health.

That fine man was shipped back to England in a bed just two years after being repatriated back in Australia.

The worst of it was, he never got to see the sweetest victory of all– being present in Australia when the recognition of the platoon he had led so successfully all those years ago was formalised.

But he did get to have his name engraved on a steel plaque on a sandstone rock in my suburb–Albion Park Rail. It was at the 'Vietnam Veterans Commemorative Walk' I'd built.

It was my final salute to him.

The unveiling of the Vietnam Veterans Commemorative Walk at Albion Park Rail, NSW:
Don Tate (foreground) with Richard Bigwood (back left);
Kevin Lloyd-Thomas (back centre); and Ted Colmer (back right).

CHAPTER 17
THE CONTENTIONS

There are 'contentions'– and then there are *atrocities*.

And, then, there *are* the photographs.

And when it came to finding an explanation for why the 2nd D&E Platoon was erased from the records, an examination of the photographs is all the explanation needed.

Like I said previously, as well as the photocopied pictures we had, Richard Bigwood had got the ball rolling, locating photographs in the 'Photographs' section within the Australian War Memorial's Collections. Colmer, too, had unearthed the same.

There are dozens of them, taken by the photographers, Bellis and Gibbons (although many by Gibbons, in particular, are marked 'Never to be Released' after he fell out with the gatekeepers of the Memorial)– not only showing men standing around looking at the bodies on the dirt road outside Thua Tich, but men dragging bodies, men inspecting the bodies, officers congratulating other officers on the success of the ambush, and so on. As well, there are photographs of the men of the 2nd D&E Platoon in action on the way to Xuyen Moc – one man standing atop an APC in one instance – fighting off a Viet Cong ambush, and then, decisively, that one showing villagers watching some of the bodies being dragged into Xuyen Moc; and yet another of the villagers congregating around the bodies when they'd been loosed into the village square.

Some of the commentary that followed the publication of these photographs revealed the 'military establishment' at its dissembling worst.

And the lowest of men, doing its bidding.

The single most important aspect of the photographs isn't *what* they depict– it's the fact that they are absolute, demonstrable proof that a *second* D&E Platoon had existed, if not a '2nd' one.

Prior to the discovery of these photographs, the Australian War Memorial maintained that there was only ever *one* D&E Platoon on the Order of Battle (ORBAT)– and that it was the one under the command of Lt Ray Woolan.

The Memorial maintained that we additional forty or so infantrymen who had just arrived in HQ Company all served in that one D&E Platoon, under Lt Woolan.

But even the simplest of men would appreciate that one infantry officer could hardly lead a platoon of some seventy men in total!

No, there were two platoons in operation. No doubt about that whatsoever.

And this was made clear in the photographs. Although only a few members of the platoon actually managed to get themselves photographed at Thua Tich, it was all that was needed to prove the existence of a unit *other* than that of Lt Ray Woolan's:

- Ted Colmer was displaying weapons that had been captured, in one;
- Richard Bigwood and another infantryman were dragging a corpse;
- Dennis Manski was staring idly at the bodies

Three of those were prepared to state publicly that they were *not* members of Lt Woolan's platoon (although Ted Colmer and a couple of others *were* retained in Woolan's platoon at a later date, after the rest of us were posted to legitimate rifle platoons).

There might have only been five members of the platoon who had been captured on film that day (Pte Len Ellecombe was photographed en route to Xuyen Moc, as well) – the rest of us employed doing standard infantry things like providing a defensive perimeter around the site, or unloading re-supply choppers of ammunition or rations, etc, etc – but five was enough.

Those five men all belonged to the 2nd D&E Platoon.

I said as much in *The War Within*:

'...What I do recall of it is the sight of the Commanding Officer of the entire Task Force—Brigadier 'Sandy' Pearson—jumping out of a chopper at first light, along with other brass, and a couple of photographers who strutted about taking happy snaps of all and sundry from every perspective. Elsewhere, a re-supply chopper brought in fresh ammunition and reinforcements…….

The cavalry boys stood around watching while us infantrymen did the cleaning up. They were hi-fiving and yahooing 'their' victory. It was the biggest thing any of us had been involved in.

It'd been one hell of a shit-fight, that's for sure. All round, the sparse, dry scrub was shredded, and bodies lay up and down the track. Riddle had us all hauling the bodies into a neat row, so he could search them.

'If it wasn't for Spooky comin' in, we'd have all been fucking killed. The bastards stuck us in front of an army,' someone said. Sounded like Pte Allen. He was spitting chips. His face was drawn and haggard, like he'd been part of a nightmare. 'We're just shit in their eyes,' he added, waving his armalite in the brigadier's direction.

The brass was oblivious to it. They were busy getting their glory shots like they'd had something to do with it.

Riddle was more circumspect about the brass invasion. He saw it for what it was and told the photographers to 'piss off' when they wanted his picture, that it was 'a load of wank'.

But there had to be a pictorial record. It's what war is about. With photographs, comes validation, and military leaders have always used it to their advantage.

On this occasion, we were blessed to have not one, but two photographers present—an Army photographer, Sgt Bellis, and a civilian one, Dennis Gibbons. And there they were, snapping away, recording the moment for posterity, and Brigadier Pearson's credit.

I'd have put my hand up for the glory shots, but not Riddle. He let others do the posing, and attended to the business at hand. Pte Ted Colmer was called over to pose with some captured RPG's. He was rapt.

'They reckoned I looked good wearing my sweat-rag,' he said. 'Pick of the bunch.'...'

Those photographs were the keys we needed.

If we could prove that those men in the photographs were *not* members of Lt Woolan's D&E Platoon, the Australian War Memorial would have to explain who the hell they were, and where they came from.

I made those points via telephone calls to Ashley Ekins and Steve Gower of the Australian War Memorial. I made it clear, in no uncertain terms, that the infantrymen pictured at the scene of the ambush at Thua Tich were prepared to state publicly that they were never part of Woolan's platoon, and that therefore they had to belong to some *other* infantry unit.

It was up to them then, to provide an explanation as to what that *other* unit was. I'm not sure that they actually appreciated the gravitas of what I was suggesting, but I was damn sure I got them talking between themselves afterwards.

I must point out one other facet of the process that needs to be understood– the whole process of validating the platoon had been a matter of trial and error.

With the exception of Colmer, we were amateurs at this detective work, after all.

At one point or another, every man involved in pursuing the matter (or even those on the sidelines like Normie Rowe) had had lapses in memory, or had got facts mixed up as we attempted to reconstruct the events of almost four decades earlier:

- Allan Roach had maintained he had been aboard Normie Rowe's APC for six weeks– but Rowe was only was present for a few days after Thua Tich. Was that name-dropping, a boastful lie, or a simple error of memory?
- Ted Colmer was the severest critic of anyone who couldn't remember aspects of their service– but he couldn't remember the name of his platoon sergeant in 4RAR or how many bodies had been strung up the back of Arrowsmith's APC. When challenged about his lapses, he was quick to point out that 'blocking out images' was part of the PTSD phenomena.
- Des Blazely thought the ambush at Thua Tich had occurred after the 'concert' by Normie Rowe in Thua Tich.
- Normie Rowe couldn't remember even putting on that impromptu 'concert' as we called it, in Xuyen Moc (but was quick to state that he had been 'encouraged to block out everything from the war' by a psychiatrist, so that excused his inability to remember it).
- Richard Bigwood got the names of riflemen dragging bodies to the bomb crater mixed up in his Statutory Declaration to the AFP.
- Major Barry Parkin got dates, events and sequences wrong– and he was an officer.

And so on.

None of them had received a brain injury like the one I had received in 1992. Nor had any of them experienced the very real trauma of being badly wounded in a bunker assault, stabbed on a city street, or been bashed with steel bars, fists, or a piece of timber like I'd experienced. None had ever endured seventeen general anaesthetics which close the body and the brain down completely, like I had. Those things, cumulatively, take a toll on the mind.

And none were subjected to the vitriol that came my way for my evidenced memory loss. But then, they hadn't written a book either, exposing corruption within the military.

No, I became the major target because what I was insinuating was that the entire Australian Defence Force was rotten to the core.

While I have included a number of validating photographs in this narrative, there are many photographs taken at Thua Tich and Xuyen Moc and thereabouts that are marked *'Never to be released to the Australian Public.'*

Like some of the supporting documents that are locked away– the 'Major Pound Enquiry' being just one of those.

There was good reason for this.

An essay by Simon Forrester of the Australian War Memorial reinforces the notion that sanitisation of documents and images from the war was rife, that the 'propaganda' we accuse others of applying to history, is just as rampant in our history:

> *'The enemy are always depicted as defeated. They are shown hands tied, blindfolded, awaiting interrogation. Although now unarmed and looking meek, they are always closely guarded, suggesting they are dangerous and treacherous. Although enemy dead are photographed on many occasions graphic images were never made public at the time of the war. Army Public Relations photographer Sergeant Chris Bellis' image taken on the morning after a night ambush against Viet Cong at Thua Tich in June 1969 is an example. [3] The contorted body of a Viet Cong wearing a light shirt and shorts, his head haloed by barbed wire, dominates the entire foreground. In the middle distance, with a second Vietnamese body, are seven Australian soldiers milling about. In the original albums presented to the Australian War Memorial by Defence Public Relations 'NOT FOR RELEASE' is written heavily over the small print of this negative. There are many similar examples to be found throughout the albums.'*

(Australians in Vietnam: Photography, Art, and the War, Simon Forrester)

This is the image he was specifically referring to– one of the bodies at Thua Tich:

Some say 'sanitisation'. I say official corruption.
Not that the veteran community wanted to hear it from me.
Sanitisation or not, the photographs just added to the intrigue.
And there were plenty more of them where those came from.

CHAPTER 18
PSY OPS

There are so many questions…

Why were the bodies removed from the ambush site at Thua Tich, and what implications did it have on the 2nd D&E Platoon?

Why weren't they buried where they were killed? (That goes for the additional five Viet Cong killed en route to Xuyen Moc).

Why were bodies being dragged?

Why were they deposited in the village of Xuyen Moc?

There are many such questions which naturally arise from seeing the photographic evidence.

All I know is, as I said earlier, prior to my involvement in the 2nd D&E Platoon, it was my experience that bodies were treated respectfully and buried in shallow graves in the general vicinity of where they were killed.

What happened to the bodies on *this* occasion was altogether another experience.

And this is where historical fact became fiction at the hands of a corrupt military.

Half the bodies located after the ambush were dragged into a bomb crater near the gates to the village, wired up with explosives, and blown up.

Make no mistake about this.

I didn't actually see the explosion. Most of us didn't. Only after we'd started moving away from the ambush site at Thua Tich, towards Xuyen Moc, did the engineers do their thing. So it actually happened *behind us*. Those of us in the lead APCs only heard the noise and a pall of black smoke rising, but the men riding in or on the APCs at the rear end of the column were much closer, and some (like Pte Des Blazely) will assert that they were showered with debris afterwards– including human remains.

It's a fact that no one present at Thua Tich saw *everything* that went down, and any man who says they did, is a liar. The ambush site at Thua Tich was extensive, by comparison with ordinary infantry ambushes. The armchair experts won't appreciate this fact but there are so many variables involved when you have a combined force of more than a dozen APCs spread out in column over at least half a kilometre, with forty infantrymen scattered across them– every man's perspectives and memories of any aspect or event, will differ.

Same when the Task Force Commander – Brigadier C. Pearson – turned up by chopper at first light. Whenever he dared set foot outside the wire at Nui Dat, it required a whole platoon of men to protect him. It was the one specific task that the D&E Platoon was tasked with, other than some escort work and general duties.

A whole platoon of men to protect the Task Force Commander in the field?

Talk about over-kill.

No one's *that* important. Surely.

But that's what most of us were doing while Pearson was getting his glory shots– providing a defensive position.

Only after he left with his entourage, did we get tasked with the job of getting rid of the bodies.

Did Pearson order it?

Or was it Major Ron Rooks, the OC of the Armoured Corps?

Or was it an off-the-cuff decision by Capt Tom Arrowsmith?

It's a moot point, and goes to culpability. But it's not for me to lay blame. There will be a time and place for that, if at all.

As it was, only *some* of the riflemen from the infantry platoon were given the task of disposing of the dead. Certainly none of the troopers present were going to be dragging bodies. Dirty business like dragging bodies and inspecting them was infantry business, and no trooper was going to get blood on his hands.

As it was, only *two* infantrymen are actually on photographic record as having dragged those bodies into the bomb crater and tying them to the back of the APCs. Richard Bigwood was one of them.

And he stated as such in his Affidavit to the Australian Federal Police when the time came.

In that affidavit, Bigwood wrote:

> *'... Marked annexure "E" is a photograph of me and private Terry Slattery dragging one of the bodies. The person I recall being Capt Arrowsmith ordered Private Slattery and me to tie 2 of the bodies to the back door of an APC. The door was in the down position and we used our toggle ropes to fasten them by the ankles to the bar inside the rear door, when the door was raised the bodies hung down on the outside of the vehicle. All the other bodies were dragged to an old bomb crater and were given an "ENGINEERS BURIAL" they were blown up....'*

(**Author Note**: Later, he altered the name of the other rifleman who assisted him from Slattery to Simpson.)

Given that it was now May 30th – Buddha's birthday – and that all parties had agreed to an official ceasefire for the day, it might be argued that the decision to blow some bodies up and transport others tied upside down to the backs of APCs during a cease-fire could be considered a provocative act– and one likely to bite us on the arse.

As it did later in the day, on the way to Xuyen Moc.

No doubt, remnants from the enemy force would have been observing these goings-on at the gates to Thua Tich with all the brass coming and going as they were, and the fanfare that went with it.

And therein, lay another crucial fact. Brigadier Pearson's attendance at the scene of the ambush just to have his photograph taken was only possible when he knew he had the protection of the generic D&E Platoon to protect him.

But *it* wasn't there that day. It was up in the de Courtenay rubber plantation. Lt Ray Woolan has confirmed this fact.

It was *our* platoon out there that day doing the defensive work– the 2nd D&E Platoon. And those photographs prove it.

And it was only after Pearson left that an order came from on high – from 'Seagull', according to the radio log – to the effect that some bodies were to be taken into Xuyen Moc.

The District Chief of the local friendly forces in Xuyen Moc– Major Le Van Que, wanted the bodies deposited in the village for 'propaganda' purposes, and 'Seagull' had approved it.

'Seagull' was (we believe) Major Ron Rooks, OC of the Australian Armoured Corps.

So much for honouring the ceasefire.

And as you'd expect when you're out degrading bodies of the dead in a foreign country on a national religious holiday when a ceasefire had been agreed to– a Viet Cong force was waiting in ambush not far down the highway to pay its respects.

It might have been a good guess by the Viet Cong which direction we'd be travelling. Or, for all we knew, the District Chief may well have even alerted the enemy of our intentions and the route we'd take that day, and what we were transporting.

It was war, after all. And although we pretended we were winning them over, we never did know the hearts and minds of the people.

The second major event was, of course, the attempted ambush of the APC column as it moved towards Xuyen Moc.

More bodies were collected.

The Viet Cong, dressed differently to the mob we'd ambushed the night before (but no doubt all part of the same congregating force) hit the moving APCs from the side.

Fortunately, they were too close, and the RPGs didn't arm– bouncing off the turret of one vehicle and exploding harmlessly between two of the APCs.

There were only a couple of enemy out in the open, at first, and as we learned later, Arrowsmith had been forewarned by someone in a 'Possum' above that an ambush was imminent– and he executed a brilliant counter-attacking manoeuvre ('fishboning') and routed them.

This action, again, was recorded by the photographers, and one particular photograph was further proof that the infantrymen on the operation did not belong to Lt Woolan's 'D&E Platoon'.

It clearly shows a rifleman – Pte Len Ellecombe – standing atop an APC shooting VC at close range. It was a precarious action which might have earned him a citation if he belonged to a regular infantry platoon and not the 2nd D&E Platoon.

And the fact is– Pte Len Ellecombe was *never* a member of Lt Woolan's platoon. Like the other infantrymen who had been captured in photographs at the earlier ambush (who also weren't part of that platoon) it was more proof that a second infantry platoon existed.

Cpl Len Ellecombe of the 2nd D&E Platoon, in action en route to Xuyen Moc

The bodies from this ambush were also strung up to the backs of the APCs.

As an aside, a pearl-handled Chicom pistol taken from one of the bodies by Pte Steve Paterson, and a pair of binoculars taken from another body were both commandeered by Capt Tom Arrowsmith for his private collection– an act that didn't endear Arrowsmith to any of us in the infantry.

Nobody wants to know the truth about what happened that day after the ambush.

According to Steve Gower at the Australian War Memorial, Capt Tom Arrowsmith's official account was that 'all the bodies were wrapped in green tarpaulins and buried'– and that was fine by him.

And that's exactly what the generals, the veteran community, and the Australian War Memorial *want* to believe.

Fundamentally, it's why the official accounts are corrupted. No blowing up of bodies. No strapping them up to the backs of APCs. No indiscriminate firing at peasants on the outskirts of Xuyen Moc.

No– such things were anathema to men who served the nation proudly.

And, having to raise those matters was anathema to us as well.

But in the end, we were forced to. The bureaucratic walls might have been crumbling slowly, but not quick enough for men who had pursued the matter for so long.

Like Normie Rowe had been back in 1987, the Armoured Corps veterans were particularly incensed– and set up a web site to attack us in retaliation. They called it 'SITREP'– and allowed contributors to leave anonymous posts vilifying us.

Man, what a hotbed of angst that was. Cowards came out in force, using pseudonyms, and tore into us from all angles. Such cowardice– but 'SITREP' showed the rest of the veteran community another side of the Armoured Corps.

I copped the brunt of it, but none of us were immune.

Normie Rowe made sure he got in for his chop as well. 'CAVALRYMAN' was his preferred pseudonym.

It wasn't until men of conscience within their own ranks saw the evil being done to fellow veterans that they broke ranks, and the truth began to ooze out.

The first chink in the Armoured Corps armour came when Paul Coleman stood up.

Coleman is a rare animal in the veteran community– a former officer and a man. Or perhaps a man first, and former officer second.

There weren't too many former officers prepared to put their hands or their heads up as we fought to validate this platoon.

But Paul Coleman did. And he was ex-Armoured Corps.

After we'd received advice from Minister Bruce Billson that the 2nd D&E Platoon didn't 'officially' exist, we asked anyone if they had *any* information about the platoon that could help us, to let us know.

One never knew where any piece of evidence could lead.

Quite unexpectedly, and from the least likely of sources, Paul Coleman sent me this advice (sic):

'Hello Don,

To the best of my recollection this operation was conducted by the 3 Cav Sqn HQ under the direction of HQ 1 ATF. I cannot remember the "seagull" at 1 ATF but the SO2 Int was Major Paul de Cure, he always accompanied the commander. It would have been on his advice that the operation would have been mounted. I think the bodies were still laying "in situ" when we arrived. I can understand your disappointment at the treatment you describe but I would be extremely surprised if Tom (Arrowsmith) would not have supported you fully. Reading the minister's letter it would appear that he hasn't even been asked for his comments! I would also be surprised if General Pearson, still living in Sydney last I heard, does not remember the incident. These two key officers may hold the key to your situation.'

That a senior armoured corps officer had now engaged us was a significant shift of fortunes, given that he was an eye-witness at the scene, and could understand our predicament in trying to validate this part of our war service.

I passed the letter on to Ted Colmer, who responded in part (sic):

'Thanks for your most candid and refreshing comments, now substantiated Paul...we appreciate and value your comments; particularly where other commissioned officers have either refused to comment, or had selected memory problems...I understand from your perspective and reality most of the bodies were still "in situ" when you arrived that Friday morning 30 May 69; I think about 1030H. In fact 3 bodies were already collected from an ambush position 500 metres south of that "killing ground" position, near the "gates" Thua Tich; earlier that morning, and centralised for searching and disposal purposes. There was nothing unusual about that routine, other than the C4 body disposal method and transportation to Xuyen Moc base!...

...we are still pondering on what the collective consensus was with the enemy intel situation by HQ 1ATF? To so suddenly deploy 2 Troop, with such enforcement and urgency [immediate assignment AO-FROG, to 3 Cav] with infantry and engineers deployed into a widespread area ambush situation, must have followed with direct substantive evidence of probable enemy contact [likelihood intel], with that movement to our north, reported by SAS, and other speculation that we're unaware of?...

...This is not about compromising anyone Paul with the "body disposal" C4 situation: or transportation and removal of corpses to Xuyen Moc. We already have sufficient evidence for that, which is not our MO. I/we have the greatest regard for Tom Arrowsmith, so we are not trying to besmirch his name or that of his gallant troopers, because we operated so well as a composite fighting force....'

Paul Coleman didn't dog it, like some. Didn't run for cover. He replied (sic):

'During my time as ADC the commanders group consisted of the Commander, the SO2 Int, the ADC, the commanders signaller and driver (for close protection) In my time with Sandy Pearson he never travelled without the SO2Int, all his operational decisions were based on Paul DeCure's advice. Again during my time the SO2 Ops (David Chinn) never accompanied the commander as his job was to mind the "shop" at HQ 1ATF. To the best of my recollection Chinn was not present that day.

I was not privy to the detail of the planning but I was always generally aware of what was going on. My job was to look after the commander's daily itinerary, his movement and security and in the circumstances I was flat out all the time just keeping up with the constant changes to each day as they unfolded.

The rapid deployment of 2 troop would most likely have been based on intelligence from a number of sources including the SAS and Sigint. It was not unusual for such an operation to be conducted by the 3 Cav HQ and, under such circumstances, "seagull" would, in all likelihood, have been the Sqn Comd Major Ron Rooks. I honestly cannot remember if Ron Rooks accompanied us that morning but logic would say that, as it was his operation, he could well have been on the Commanders chopper (Albatross 05) that morning. His HQ was only 100m from the chopper pad.

I am aware that "engineer" funerals did occur, particularly when people were short of time and had to move on quickly. Except for the major actions there were certainly no battlefield burial parties and the smaller independent ops had to make do. During my time in 2 Troop we always returned bodies to the closest RF/PF *post. Nobody liked carrying them inside the vehicles, as we had to sleep inside, and carrying them on the trim-vane was most unpleasant for the driver; so movement of bodies was always a problem (if they were particularly badly knocked about by .50cal they were difficult to pick up) There had been a row previously when bodies had been dragged behind vehicles; so it was a difficult situation that remained unresolved.*

I see on a separate email that we now have a contact number for Tom Arrowsmith; I am confident that he will support your case.'

He was wrong about Arrowsmith; he didn't support our case, but then, we didn't really expect him to.

Not once did Arrowsmith ever speak publicly.

In fact, with the exception of Major George Pratt, not one single officer intimately involved in any of these matters spoke a single word in public. It didn't matter how outrageous we were in provoking them, or pleaded with them, they steadfastly refused to comment.

The significant aspect of Paul Coleman's letter was his revelation that *'engineer funerals did occur'* and his confirmation that *'bodies had been dragged behind vehicles'* previously.

These were substantial comments by Coleman.

In short– he shot down those cowardly elements within the Armoured Corps like Normie Rowe who had been tearing us apart for suggesting such acts had occurred at Thua Tich and that the Armoured Corps were involved.

We hadn't dishonoured the Armoured Corps at all. Just broken through their wall of silence.

Then, we found a story in Brisbane's *Sunday Mail* about an Armoured Corps trooper who claimed to have treated enemy bodies roughly– a year after Brigadier Pearson's edict about treating bodies with dignity.

Trooper Zev Ben-Avi maintains that at a pre-Operation 'pep-talk', two officers from the Armoured Corps spoke to the men of his Troop and demanded more 'kills' to add to the Corps' body count.

The more 'kills', the more prestige, you see.

All quiet when drums cease

WHAT price a life? I'm not sure but a Queensland Vietnam veteran has put a value of $25,000 on a body.

Zev Ben-Avi — former commander of an armoured personnel carrier, life member of the Vietnam Veterans' Motorcycle Club, returned servicemen's advocate and all-round pest so far as the Government is concerned — is claiming $200,000 for the delivery of eight bodies in the Cam My rubber plantation in Long Khan Province on July 4, 1970.

A few veterans of my acquaintance would write off Zev as a grandstander and a mischief maker, but his story is a terrible reminder of the bizarre nature of the Vietnam conflict.

Zev is mightily miffed by the fact that he is involved in a long-running blue with the Veterans' Affairs Department over a disputed pension adjustment.

He is so miffed that he has challenged interpretation of the "statement of principles" on post traumatic stress disorder.

He argues that the guilt associated with being the perpetrator (under orders) of a "stressor traumatic event" has been as disabling as any other injury or experience covered by the statement of principles.

He has written to Prime Minister John Howard and a bunch of his ministerial flunkies claiming the $200,000 "to compensate for the pain and suffering caused ... whilst an employee of the Australian Government under direct orders of superior officers (named in the letter) who both ordered that the bodies be produced whilst on operations".

"The pain and suffering is the mental anguish and guilt from having been the perpetrator who carried out those direct orders," says the statement of account.

He says that before an operation in 1970, two officers had "stressed that the squadron needed more 'kills' to ensure that a better 'body count' would make the squadron (and 1 Troop, in particular) look better performance-wise".

To cut a horrible story short, his armoured personnel carrier surprised a group of eight North Vietnamese (who were expecting a diesel truck, not more than 12 tonnes of angry armour) and he raked them with machine gun fire.

The bodies, some with up to 20 wounds, were pretty badly torn about but, he says, he was ordered by an officer to "organise the searching of the bodies as a reward for having just killed them".

The officer, he claims, "was like an excited small boy after the contact as I had restored the 'honour' of the troop with these important kills".

Then he was ordered to bury the bodies.

SOLDIERING ON: Zev Ben-Avi (above) the activist and (inset) on his APC in Vietnam

"We drove one of the APCs rapidly, then slewed on one track to dig a hole," he says. "We loaded the bodies into the hole and then drove the APC next to the hole, slewing so that the track sprayed dirt on to the bodies, thus burying them.

"I can remember that both myself and the crew were laughing hysterically.

"The dead enemy all had photographs of family and friends on them.

"They were all human beings. That we, and I in particular, did not treat them as such is something that I have had to live with for over 30 years.

"No officer, no general, no bureaucrat and no politician has blood on their hands — I do.

"I have to live with what I did (under orders) to make the body count ...

"I have never been compensated for the mental anguish and guilt caused by my actions under orders because there is no Repatriation Medical Authority statement of principles to cover the perpetration of acts of violence that lead to mental anguish and guilt."

This is an abbreviated version of a long and terrible account of modern war.

It's not a pretty story and it's not one you'll read in the official histories.

A stunt, an exaggeration, a load of new-age nonsense, or the bleating of an aggrieved man?

I make no comment except to commend Zev's words to some of those who feel all hairy-chested as the Government once again beats the war drums.

And if you really think governments always match their passing martial ardour with ongoing concern, compassion and understanding for those who serve their country, I think you'd make great cannon fodder.

sweetwords@ozemail.com.au

Zev Ben-Avi accomplished that. According to his version of events, his troop of APCs killed twenty Viet Cong in one hit. (I haven't verified the truth of that).

It was what happened next in his story that interested me.

Ben-Avi says that he dug a rough mass grave by slewing away the earth with the tracks of his APC, and after the bodies were thrown in, covered up with sprays of earth slewed over them– as he and his crew 'laughed hysterically'.

'They were human beings,' he said, 'with photos of family and friends'.

He claims that the manner of the body disposal was done without the 'dignity' demanded of Australian soldiers by Brigadier Pearson only a year earlier.

It was a 'stressor-traumatic event' Ben-Avi claims, 'the equal of other injuries or experiences' and was demanding a $200,000 compensatory payment from the government for the 'pain and suffering' he endured as a result of those officers' expectations of him.

The article appeared in 2006.

I don't know how successful Ben-Avi was in prosecuting that claim, but we rejoiced.

Allan Stanton was the driver of Capt Tom Arrowsmith's APC.

In 2009, he learned that he had a serious, life-threatening illness, so he determined to set the record straight.

His memoir– *'Before I Forget'* (Sid Harta Publishing) was published about a year after mine was.

His memoir pulled no punches either. He had nothing to lose.

He wrote (sic):

> 'The Arrow (Capt Tom Arrowsmith), like me, did not want the bodies in the cargo area of our carrier, so it was decided to take five bodies, tie them together and hang them by their ankles from the back of the carrier for the trip back to Xuyen Moc.
>
> Before leaving the ambush site we had one further task to perform- dispose of the other six bodies. We dragged them to an old bomb crater just to the side of the old gates of the deserted village. Along with the bodies were placed explosives, hand grenades, a number of Claymore mines, a few gallons of petrol and a long fuse cord.
>
> The fuse was lit and about five minutes later the explosion of our crude burial could be heard......'

And (after the second VC attack on the way to Xuyen Moc)...(sic):

> *'There was now one more task to perform before our return to the Dat- take the bodies of the five VC still hanging from the back of Two-Alpha-Zero (Stanton's APC) into the village square. I knew they were still there by the shocked looks on the faces of the locals as we drove through the village...*
>
> *The bodies were cut from the carrier and left with the village chief to do what he wanted with them.'*

The suggestion that we had lied about the treatment of those bodies had been dispelled; the "official" line that the bodies had all been wrapped in 'green tarpaulins and buried', was put to rest.

There was no apology of course from the cowardly elements within the *'wankie tankies'* as the infantrymen called the Armoured Corps. They'd wanted our hides, and more for raising the issue.

The remaining point of contention concerned the incident that occurred as the troop of APCs was travelling at speed towards Xuyen Moc.

This was the incident I had written about in that article by Mike Cordell, published in 1987, where I had recalled seeing a woman and child being killed.

Proving this would be even trickier because there's a big difference between degrading corpses, and shooting innocent civilians– shades of grey. Like the difference between murder and manslaughter.

Getting anyone to validate that allegation wasn't going to be easy.

Although Jim Riddle – resident in England when this matter erupted and unaware of any of the controversy – hadn't hesitated for a second in validating it. He'd written (sic):

> *'... I recall the girl who was killed at the ambush... and there was another on the way back, after the ambush, when the tracks were in a panic and heading at speed while firing at people in the fields... on the way to Xuyen Moc ...'*

And when Ted Colmer underscored it by admitting that we had 'brassed up the villagers en route to Xuyen Moc', the third contention was now out in the open.

Armoured Corps types ducked for cover. Again.

At Army Headquarters in Canberra, the photographs taken by Bellis and Gibbons were a sensation.

Lieutenant General Daly, Chief of the General Staff, was apoplectic.

Five weeks later, Major General Stuart Graham wrote to Maj Gen R. Hay (Commander Australian Forces, Vietnam) that the photograph apparently showing bodies being dragged behind the APC *could cause immeasurable harm to the image of Australian soldiers in Vietnam.'*

I'll say.

I only became aware of how outraged the top brass had been when I received an email from an anonymous source calling himself 'SeptemusPrime' that revealed exactly how the brass had reacted. The information provided, and the author's knowledge of specific personnel and their roles, would only have been known by a few, select officers. It read (sic):

> *'The occurrences which were documented by Don Tate in his book 'The War Within' did indeed occur. I happened to be working at AHQ in Canberra shortly after the event and I can tell you the incident caused quite a stir, especially within the ranks of the Australian Army Public Relations Service.*
>
> *I recall a mad scramble headed by Lt/Col Lance Logan, the CO; and Major Ross McKenzie (2IC).*
>
> *I was informed of the incident by Captain Eric Barnett, well after the fact. The incident was common knowledge by all members of the AAPRS. A complete statement of denial was written at that time at the highest level at AHQ to thwart inquiries from journalists and news organizations should the incident become widespread public knowledge. Lt/Col Logan oversaw this.*
>
> *The Australian Army deliberately destroyed documentation, falsified documentation and intimidated witnesses to cover up certain unsavory acts and atrocities committed by Australian soldiers in the field in South Vietnam.*
>
> *16mm cinefilm and 35mm photographs did exist showing an APC towing dead suspected Viet Cong through a muddy field. I saw the film myself before it miraculously 'disappeared' from AAPRS custody. It was not something anyone could ever forget after viewing.*
>
> *The AAPRS was charged with the processing and release of all 'official' media activity concerning the Army's role in Vietnam.*
>
> *Those images deemed un-PR-like, were censored and listed NFR (not for release). Images showing death and destruction were always marked NFR. Images*

of Diggers receiving awards, doing good deeds for the local population, attending to the medical and nutritional needs of villagers were always good PR and released for publication. The AAPRS was highly active in controlling information, anything portraying Australia's involvement in Vietnam in a 'positive' light was deemed 'good' PR.

The people of Australia owe Don Tate a huge apology. Those most vocal in shouting him down should be suspected as either stupid, insane, or perhaps part of the cover up, which has continued far too long.'

Too late, I'm afraid.

The jury wasn't only out– it had delivered its judgement against me, and gone home to bed.

CHAPTER 19
THE WAR WITHOUT

An amusing aspect of the whole shebang, yet a significant plank in the battle to prove the 2nd D&E Platoon existed, centred on a relatively minor matter– whether or not Normie Rowe put on a 'concert' in Xuyen Moc or not, a day or so after the events at Thua Tich.

In the greater scheme, it was a total irrelevancy, but because I had referred to it in *The War Within*, it became a matter of contention and credibility.

And since Normie Rowe told everyone within earshot, or on the web, that he *hadn't* put on any 'concert' at Xuyen Moc, he did the dirty on me for a second time.

But how was I to prove it?

What I had written in *The War Within* was (sic):

> '*We all got drunk that last night in Xuyen Moc, and Rowe put on an impromptu concert. He commandeered a guitar from a local police sergeant's daughter in his usual arrogant manner, and got up on a board slung between two barrels filled with ice and Vietnamese beer. He sang a few of his hits.*'

Rowe had been following the debate about the 2nd D&E Platoon for years, and had been one of those leaving vitriol and slander on various web sites. And when he read or heard about this supposed 'concert', immediately denied it. He sent an email to a fellow blogger, 'Bomber' Bob Gibson, dated 18th May 2007. Gibson (who was later outed as one of the more outrageous *wannabees* in Australia) made sure it did the rounds.

Rowe wrote (sic):

> *'Oh for fuck's sake, they almost had me until it got to the piece about me. Fucking Concert in Xuyen Moc? Bullshit. If there was a concert in Xuyen Moc, it wasn't me. I never did a concert on Xuyen Moc ever or any other place but Vung Tau and the Dat, plus a TV telethon for orphaned kids from Saigon just before I came home. How I could've been amongst this lot dismays me. Tom Arrowsmith was with 3 troop, I was with 1 troop. I never worked with any other troop leader but Captains Parker and Lawrence.*
>
> *Once again, if these people want others to believe them, they'd better stick to the facts as recorded, not by over embellished "I was a hero" memories.*
>
> *I'm not saying that any or all, of this story as I read it is a lie. I'm just wondering why I was involved at all. Is it to get more people interested by the use of my name? I'm sorry to do this but it all smacks of medal hunting'*

In the first instance, Rowe's own memory failed him. He stated that Capt Arrowsmith had led '3 Troop'. This was incorrect. Arrowsmith actually led *2 Troop*.

That's a critical error to make by a man who actually belonged to the Armoured Corps and who worked in close proximity to other Troops. It says something about memory, that's for sure. But, even though any error of fact I made became headlines and a source of ridicule, I never made an issue of Rowe's lapse. Nor did anyone else.

But, it wasn't the central issue.

The 'concert' was.

In my naiveté, it was an inappropriate word choice. But young men like we were in the day called it a 'concert' because most of us had never seen a real concert. Not before Vietnam, and not in Vietnam. So when word got around that Rowe was putting on a 'concert' that night, the word stuck.

What it actually was, was a sing-along led by Rowe that night– just a few songs belted out into the night air of Xuyen Moc.

One can be amazed that such a minor matter even became a bone of contention.

But a lot of ink was used castigating me for saying so.

Yet– every man from the 2nd D&E Platoon who was there on that night absolutely recalled it, and confirmed it. Some of them also referred to it as a 'concert'.

Such an advice came from former 2nd D&E Platoon member, Steve Paterson, via Allan Roach (sic):

> '*Thanks Allan for jogging my memory on the Normie Rowe incident at Xuyen Moc.*
>
> *My recollections are that we had an informal nontac night in the market square. The produce warehouse became the venue for what was to have been a welcome for us all from the local villagers. The Vietnamese sargeant of the police and his little 16 year old daughter opened the show with her French acoustic guitar and began singing us traditional songs of welcome, which Normie Rowe in his brash and insensitive way overrode and commandeered the guitar, retuned it to suit himself and belted out Que Cera Cera and other numbers, much to the confusion of the locals who were too polite to try and explain what they were doing. ...My memories of the man was that his nature always tried to hog the limelight (in short a fucking big note artist) who should have been taken down a peg or two.*
>
> *Feel free to pass this on to whoever.*'

(**Note:** I deleted a particularly interesting couple of sentences about another habit of Rowe's from this letter...... out of courtesy).

Why Rowe maintained that he *hadn't* put on a performance of any sort in Xuyen Moc is for him to explain. Personally, I think a denial was the coward's way out. He didn't dare stand apart.

He certainly never apologised to me. He wasn't man enough for that.

Worse, years later, was his statement to journalist Frank Walker that he had 'tried to help Jim Riddle get back to Australia.'

Normie Rowe had never lifted so much as a finger to assist him.

Nowhere is the symbiotic relationship between the highest echelons of the military 'establishment' and the basest of individuals more manifest than that involving the office of the Chief of Army and a convicted paedophile– Keith Tennent.

Tennent was the 'establishment's 'go-to man'. As the 'administrator' of one of the cowardly web sites, he caused me considerable distress.

For some inexplicable reason, despite a sordid civil offence where he had pleaded guilty, and a premature discharge from the army as a consequence of that offence, he had attained a position within the veteran community where he exercised considerable influence. Some of his work was veteran-related and earned him credit; but at the same time, covertly, he was also a key figure in distributing vitriolic comment on various off-shore web sites. He discredited fellow veterans who dared voice any criticism of the military.

Just why and how he had earned favour with the military establishment was beyond understanding– especially given his antecedents. Yet not only had he gained favour, but *darling* status.

Tennent sent me a letter gloating about how 'connected' he was, and attached a document purporting to show that the Chief of Army was prepared to allow 'mitigating' circumstances into his service records as the reason for his discharge.

That done, Tennent then ensured that *his* service records, and the mitigating factors for his discharge – all the sordid details – were locked away in the National Archives, well away from prying eyes.

And from that position, Tennent was allowed free rein to continue his dirty work of shredding the reputations of genuine men on the web sites he was running with Bob Buick. He had already muddied the reputations and character of many others prior to my arrival on the scene– using on and off-shore web sites as their vehicles.

I just joined the list of targets.

One can only conclude that Tennent was acting on behalf of the military 'establishment'– charged with silencing me. When it dawned on them what damage my allegations of foul deeds and corrupt behaviours would have on the 'Anzac heritage', out came the blowtorch.

Together with the aforementioned Bob Buick, the pair used a variety of pseudonyms to hurl insult and slander– apparently assured that no police agency would come after them. Any argument I raised in response, or in my defence, was ignored.

Not posting my responses and counter-argument, or contorting whatever I said, or manufacturing comment I was supposed to have made was cowardice of the worst sort, from the lowest of men.

But what Tennent represented, in many men's eyes, was a true reflection of a significant component of the veteran community's underbelly– fraudsters, wannabees, criminals, thugs, and cheats. All pretending to be holier than thou.

They were outed slowly– one by one.

And their names put up in lights in another place.

But the manner in which they had been used in the internecine battle between the military 'establishment' and us rabble-rousers accused of threatening it, was nowhere more manifest than in examining how Keith Tennent's paedophilia was allowed into his service records as being 'PTSD-related'– by the Chief of the Army no less.

Here is that proof:

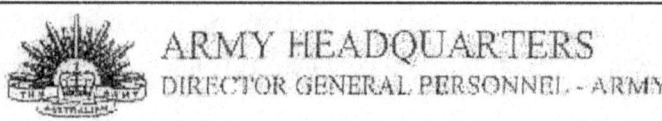

ARMY HEADQUARTERS
DIRECTOR GENERAL PERSONNEL - ARMY

R8-9-025 RUSSELL OFFICES CANBERRA ACT 2600

PE 98-19304
DGPERS-A 5500 /00

Mr K.J. Tennent
5/146 Fitzroy Street
ROCKHAMPTON QLD 4700

Dear Mr Tennent

I refer to your letter of 5 July 2000 to the Chief of Army requesting a review of the reason for your discharge from the Army. Lieutenant General P.J. Cosgrove has asked me to reply on his behalf.

Receipt of a copy of your letter of 28 May 1999 has clarified the grounds for your request that the reason for your discharge from the Army be changed. You state that the incident that occurred in August 1975 resulted from your experiences while on operation service in Vietnam.

This does not alter the fact that your offence resulted in a civil conviction and consequently the reason for your discharge from the Army must stand. However, should you wish to forward a statement of mitigation, I would allow this to be included in your file.

Yours sincerely

L.C. GORDON
BRIG
Director General Personnel - Army

10 August 2000

Yet the same powers didn't see fit to support the forty men of the 2nd D&E Platoon fighting to validate their honourable service in the war?

Veterans across Australia were more than bemused at the double-standards.

I've even copped it from an ex-general– Steve Gower, Director of the Australian War Memorial. Gower is a blue-blood when it comes to the military. He's one of the few ex-officers game enough to enter the fray under his own name.

We've had our battles.

It was him who told us that his 'researchers' hadn't been able to locate any of the significant officers involved in the 2nd D&E Platoon matter. But *we* did. It was Gower who told us his 'researchers' had been unable to locate any evidence that the 2nd D&E Platoon existed. We found it.

And when Kelly announced that the government was formally acknowledging the existence and operations of the platoon, Gower simply refused to accept it. The gatekeeper of the nation's most prestigious military museum will not be told what to do by politicians, you see.

Or by ex-Privates who write books.

So Gower decided to throw some rocks, as well.

Like I said, I had donated rare, colour movie film of my time as an infantryman to the Memorial in 1993, valued at about $90,000 by independent valuers.

But quite out of the blue, Gower decided to join in the rock-throwing, and sent an email into the veteran community about the worth of my films. He didn't use AWM letterhead; and didn't think a personal phone call might have been more appropriate.

No– he opted for a plain old email and addressed it to a variety of 'postmen' within the veteran community so as to secure maximum exposure. One of those 'postmen' was Keith Tennent– the same former artilleryman who had had those 'mitigating circumstances' allowed into his service file by the Chief of Army, and the same man that most normal men would steer clear of.

One really does need to think long and hard on that connection.

Tennent had an extensive email network, though– and Gower exploited that.

I'd asked Gower a series of questions about the AWM's role in the investigative process– especially the fact that the institution hadn't been able to locate certain key individuals, and in light of revelations by Allan Stanton of the Armoured Corps which confirmed that the bodies from the Thua Tich ambush had been blown up, and strung upside down to Arrowsmith's carrier. Specifically, I asked– why was the AWM maintaining the line from Arrowsmith that all the bodies had been *'wrapped in green tarpaulins and transported elsewhere'* when they clearly hadn't been; and why was it that the AWM was unable to locate the *'Major Pound Enquiry'* – an Army document which we, and many other veterans, considered to be the Holy Grail of the matter.

You see, over time, the 'Major Pound Enquiry' had gained a life of its own. Ministers, like Mike Kelly MP had referred to it; but the AWM and the Defence Force were both unable to locate it; while Pound himself seemed to have had 'no recollection' of ever conducting it.

Curiouser and curiouser, indeed.

In fact, the actual title of that document was *'Defence (Army) Investigation Xuyen Moc 1976'* – and was eventually located only recently, albeit, hidden and disguised within the National Archives. It contained documents that could only be regarded as the 'Gordon Pound Enquiry' component. It was incomplete.

Surprise, surprise.

What was even more interesting was that Major Pound had been chosen as the officer to conduct the enquiry. It smacked of duplicity. There happened to be another officer in Darwin at the same time as Pound was, and who might have been a much better choice than Pound to conduct that enquiry. It was Major Gary McKay, an author and a hero of the Vietnam War– an infantryman decorated for bravery with the 4th Battalion on its second tour.

So why Pound, and not McKay?

It is a question well worth asking, especially since Maj Gordon Pound had been a member of the Civil Affairs Unit that was vitally involved in a number of projects in Xuyen Moc, of all places. These included: mortuary; construction projects; water supply; village dossiers; Viet Cong activity in Xuyen Moc; and other things.

As such, Pound would have had an intimate knowledge of the 'body disposal' issues in Xuyen Moc in 1969– and therefore, and this should be apparent to all, an obvious conflict of interest.

So why was he chosen to conduct that enquiry?

At least McKay had no vested interest in the matter. Or at least, that's what we thought, despite his name cropping up in discussions time and time again in respect of the vitriol being spewed out against us. However, his close association with various institutions and individuals known to be involved puts him in an invidious position, and should he be found to be involved will damage the credibility of the Defence Force more than any other thing. Time will tell.

Our investigations continue.

But back to Gower.

Gower was dismissal of my concerns. In his opinion, there was *'no official line, no protection of people, no 'corruption' nor hiding of records'*. He considered my comments *'derogatory and defamatory',* which *'couldn't go on in the interests of a civilised relationship'*.

But then he added (sic):

> *'...I will go on to another subject, your donated film material. You have said on several occasions you donated private movie film valued at $90,000 to the Memorial. I understand in 1993 the Memorial was pleased to get the donation but, no Don, two independent valuers assessed the film at an average of $5,186. Could you please use that figure in future. That's what you used for the Tax Incentive for the Arts Scheme, isn't it?'*

I was more than bemused by that statement, especially knowing it had been disseminated widely.

But of course, that was the purpose. This was how the military 'establishment' worked. I mean who were veterans more likely to believe– the ex-infantry Private who was wreaking havoc in the veteran community with allegations of atrocities and corruption of records, or a well-heeled General who was the Director of the nation's most significant War Memorial?

The only way I could defend myself was to post the valuations on the internet for all to see.

The actual valuations were $81,270 and $103,200 (an average of $92,000). They were carried out by Graham Shirley P/L of Balgowlah, NSW; and by Dominic Case of Eastwood, NSW.

The war Memorial's Curator of Film – Antony Rudnicki – described the films as 'virtually unique.' He wrote (sic):

> *'Tate's film provides the only footage available of the 4th and 9th Battalions in action in Vietnam...I was reminded of the detail and unselfconscious quality that shines through the best of Damian Parer's camera work from World War 2...(they) take the viewer on a powerful journey made all the more remarkable by the realisation that its cameraman had the courage to keep filming at times when others might have put the camera away...it is a keenly observant insider's view of the Vietnam War..'*

Those valuations are held by the Australian War Memorial.

The $5,186 figure Steve Gower had focussed on was the tax-write off I received for the donation.

I referred Gower's rather indelicate attempt to discredit me to the Minister for Veteran Affairs, the Hon Alan Griffin MP– but like most things that went into that Minister's 'IN' tray, it went unanswered. He had copped a caning from all sides about the whole 2nd D&E Platoon issue over a long period of time, and it got to him in the long run.

In the end, Minister Griffin found veterans too volatile, gave the Ministry away altogether, and bolted for the hills.

They attacked me on the character-front too.

Mind you, I'd given myself quite a serve in *The War Within*, so I should have expected a backlash of sorts.

One of the more curious attacks was to the effect that I was a 'fake TPI'. That is to say, I did not deserve my war pension based on total disablement.

When I say it was a curious comment, it's because I'm one of the very few men who was actually *physically* wounded from the war– the greater bulk of men relying on psychological disability as the basis for their claims.

It didn't occur to most that the man who was physically wounded most likely *also* suffered from PTSD– a double disability, if you like.

Regardless, the physical wounds were enough to contend with. I think some were embarrassed by the fact that I was wounded in the war and they weren't, and I had the scars to prove it, whereas they had to resort to pretence.

I had been left with a hip joint held together with steel pins and rods– a disability classified by two orthopaedic specialists as being worse in effect, than a double amputation. The consequences of having an immovable hip joint as far as damage to other joints and the back was concerned, was lost on the majority of my critics.

But it was just another angle to flay me from.

Sticks and stones stuff from little men.

At the time of writing, I have endured my 17th operation since being wounded forty-four years ago, and have only recently learned that osteomyelitis is now profuse in the bone.

That is my lot in life.

While most other veterans live lives of relative physical good-health, I still pay the piper for my decision to go to war– and am mocked for it by fellow veterans.

Like I said, so much for the 'Anzac' spirit.

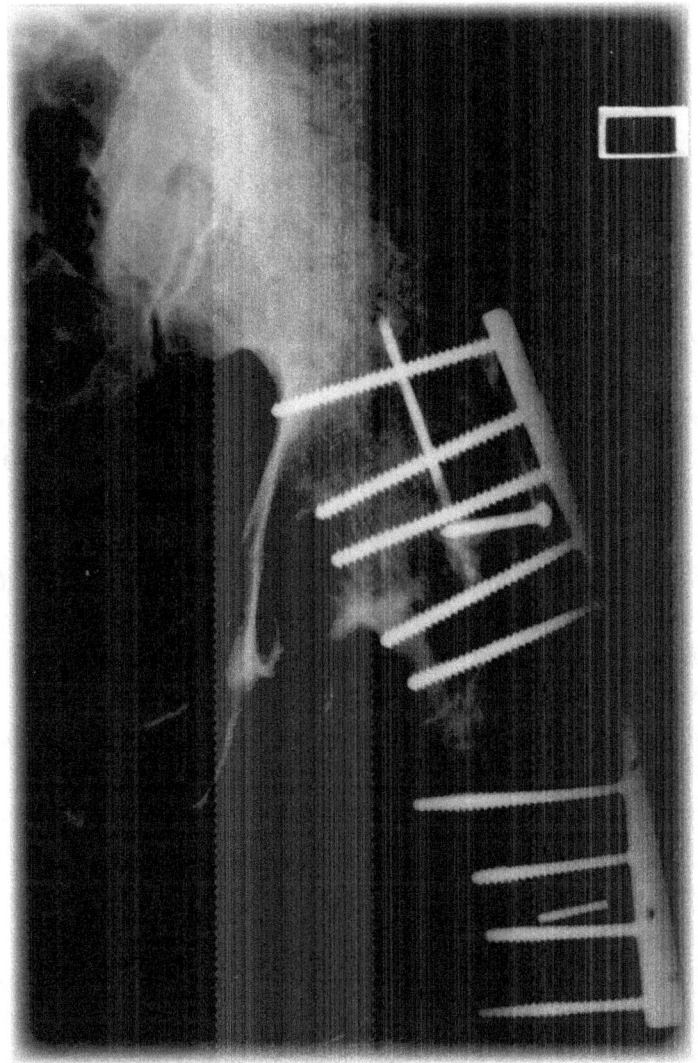

After the wound, my leg was connected to the hip with a series of steel bars and screws.
Despite being told I would be most unlikely ever to play sport again,
I played First Grade cricket- opening the bowling and batting.
In the process, I set Club and Association records.

Of more import were the words of a man who recently said he had been an officer in Vietnam, who had attended one of my author talks, and felt compelled to make his own enquiries about me. He advised veterans of his findings in a lengthy document. He gave no name, but this is an extract from it (sic):

'......As to his memoir, The War Within, and his observations about the military in general, about officers, and about gallantry medals and so on, I make only this point that his comments mirrored mine, at times, and I am sure they mirrored those of countless others who experienced the army life. As a young subaltern, I often had similar thoughts about my superiors, and their motives.

While my opinions altered with maturity and experience though, Mr Tate's didn't. But this was to be expected of a man whose wound was such that it excluded him from furthering a career in the army where such views may well have altered.

Nevertheless, in writing a narrative from the perspective he chose, that is, his particular, somewhat narrow viewpoint of the world, his words echo that of all ranks (including us officers) and he must surely be congratulated for the honesty of thought he presents, not flayed for it. Equally, as Mr McKay noted, his ability to explain how war experiences affect a man and results in PTSD, is of some considerable import.

Mr Tate's naivety is not confined to his experiences in Vietnam in his tome, and I'm sure those who read 'The War Within' could only have found it a work of great consequence and most considerable literary merit, especially given the circumstances of his upbringing, and his most basic education.

I must say, I find it somewhat ironic that this man laid his life bare, all his failings and weaknesses, doing so with the most remarkable honesty, and rather than applaud him for it, many of my fellow veterans have used those admissions against him. He has been mocked and ridiculed for them, yet it was he who freely admitted them!

How can this be?

He did not brag or boast of military exploits like so many others have done. He claimed nothing grand about his life. Indeed, his memoir follows the travails of a man simply attempting to be a better man than he might otherwise have been, given the circumstances of his family and the environment in which he was raised.

I have read, and watched, this man being ruthlessly attacked and been appalled at the damage done to him, and no doubt to the sales of his book.

There has been a travesty done here to one of our own....'

If only they knew *how* much damage.

CHAPTER 20
Now the squeeze

In early 2007, we took the bit between our teeth and all but demanded a meeting with the Australian War Memorial.

We had kicked up such a furore, used the media to advantage, and showed a tenacity that probably wasn't expected of us– so the AWM really had no option but to hear us out.

They agreed, but with one stipulation– I could bring two others, but neither Ted Colmer nor Jim Riddle were welcome.

I could understand why they wouldn't want Colmer near them, but not why Jim Riddle wasn't considered relevant.

Colmer's verbal and written abuse of various officials within the AWM had concerned Gen Steve Gower, while Gower considered the attendance of Jim Riddle to be just one infantryman too many in his presence– despite Jim Riddle's significance to the whole damn matter.

I was incensed. I told Gower that Riddle was a key figure, so important to the matter that he *should* be there, and that as far as Colmer was concerned, he had been ferocious and diligent in his investigations and had uncovered a lot of the evidence, and also deserved a place at the table. In my opinion, I thought Colmer was probably the best bet because Jim Riddle was seriously ill in Queensland. I added that if Colmer *wasn't* welcome, none of us would be, and we'd continue our campaign in the media and on the internet.

Gower caved in. He reluctantly agreed to Ted Colmer's attendance– but was adamant that Riddle wasn't to attend.

As it turned out, I pulled the wrong rein.

Colmer's mental condition was deteriorating, and was palpably obvious. He had serious issues. But then, Jim Riddle in full flight was a formidable sight too.

Whatever, it was a done deal. Four of us were to state our case at that bastion of military history– the Australian War Memorial in August 2007.

By that time, our passions were inflamed; discussions with representatives of the AWM, fellow veterans, and even between each other, had become vitriolic.

There is only so much frustration and rage a man can bear– and we'd all reached that point.

Kevin Lloyd-Thomas wrote to us all just prior to our meeting with the officials of the AWM, added some information that was important, and urged propriety.

He wrote (sic):

> 'Since last Thursday, 10th May, as Don and Ted know, Helen Withnell referred me to Ashley Ekins. I left a message to talk to Ashley and to let Don and Ted know that I had found Ray "Mick" Woolan, also leaving a message for him to call me in regard to this matter.
>
> Ashley returned my call on Friday morning and we had what I believe was a frank, forthright and very worthwhile discussion. The key elements of that conversation are these:
>
> 1. Ashley had also found Mick Woolan. They spoke last Sunday week, 6th May. During that conversation, Mick confirmed that, among other things, he had not been involved in the ambush at Thua Tich as he was around the area of the Courtney Rubber.
>
> 2. I made Ashley aware that I too, had found Mick Woolan and was awaiting a return call. This call came on Friday afternoon. I will come back to this in a moment.
>
> 3. Ashley advised me that he had also tracked down George Pratt and Tom Arrowsmith. At that time he was awaiting a return call. We agreed it would be very helpful if they were prepared to talk openly about the events and the action around the time of the 2nd D&E Platoon in which we fought. We need to be very clear though, that neither one of these two gentlemen may be prepared to discuss these matters. If this is the case, it will be up to us to pursue this on our own. I forgot to ask Ashley if Brigadier Pearson was still around...it would be of value if he would confirm our theory behind the forming of our Platoon.

As I write this, I don't know if Ashley has been able to speak to either one of these gentlemen.

4. We agreed on this theory. That is, the SAS had reported on very significant numbers of enemy troops and troop movements. We were left over from 4RAR and had had front line experience, why not use us as a highly mechanised ready reaction force? That's what happened, and the rest we know, so no point in repeating it, except to say that, even though we had a Section structure, there was no Platoon Commander and no promulgation of an official 2nd D&E Platoon. Jim Riddle was one Section Commander, I was another, I don't recall a third one, although there may well have been.

*(**Author Note:** In fact, there were two others- Howie; and Ellecombe.)

5. I put forward the idea, and Ashley supported this, that we should convene a meeting, at the earliest possible opportunity, of all the interested parties. This should be at the AWM.

The objective of this will be to confirm that we did exist, we did what we said we did, and that the official history WILL record this. All that is being sought is RECOGNITION of what happened, who did what, and the part they played in it.

It will enable Ashley to outline the process he has gone through to ensure that the historical record is as correct as it can be, given that, no matter how hard we try, there will be some gaps. Hopefully, at that meeting we will have the company of Mick Woolan, George Pratt, Tom Arrowsmith and whoever else played a part, to clarify and corroborate what is on the record, what is not, and what is in some doubt.

As of this morning, I have had a conversation with Helen Withnell. She tells me that this proposal of a meeting is in the process of being organised and in the next day or two, someone will be in contact with each of us. She also made me aware that this matter is in front of the appropriate Federal Ministers and they will be kept informed.

On Friday afternoon Mick Woolan returned my call. We had a very good and very friendly conversation. He confirmed that he had been speaking to Ashley Ekins and had provided as much detail to him as he could recall, and was comfortable in discussing this matter.

Mick told me that, although he was aware of us, he was not in command of us, nor could he recall if there was any other officer involved. That is, there were no other subalterns attached to HQ Coy involved in any operational activities. He also said that he felt he was vaguely aware that there were a couple of significant actions around Thua Tich but at that time he and his platoon were operating around the Courtney Rubber.

We agreed that all this was a long time ago and it is sometimes difficult to remember all the detail. He told me that he really became aware of the size of the ambush we pulled off when he was in a barber shop in Katoomba about fifteen years ago and read about it in a magazine!! We talked about the names of operations and how difficult it was to recall which was which and actually where you were. I certainly can't recall them, and I think most of the time, most of us probably couldn't, not that it really mattered. It was all about self-preservation.

So that I could clarify things for the rest of us, I specifically asked Mick if he had seen any emails in regard to this matter of a 2nd D&E Platoon. He said he had not. To me, this is good news. It's good news because he will not have seen any comments about his Military Cross. I believe that this is NOT a matter for us to discuss or speculate on. Mick was not OUR Platoon Commander so we don't know. Whoever recommended him for his decoration probably did so for all the right reasons. No more to be said. ...

A couple of observations and ideas:

I believe we should now take the heat and emotion out of this discussion. I am calling for us all to become cool and calm again.

This proposed meeting is CRUCIALLY IMPORTANT to all of us as we are ALL stakeholders in this. To be treated with trust, dignity and respect is a two way street.

I have no doubt that Steve Gower and his people, including Ashley Ekins in particular, and Helen Withnell, have the same desire as we do. They WANT us to have the recognition we so thoroughly deserve. Ashley Ekins WANTS to write a history that IS correct in as much detail as possible. We can and MUST help him do this. We were there, we did this, it all happened, and what we did and saw is the TRUTH. This cannot be taken away from us.

Why would anyone want to write a history that isn't true, a history that could be challenged???..doesn't make sense...does it??

It is my view that we, and our exploits, will be given all the credit that is due to us. We were an EXTREMELY SUCCESSFUL and effective unit for the very short period of time we were in existence, and the records show this. This is WHY we WILL get the RECOGNITION we deserve.

I believe we should keep the politicians RIGHT OUT of this. They have nothing to contribute except divisiveness, ideological rhetoric, self-glorification and point scoring mumbo jumbo.

There are some things that should stay on the battlefield. This applies to those VC and NVA who died in that ambush and the bodies that were taken in to Thua Tich. Even though it DID happen, it has the potential to open a can of worms. We don't need a bunch of do-gooders accusing people of war crimes. Not sure how we handle this.

So what about the media??...personally, handled the right way, I think this is a real human interest story and should be told, an opportunity to get very good publicity for the AWM and its people, to raise the profile of the veteran community, to encourage people to come forward and provide information so that the true history of events that shape the nation can be told.

I think we should do it but make sure that it is apolitical…

…I will very much look forward to a meeting in Canberra.'

It was something of a historic meeting we had.

In itself, that meeting was a victory. We were told that never before had any ordinary soldiers ever forced the Memorial to a discussion table about any matter– let alone four raggedy-arsed, ex-Privates doing it.

'Well, what have you got?' asked General Steve Gower.

The formalities of the handshake being over, we were straight into it.

'This,' I said, handing him the extract taken from the Engineer's Narratives that Adam Rainford had located, 'proof that there were two D&E Platoons in existence, and operating parallel to each other. And one of them was ours.'

R May 69	COMMANDERS DIARY NARRATIVE	OFF
	EVENT OR INFORMATION	
1.	A small group of instructors and boat operators from 1 Tp carried out watermanship training for the new ATF D & E Pl in an area near the SONG CAO MAY bridge. The Sqn also provided Mk 1 assult boats and motors.	

Gower took the document and read it, raised his eyebrows, and without saying a word, handed it to Ashley Ekins.

Both men's demeanour changed instantly. I could've sworn Ekins' jaw dropped.

'And if there were *two* D&E Platoons,' I added, 'it stands to reason that one had to be called something different to the other, and 2nd was a likely choice.'

Steve Gower was an impressive man. Typical, old-school officer. Immaculately dressed, and straight of back. He hadn't been actually involved in tackling the enemy in Vietnam, but had at least been in the 'J'. If I recall correctly, I think he said he was a forward observer for the artillery– but don't hold me to it because it's neither here nor there.

'Anything else?' he asked, coolly.

I had nothing more, myself. All that I had gathered had also been gathered by Colmer, and given his previous employment, we'd left it to him to prepare for exactly this moment. I figured he'd have it all organised and shipshape.

I turned to him. Colmer had brought an old battered suitcase with him– full of the documents he had unearthed and annotated. He opened it, and started to search.

'The first document is Brigadier Pearson's authorisation for the 2nd D&E Platoon to conduct live firing at Baria,' said Colmer, rattling through his sheath of papers. 'It had to refer to the *new* D&E Platoon because the other one was out on Operation *Mailed Fist*.'

We waited for him to find it. And we waited.

We waited for five minutes. And still he couldn't find that damned document.

'Let's move on,' said Gower– and with that, he basically sidelined Ted Colmer for the duration.

Little else of significance came from the meeting.

Gower handed me two foolscap pages at one point. It had a list of records held by the Australian War Memorial.

'That is a list of every record held by this place,' said Gower, 'where any reference to a "second D&E Platoon" could exist. Our researchers have examined every one of them. We have not found one single reference to your 2nd *D&E Platoon*.'

I should have told him that they had obviously missed that three-minute interview conducted by the ABC in black and white that Ted Colmer had found right under their noses months earlier. Capt Tom Arrowsmith had waxed lyrically about the ambush at Thua Tich and the subsequent attempted ambush of our combined force as we moved from Thua Tich to Xuyen Moc. The thing that intrigued us about that interview was that he never mentioned the involvement of the 2nd D&E Platoon (other than a reference to the section at the listening post being his 'scouts') and didn't mention the treatment of the enemy dead– especially about those bodies slung up to the back of his APC.

But we made it clear that somewhere in Colmer's suitcase there existed enough primary evidence to prove that the 2nd D&E Platoon had existed.

Gower and Ekins listened.

Afterwards, Gower brought out a plastic bag full of notes and handed us an amount each to cover our petrol expenses for coming down to Canberra.

I couldn't help but feel it was a bribe of sorts. You know– to sweeten us up, and get us out of his hair.

And that was it.

We'd formally stated our case to the gatekeepers.

A day or so later, we received a summary of that meeting from Steve Gower. He didn't send it himself– he sent it via Ashley Ekins.

It read:

'Meeting at the Australian War Memorial, Friday 18 May 2007
The intention of this e-mail is to agree upon the outcome of a meeting with Mr Don Tate, Mr Ted Colmer and Mr Kevin Lloyd-Thomas (representing a group of the former Defence and Employment Platoon (D&E Pl) of HQ 1ATF), and Australian War Memorial staff, including Director Steve Gower and Ashley Ekins, Acting Head and Senior Historian, Military History Section.

The AWM team believed:

• Ashley Ekins, author of the final volume of the Vietnam War official history, Fighting to the Finish (anticipated release in August 2008), assured the veterans that the combined infantry—armour night ambush near Thua Tich on 29/30 May 1969 by soldiers of the D&E Platoon and 2 Troop, B Squadron, 3 Cavalry Regiment, is to be covered comprehensively in this volume.

• Ashley also assured the D&E Pl veterans that their platoon, which was a sub-unit under command of Headquarters Company, 1st Australian Task Force at Nui Dat, would be identified in the history as a discrete group. Although it is not possible to refer to them as the "2nd D&E Pl" or "No. 2 D&E Pl", since no official evidence of such a platoon exists in the 1ATF establishment table, rolls or order of battle, their operational service and their actions in a particular operation (Operation Garry

Owen) will be attributed to a group who called themselves unofficially the Second D&E Platoon.

• *An assurance was given that the history will record that their sub-unit comprised mostly soldiers who were posted as reinforcements from 1ARU to 4RAR in early 1969 (Feb/Mar 69). When 4RAR returned to Australia in May 1969, they remained on the strength of 1ATF, held over as supernumerary to establishment and posted to HQ Company 1ATF. From about mid-May to mid-June 1969, they served with D&E Pl, possibly as a single rifle section under command of a junior NCO. In mid to late June 1969, most were subsequently posted to 9RAR and served out their tour in Vietnam with that unit.*

• *It was requested that, if possible, the veterans provide the AWM with a brief (one or two paragraphs) personal account of the night ambush at Thua Tich to assist in the description of the action (any use in the official history to be attributed to them).*

I believe this was a most worthwhile meeting and thank all those who attended.
Steve Gower'

In all that, only one clause grabbed my attention– *"...served with D&E Pl, possibly as a single rifle section under the command of a junior NCO..."*

A 'single rifle section'?

Was he saying that the thirty-nine men comprised a 'single rifle section'?

Given that he was a former army general, I think it said much about the quality of the officer corps if one ex-general seriously considered that thirty-nine men constituted a 'section'. Most properly-constructed *platoons* contained about forty men, divided into three sections each of about ten men.

God help us if Gen Steve Gower was the judge and jury.

As I was inclined to do, I immediately wrote back to Gower and Ekins (sic):

'Now gentlemen, I believe we had a cordial, and relatively amicable meeting today, and I believe we achieved certain objectives. But, right from the outset, we have battled to have the truths of this matter fully revealed, and we cannot accept any distortion of the truths already established at the meeting today.

We chose to let some very contentious issue rest for the time being (the medal won by Woolan; the disposal of the bodies with C4; and the manner in which bodies were taken into Xuyen Moc). These dogs bark. I cannot speak for every one of the 39 men who were involved in this platoon– but I am adamant that half-truths are unacceptable. I am sure that when the men of this "second D&E Platoon" are told that Arrowsmith's latest version of events is that all the bodies were wrapped in "tarpaulins" and neatly stacked on the sides of APCs before being transported elsewhere for a decent burial, they will be sick to their stomachs– and wiser, more knowledgeable veterans of considerable rank and experience will make mincemeat out of that claim as well, to everyone's detriment.

Mr Gower, as a former officer yourself, of high standing and repute, you must be sick, yourself, to be witnessing a disgraceful cover–up. I have said for many years, in a variety of publications and forums, that those bodies were blown–up, and that Arrowsmith received a severe reprimand. You must be aware that no one has ever challenged that account in 30 years– Arrowsmith would be very unwise to try to do so now.

Similarly with Woolan– there are men who served under him (and even Woolan himself) who wonder why he earned a MC– and we were hoping he would have been man enough to publicly state that he and his platoon were elsewhere (and not leave it up to us to prove it!) But he wasn't such a man. He is of the same ilk, apparently, as Arrowsmith.

Finally, if we cannot be given the title "2ⁿᵈ D&E Platoon" (and given that you state we call ourselves such, why then can't we be recognised as a platoon of men who called themselves "Sabre Force"? Then it would most certainly be a discrete force, and allow ourselves to be distanced from Woolan's mob, once and for all. Regards, Don Tate'

Neither man responded. I think they thought the less said, the better.

We had little more to do with the Australian War Memorial after that. Didn't seem any point.

As far as I could see, what I was witnessing was the deliberate falsification and misrepresentation of national records and archives by senior ex-officers and those governing the Memorial. If one was so inclined, one might find an argument to suggest that it was tantamount to perjury.

Certainly, the actions of some of the AWM staff involved in this matter does not reflect well on their corporate governance, and there is no doubting the fact that there might have been deliberate perjury and/or the falsification of records contained within some of the Collections that may warrant some sort of independent judicial investigation.

There may also be a need to consider the questions of a perceived conflict of interest by some of the senior personnel of the Memorial.

Certainly, if nothing else, the protocols need to be examined as to the capacity of those individuals who are charged with the responsibility of objectively ensuring the accuracy of what *others* purport to be 'accurate records' to actually comply with their charter. And at the same time, to ensure that the AWM's assertions that what is marketed as *accurate* national historical records, accounts, and documentation *is* truly accurate– not just what they think the public wants to see, or believe.

Having dealt with some of the staff personally, of particular concern to me is that some of the academic staff present themselves and their interpretations of custodial records as being above question or challenge– perceiving themselves to be the 'intellectual gatekeepers' of our national military heritage.

How dare men of lesser rank than them challenge or correct the AWM perspectives of fact and fiction– effectively denying those who actually fought the war at the coalface a voice, or an opinion?

Any such judicial investigation might well include concerns about perjury and conspiratorial acts to create (by misrepresentation) after-action accounts that result in rewards for 'bravery', where that which is described either *didn't* occur at all, or were significantly embellished by non-present 'witnessing' officers (as per the Bob Buick award at Long Tan) for questionable motives.

Some sort of investigation at the political level is way overdue.

Shit happens in war. And senior officers and politicians are quick to cover them up.

Take the matter of To Thi Nau. She was the self-confessed head of the communist Military Proselytising Committee in Hoa Long.

A platoon led by 2Lt John O'Halloran had detained her in a cave in the Nui Dinh Hills, wedged into a crevice in the roof 'like a spider suspended from the roof'. She spent the night tied to O'Halloran, who told her she would be shot if his men were attacked.

She was delivered safely to Nui Dat and dragged blindfolded to a tent where two Australian officers 'interrogated her'. Peter Barham – a SAS Sergeant, and interpreter – witnessed her having to endure water torture, and threats of having her nails pulled out and objects thrust into her orifices, and the like. It was harrowing for her, and equally so for Barham having to witness it.

Only recently has Barham admitted witnessing the torture. It destroyed him psychologically.

An investigation by the Task Force Commander of the day resulted only in the denial of the matter by Barham and two officers, although Warrant Officer Ken Borland was subsequently removed from further duties.

The officers then lied to a parliamentary enquiry.

Surprise, surprise.

CHAPTER 21
PUTTING UP

With the evidence mounting, and the wind at our sails (despite not getting anywhere at the Australian War Memorial) it was time to put up or shut up.

Now we needed to put it direct to the politicians.

Collectively, we agreed on the basic facts, worked up a letter containing them, and sent the whole thing direct to the Minister for Veteran Affairs, Mr Bruce Billson MP, on the 27th May 2007.

Copies were sent to other parties with a vested interest, as well– including the national historian.

This is that letter:

> *'Re: The omission of the "2nd D&E Platoon" from official records of the Vietnam War*
>
> *We, the undersigned- all veterans of the Vietnam War, wish to bring a very serious matter to your attention- the omission from the official records of the Vietnam War of a discrete platoon of infantrymen that operated in Vietnam between May and June, 1969, but which does not exist in the "official" military records of the war.*
>
> *You might already be aware that this platoon recorded significant successes against the enemy in its short life, without a single casualty of its own- due mostly, to the professionalism of the platoon's unofficial leader- Cpl James Riddle.*

I am sure you are already aware that this matter has been the subject of intense debate within the veteran community for some time, and that representations have already been made to various government departments and leaders, and culminated in a frank, open discussion with senior officials of the Australian War Memorial on May 18th, this year. At that meeting, chaired by Maj. General Steve Gower, the official historian of the war- Ashley Ekins, accepted the evidence we provided him with, and has stated that he is prepared to acknowledge the existence, and exploits, of this platoon in the official histories due for publication next year.

Nevertheless, you would be aware that the lack of an official title for this platoon (still only referred to as "a discrete infantry force") has had a significantly negative impact on the men who served in it- from outright condemnation by fellow veterans, personal character assassination, and the denial of benefits under the DVA legislation- there being no basis of any claims based on this particular platoon's experiences in the war, simply because no records exist to support it.

We trust that given the AWM's formal acceptance that the 'discrete' force DID exist, it is our demand that somehow, this 'discrete force' be formally named, and officially recorded in the military records, and that our individual records be amended accordingly, albeit 39 years late.

The Facts of the Matter

It was our belief that the platoon was called the "2nd D&E Platoon". It was a title given to us by a Major George Pratt, on or about, the 10th May 1969, when some 35 of us transferred over from the 4RAR following the completion of its tour. (A "D&E Platoon" already existed- thus the "2nd"!) However, for some reason, it was never formalized on the Task Force structure.

All of us were reinforcements. All of us were regular soldiers. (The remaining reinforcements from the 4th Battalion- all national servicemen, were either sent home early, or placed in the other battalions.)

To the best of our abilities, we have examined the official rolls (from the 4RAR; 1ATF; and the 9RAR) and have compiled a list of the men we believe were members of this "2nd D&E Platoon". (Author Note: These names were listed in the letter, and appear elsewhere in this narrative.)

I attach a simple overview of the matter as best we can put it together. I have provided names, dates, and enough specific history to ensure there is no doubt of the validity of this platoon's existence.

> *I am sure your own skilled researchers will have no difficulty in filling the gaps.*
>
> *While anecdotes and personal accounts might not be the normal tools of a submission like this, I also include them here as supplementary material, due to the absolute lack of official records.*
>
> *I trust that you will appreciate that it has taken us 38 years to prove the existence of this platoon- and the process of validation (from our limited access to records) has been difficult. Each of us has suffered in some respect- some, very deeply. Having served your country in a time of war, then have the integrity of your service questioned, has caused us great distress.*
>
> *We look forward to your response.'*

As well as myself, it was jointly signed by Kevin Lloyd-Thomas; Richard Bigwood; and James Riddle, and the evidence we had found to that point, was attached.

On the 10th August 2007, Billson replied, after a few months of 'investigation':

> *'Only a single D&E Platoon was recorded in the 1ATF "Order of Battle" and establishment records. There was no authority to raise a "Second D&E Platoon", as only one was required by HQ Company, and it already existed on the 1ATF establishment.*
>
> *The creation of a Second D&E Platoon would have required the appointment of an officer to command it, and this would be recorded on the HQ Company 1ATF establishment table. It would also be recorded in the official "order of battle" of the Australian Army in the Vietnam War (reproduced as Appendix B of the official history: "Australian headquarters and units allocated for service in Vietnam, 31 July 1962 – 1 July 1973").'*

There were two interesting comments in that letter that raised more questions:

- that there was 'no authority' to create a second platoon because that would require an officer to be appointed
- and that an officer would have had to lead such a platoon if it had been created, and such an appointment officially recorded

Yet, an officer *had* initially been appointed– Lt Barry Parkin

Did that mean that the appointment of Parkin had only been a token gesture to give the platoon members a degree of security, or pretend some semblance of legality?

Why wasn't that appointment recorded in accordance with protocol?

There was something very wrong here, and we infantrymen were the meat in that sandwich.

We were enraged.

It was obvious that Billson had simply been played for a fool by the armchair generals who had advised him.

How was it possible that he could ignore the plethora of evidence we had uncovered?

But when we thought on it, we realised it wasn't hard to do– he was, after all, the most junior and inexperienced Minister in the Howard government. He could be forgiven for having had the wool pulled over his eyes by experienced army officers keen to ensure that this platoon *didn't* get recognised.

Especially when they were hell bent on protecting their mates from charges of corruption of historical documents, and being involved in dark deeds.

On the 27th August 2007, I wrote back to Minister Billson MP (sic):

'I am in receipt of your letter dated 10th August 2007.

There are a number of issues in your letter I wish to address. I will do that in due course.

But right from the outset, I want you to be aware that you have been lied to. I have IN MY POSSESSION proof positive that a second D&E Platoon was created- and I will present that at the appropriate time for all the world to see.

What should concern you as a government minister, is that this matter has been the subject of deliberate deceit and lies for almost 38 years- and that those who have much to be embarrassed about are behind those lies.

Do you not see the dilemma you place the 35 men involved in this platoon in? On the one hand, you accept that the platoon operated as a unit, yet because there is no official history of it, those men are UNABLE to use the activities they were involved in during that platoon's activities as the basis of any pension claims. Simply- DVA investigators will send them packing, as they have in the past.

You cannot acknowledge the existence of a 'discrete infantry force' where the names of the men are not acknowledged- ANY infantryman can put up his hand and claim to have belonged to it.

> *I appreciate that you are under pressure, but the absurdity of the arguments you present in your letter leave you open to significant attack not only from veterans, but from politicians on the other side.*
>
> *I trust, sir, that you go back to the 'commanders' and 'former soldiers' who you relied on to investigate this matter to start telling you the truth- because the truth will out'*

But there was nothing more from Minister Bruce Billson MP. Like Pilate, he washed his hands of the matter. I was disgusted to learn, later, that Billson's letter had actually been 'crafted' by a 'team' within the AWM, using information provided by Ashley Ekins, the historian.

Meanwhile, I had been granted a two-hour meeting with my local Member of Parliament– Ms Jennie George MP, and given the opportunity to outline the case for the recognition of the 2nd D&E Platoon.

Jennie George was nobody's fool. A long-term Labor politician, she had marched in opposition to the war back in the 70's, and like me, had gone on to become a teacher.

She and I had clashed swords in earlier times about other matters, and she knew I was on the opposite side of the political divide, but to her credit, she allowed me two hours to make my case – a far greater hearing than any other of her constituents would get for any other matter.

After the oral presentation, I gave her the outline in detail, in writing, and included all the evidence we had collected.

On that document (forwarded to the Army History Unit) I stated quite clearly that I had no full recollection of the ambush.

It was exactly as I had said in *The War Within*, and had always maintained. Except for those few images I had (which I had previously published in various articles) I pretended nothing.

No bullshit. No pretence of any sort.

You can't be more honest than that.

Ms George listened intently, and though she didn't necessarily grasp all the military aspects, she certainly got the whiff of maladministration and corruption.

She said she would personally further the matter with her colleagues in Canberra.

For the very first time, I was sure we would be getting a fair hearing in the corridors of power.

CHAPTER 22
THE CORRUPTIONS

Probably the most telling aspect of this whole matter was the deliberate corruption of documents that took place.

While there might be excuses for maladministration, there should be no room for error when it comes to historical documentation.

And certainly not when that documentation pertains to individual service histories upon which the Department of Veteran Affairs relies when it comes to the question of war pensions. What a man does in the war (or doesn't do) determines the amount of pension he might be awarded as far as relevant disability is concerned.

So if 'official' documentation has been falsified – be it accidentally or deliberately – by officers in Central Army Records or some incompetent clerk, it is the veteran who pays. It is he who must battle the bureaucracies to correct them.

And that is no easy task.

Take the document that purports to show the movement of the 4RAR leftovers to HQ Company of the Task Force:

```
                    AUSTRALIAN MILITARY FORCES
                    NJK                              RESTRICTED
                                              ROUTINE ORDERS PART 2
21939       COMPILED FOR              RA INF                          ISSUE No:    INF  4045
12447
72116       DISTRIBUTION: LIST    'A' Plus Aust Records Det VIETNAM   DATE OF ISSUE: 22 MAY 69
0658              RO2      51306.     400      4045    69  V
```

EDP LINE No.	CORPS SHEET	PERSONAL PARTICULARS			KEYWORD	PARTICULARS OF OCCURRENCE		ENTRY No.
		4 RAR						
					UNIT	following now 6 RAR	14 May 69	
						AND		
					POSTING	as shown	14 May 69	
		2274919	Pte	D.W. EDMONDS		Dvr ECN 109		28,29.
		312567	Pte	G.J. HYDE		Mortarman ECN 238		20,21.
		312589	Pte	R.J. CLARK		Mortarman ECN 238		18,19.
		61925	Pte	A.E. MILLAR		Mortarman ECN 238		19,20.
		6410251	T/Cpl	M.W. McEWEN		Clerk Admin ECN 074		35,36.
					UNIT	following now 6 RAR	14 May 69	
						AND		
					POSTING	Rfn ECN 343	14 May 69	
		111814	Pte	R.H. APPLEBY				22,23.
		154459	Pte	R.C. ELLIS				18,19.
		156504	Pte	G.W. BEH				20,21.
		175509	Pte	D.N. MANSKI				19,20.
		1201633	Pte	C.J. FAHY				29,30.
		1201677	Pte	O.W. SCHULER				23,24.
		1201907	Pte	D.W. TATE				21,22.
		1202046	Pte	H.G. BROWNING				23,24.
		1202112	Pte	R.J. ENRIGHT				21,22.
		216853	Pte	K.G. LLOYD-THOMAS				32,33.
		218496	Pte	R.J. RICKERT				27,28.
		218512	Pte	E.W. COLMER				17,18.
		218523	Pte	D.R. MOSS				14,15.
		218527	Pte	R.A. BIGWOOD				21,22.
		218536	Pte	C.R. EBSWORTH				20,21.
		218602	Pte	R.J. CAIRNS				16,17.
		2184228	Pte	B.J. CANNONS				19,20.

Checked by.   RECORDS OFFICER

UNIT SERIAL

Two of the men from the 2nd D&E Platoon who were prepared to fight for the platoon's validation: Cpl Kevin Lloyd-Thomas (left) and Pte Richard Bigwood (in a captured NVA helmet)

That document states quite clearly that as of the 14th May 1969, the men listed had been re-posted from the 4th Battalion to the *6th Battalion*!

Yet none of us ever set foot in the 6th Battalion, and what's more, most of us were down at Baria hunting for fish by the 14th.

So that army document is demonstrably false.

The question is– why?

You cannot 'officially' falsify the movement of soldiers in war zones or the dates it occurred unless the organisation is manifestly incompetent, or attempting to hide something.

But the corruption doesn't end there.

Take this next 'official' document. It's not completely legible, but it is dated 17th July 1969– well after 2nd D&E Platoon had been disbanded.

AUSTRALIAN MILITARY FORCES

RESTRICTED

ROUTINE ORDERS PART 2

COMPILED FOR: RA INF
ISSUE No: INF 5727
DISTRIBUTION: LIST 'A' Plus Aust Records Det VIETNAM
DATE OF ISSUE: 17 ... 69

LINE No.	CORPS SHEET	PERSONAL PARTICULARS			KEYWORD	PARTICULARS OF OCCURRENCE	ENTRY No
		4 RAR					
		Ref INF 4045/69/-			UNIT	under particular of occurrence column amend 6 RAR to read HQ 1 TF	
		2274919	Pte	D.W. EDMONDS		Went to 9RAR	
		312567	Pte	G.J. HYDE		" " 9RAR	
		312589	Pte	R.J. CLARK		" " 9RAR	
		61925	Pte	A.E. MILLAR		" " 9RAR	
		111814	Pte	R.H. APPLEBY		" " 9RAR	
		154459	Pte	R.C. ELLIS		Went to 1ARU not 9RAR	
		156504	Pte	G.W. BEH		" " 9RAR	
		175509	Pte	D.N. MANSKI		" " 9RAR	
		1201633	Pte	C.J. FAHY		" " 9RAR	
		1201677	Pte	O.W. SCHULER		" " 9RAR	
		1201907	Pte	D.W. TATE		" " HQ 1TF	
		1202112	Pte	R.J. ENRIGHT		" " 9RAR	
		216853	Pte	K.G. LOYD-THOMAS		" " 1ARU not 9RAR	
		218496	Pte	R.J. RICKERT		" " 6RAR not 9RAR	
		218512	Pte	E.W. COLMER		" " HQ 1TF not 9RAR	
		218523	Pte	D.R. MOSS		" " 9RAR	
		218527	Pte	R.A. BIGWOOD		" " 9RAR	
		218536	Pte	C.R. EBSWORTH		" " 9RAR	
		218602	Pte	R.J. CAIRNS		" " 9RAR	
		2184228	Pte	B.J. CANNONS		" " HQ 1TF and 5RAR not 9RAR	

Checked by: ....

UNIT SERIAL

Only now, it shows an amendment.

The reference to '6RAR' has now become *'HQ 1TF'*.

That is to say, *after* the platoon had done its job, and hadn't suffered any casualties, and *after* the officers had got their medals, and *after* the platoon had been disbanded, the truth of the whereabouts of those thirty-nine men for that month or so could be put on the official record– stuck in the 'D&E Platoon' of Lt Ray Woolan.

It was a good ploy, and they almost got away with it.

But their capacity to deceive becomes transparent when the next document is viewed. It records *my* movements (after being wounded) as 'HQ 1 TF'. The fact was, by then, as earlier documents show, I had been transferred to the 9th Battalion on the 14th July– as per the official Roll Book of HQ Company.

(Those Roll Book pages are in the Attachments).

EDP LINE No.	CORPS SHEET	PERSONAL PARTICULARS			KEYWORD	PARTICULARS OF OCCURRENCE		ENTRY No
NOTICAS FROM	Action	HQ 1 TF						
9RAR	Bunker Sys	1201907	Pte	D.W. TATE	CASBC*	Wounded in Action LONG KHANH PROVINCE VIETNAM	19 Jul 69	23
					MED	adm 1 AUST FD HOSP VUNG TAU VIETNAM	19 Jul 69	24
1TF	Mortar Exp	216965	Cpl	T.R. YEO	CASBC*	Wounded in Action BIEN HOA PROVINCE VIETNAM	19 Jul 69	40
					MED	adm 24 EVAC HOSP	19 Jul 69	41
1TF	Mortar Exp	44683	Pte	R.W. STRAPPS	CASBC*	Wounded in Action BIEN HOA PROVINCE VIETNAM	19 Jul 69	26

(Note: This is exactly as I received this document from CARO, except that it is truncated).

Years later, I received a letter from an officer, 'D.F. Gibson' on behalf of the CO of Central Army Records. It was in response to my querying them about the obvious discrepancies regarding my service with the 9th Battalion.

He maintained that there was 'no record' of my having been posted to that battalion, and had had the temerity to use the 9th Battalion's unofficial record of its tour as further 'evidence' of this.

This is an extract from Gibson's letter:

> Dear Mr Tate,
>
> 1. I refer to your recent enquiries to this office concerning your service with the Australian Army in Vietnam.
>
> 2. Records held by this office indicate that you saw special service in Vietnam (Southern Zone) from 23 December 1968 until 22 July 1969 when you departed Vietnam as a result of your being wounded in action on 19 July 1969.
>
> 3. Records held by this office indicate that you were officially posted to the following units during your period of service in Vietnam:
>
> a. 1 ARU - 23 December 1968 to 26 January 1969;
>
> b. 4 RAR - 27 January 1969 to 13 May 1969; and
>
> c. HQ 1TF - 14 May 1969 to 22 July 1969.
>
> 4. Copies of the Infantry Routine Orders Part 2 covering these posting are attached for your information.
>
> 5. Unfortunately this office has no details to confirm that you were posted to the strength of 9 RAR. Routine Orders for other soldiers posted from 4 RAR to other units from 30 May 1969, when 4 RAR returned to Australia, have also been checked and it has been found that those who went to 9 RAR are clearly recorded. Unfortunately your name does not appear as one of those posted to 9 RAR. A Routine Order Part 2 clearly shows that you were posted to HQ 1TF from 14 May 1969.
>
> 6. That aside however, information is held by this office to indicate that 9 RAR did raise some sort of notification to advise that you had been wounded in action in Long Khanh Province on 19 July 1969. Unfortunately however, HQ 1TF raised the official Routine Order Part 2 to record you were wounded whilst 9 RAR only recorded members of their unit who had been wounded in the same action, making no reference to your name. Copies of these documents are attached.

Gibson's letter was manifestly in error.

So, according to that document, 9RAR *'only recorded members of their unit who had been wounded in the same action, making no reference to your name."*?

Yet clearly, that I had served with the 9th Battalion is obvious from documents posted earlier in this narrative– not to mention in about eight minutes of colour film I captured.

No, the degree of maladministration of my service records was so severe, I could only conclude that there had to be more to it. That my antagonists had all sorts of administrative errors to use to their advantage, assisted their opportunity to discredit me.

The Army had given them plenty of ammunition.

CHAPTER 23
THE LEVER

You can waltz around with politicians and generals, or you could go to the one department within the military that has a responsibility for the accurate recording of history– the *Army History Unit*.

No bureaucrats; no fools.

So, even as Ms Jennie George was furthering the matter in Canberra, we focussed our attentions on engaging the Army History Unit for its opinion– a two-pronged attack.

We found an ally in Colonel Bill Houston who headed up that institution, although I admit we also tested *his* patience at times.

He was a pragmatist who understood well the sanctity of the historical record; and we were now irrational at times, aggressive, impatient, and spoiling for a fight. There were some intense phone calls.

After examining all the evidence though, Houston didn't hesitate in advising us that he was in 'no doubt that a second D&E Platoon existed'.

But he wasn't about to declare that a '2nd D&E Platoon' had existed.

There was a subtle difference.

Ted Colmer upped the ante.

The elephant in the room had always the matter of those 'atrocities' that had been committed. And the longer we were denied, and the more frustrated we became at the bureaucratic recalcitrance we were up against, the more tempted we were to throw them into the debate as a bargaining tool.

Colmer had already dipped his toe into that pool.

Early in the piece he had examined the legalities of the matter, and deduced that by *any* definition the actions of the combined force at Thua Tich all those years ago had contravened the Geneva Conventions.

An earlier email (September 2007) made it abundantly clear that Colmer would use the 'atrocities' as leverage, for advantage. He tried it with Minister Billson after we were unsuccessful arguing our case at the AWM. He wrote (sic):

> *'... I submit in accordance with all evidence that movement and placement of our 2nd D & E Platoon, together with elements of 2 Tp B Sqn, 3 Cavalry Regiment, under the leadership of Captain Thomas Arrowsmith MID MG, with the inclusion of a 5 RAR Mortar Section, and Combat Sappers, was specifically orchestrated for the purposes of conducting a large scale linear ambush placement in that Thua Tic District. I submit that it was predicted that our platoon, as a composite force together with cavalry elements, were purposely exposed to a large scale encirclement of enemy forces at Thua Tic; and not as you have explained Sir, and intend to include in your Final Volumes: Fighting to The Finish? for publication as I understand in August of 2008.*
>
> *In conclusion, I will not touch upon the other **extremely serious and contentious matters**, but expect that the Minister For Veterans' Affairs, will now finally provide our platoon members with closure, under the auspices of offering our membership the due dignity we all deserve; and thus proceed to accept our 2nd D&E Platoon promulgation forthwith....'*

But to his credit, Billson wasn't swayed by Colmer's threat to *'touch upon the extremely serious and contentious matters'*.

Colmer tried the same tactic again with the officials of the Australian War Memorial when he threatened legal action against both men– the Director, Gen Steve Gower, and the historian, Ashley Ekins. In the same rant, he let his opinion of various officers patently obvious (sic):

> *'My research has revealed their contravention (Thua Tich & elsewhere) under Part: 1, Article 3- Fourth Geneva Convention (or GCIV) with Article 3, stating with reference to combatants who are 'hors de combat' (out of the fight) due to*

their death from the ambush, with (a) & (c) inter alia, relating to mutilation, and degrading treatment, irrespective of whether they are dead or alive! The Australian Military (Commonwealth) Law at the time would have also considered this treatment prohibitive, and subject to Court Martial.

There is no statute of limitations with such serious breaches.

*With Ashley Ekins' most determined analysis of this matter flawed and totally fabricated, has now prompted to me to now consider proceeding with actually committing myself to compiling a "Brief of Evidence" that I will forward to the Federal Police. If Ashley Ekins continues to insist that we were never part of D & E Platoon, then **I am prepared to touch on the atrocities**, that he personally insists didn't happen. With that attitude as a spokesperson for the AWM- remember, Gower, and Withnell were present as involved representatives of AWM, 18 May 2007; and by such presence, and lack of protest, corroborating Ekins' assertions, irrespective of remaining mute, are also equally as complicit to the actual allegations (by common purpose) if proven per se, by, a); "Perverting the Course of Natural Justice" which is still valid at common law, indictable to 20 years imprisonment, and thus, b); "Perjury" when they lie under oath before either a Federal Police Investigation, or at any proceeding Court venue, under oath, inter alia.*

Ashley Ekins' particularly, is now in a most precarious position, criminally (and perhaps civilly) liable at Law by any Federal Police, or Private Civil Investigation. (Ekins' Professional Misconduct also Amounts to CORRUPTION - with Federal Watchdogs, and the Commonwealth Public Service, available for complaint and such pursuance. (and perhaps civilly by exacerbating our PTSD, which in my case I can attest to being legitimately exacerbated since 18 May '07). Your mental suffering Don, may well have been longer and more sustained with this particular matter!

With your meeting with Pearson, I now don't believe for one minute that he can't remember, and retract my earlier statements, after actually just recently discovering, with reference to the June Narratives that Major Chinn, GS02 OPS was referred to as SEAGULL, and if Pearson's memory serves him that well to actually stab part of his Intel team in the back, then his memory is selective and fabricated! This evidence, as discovered, confirming Pearson, Rooks, Chinn and Arrowsmith's complicity will be included in my Statutory Declaration, that I will complete at some stage Don, given that I am already past page 50, and expect it to gather more than 200 pages? I also believe, that at Law, (Maj-General) Daly himself is complicit, by not acting in accordance with his obvious knowledge (mens rea) and non-action (actis reus). The doctrine of Law with these matters does not somehow change because of actions perpetrated in a Theatre of War!

Yes– the 'atrocities' had become leverage, as well as a subtle threat to place Brigadier Pearson's role in the affair front and centre– a tactic we had previously hinted at, but been reluctant to do. No point in dragging down such a revered figure if we could avoid it.

Bureaucracies were altogether another matter.

Colmer had clearly set out the legal definition, the jurisdiction, and the ramifications of the 'atrocities' committed on May 30th 1969; threatened to forward a statement to the Australian Federal Police in which he threatened to 'touch on the atrocities' and alleging that senior ex-military officers were 'complicit'; and named them.

Threatening to use that leverage moved us in a whole new direction.

And not everyone was pleased. Not everyone was as big and bold as they were forty years previous. Time had dulled their spirit for a fight.

Allan Roach and Dennis Manski withdrew all support– while Kevin Lloyd-Thomas was vacillating.

Allan Roach said (sic):

'……You had a round table conference at the AWM that was, I believe, more successful than you could have hoped for (and that I certainly thought it would have been). It appeared from your reports that Ekins and Gower at least made an effort to find some "common ground".

Did anyone really expect the details of the "burial" or the "toggle rope incident" to go to print..and I for one wouldn't be real comfortable with that, particularly with the Parker/Gillson discovery just recently. That is not having a go at anyone directly involved, if I was standing somewhere else it could well have been me..that's just the way it is.

Incidentally, Woolan won't be the first (or last) to receive a medal that not everyone agrees with. It wasn't his choice, and I don't know that it's up to "us" to comment.'

Richard Bigwood made good his promise to provide a Statutory Declaration which was sent to the Attorney General, and then walk away from the battle and let it be. Time, and family, and an inherent desire to be part of the veteran community and not isolated from it, were his considerations.

As for me, well I had a book to launch and promote– the publishing contract with Murdoch Books had been signed, and *The War Within* printed and about to hit the bookstores. While it contained things I wasn't proud of as a man or as a human being, writing that memoir was the greatest achievement of my life, and given that I'd had a reduced working life as a result of the war wounds, it *had* to be my priority.

It was serendipitous that the fight to validate the 2nd D&E Platoon married up with the launch of my book.

I determined to use the one as a promotional opportunity– similar to how Bob Buick had used veteran controversy about his illegal wearing of the LS&GC Medal in 2000 to further *his* book sales.

What was good for the goose, and so on.

The 'atrocities' were a weapon of last resort.

Colonel Bill Houston of the Army History Unit wasn't a man who could be pushed around.

He examined the evidence, and found it wanting. It was a setback.

I found Houston to be a considered, intelligent man prepared to do the right thing, and not one likely to be anyone's fall-guy. He was his own man.

As he struggled with the matter, aware of the storm that raged within the veteran community, I made my opinion of him clear to all (sic):

> *'Guys...I just had a very long, reasoned, intelligent conversation with Bill Houston. He is on our side- but handicapped (as everyone else has been) by the lack of formal paperwork. He acknowledges that he has ABSOLUTELY NO DOUBT WHATSOEVER that this platoon existed, and did what we said it did. He did not know (and was very surprised to hear) that there were photographs taken at Thua Tich and Xuyen Moc showing Pearson, Rooks and co on site (Ted...you might be interested in Bill's statement to the effect that there is no record of Pearson's flight out that day..??); nor was he aware of the 2 min interview with Arrowsmith held by the AWM. I told him that if the AWM doesn't supply it, Ted- you would. (Or at least tell him how and where you found it) He was VERY interested in that interview.*
>
> *He said it was the first time he had heard we'd been divided into rifle sections, and asked me who those section-commanders were (I could only recall Ellecombe;*

Manski; and Kevin Lloyd-Thomas..I thought there was one other)...(Gower's statement that we'd been divided into a "single rifle section" has proved a difficult hurdle to overcome, so he was appreciative of my explaining the sub-division under Riddle, as best I could recall)

He will be pursuing Pratt's official letter to Adam Rainford (and that alone might prove to be the key document) insofar as we have a relatively senior officer publicly declaring that he formed (and named) the 2nd D&E Platoon.

He then asked me what we wanted..and off the bat, I told him:

- formal acknowledgement that the 2nd D&E Platoon existed

- that the record of its activities be detailed

- that our individual service records accurately contain this info……I repeat, he is on our side.'

Ted Colmer then sent him a list of *all* the references to 'D&E Platoon' he had located in every army record between May 12th and mid-June of 1969.

It was so comprehensive, that even the stupidest of men had to realise that no *one* D&E Platoon could possibly have been responsible for them all, and when that information was sent around the 'net, veterans began to suspect that validation of the platoon was a *fait accompli*.

In March of 2008, Colonel Houston put paid to that, replying directly to Colmer:

'Thank you for the list of references. I had found sufficient to realise that there were two elements operating that were called D&E Platoon.

I must add, however, that my reading of all the material I can find suggests that the platoon that was attached to 2 Troop, B Squadron, 3 Cavalry Regiment was never intended to be more than an ad hoc organisation. It seems clear that a number of people from 4RAR were moved to HQ Company into a holding element, with the intention of redeploying them to other battalions later. While they were with Headquarters Company, a job was found for them, essentially as Assault Troopers with the cavalry.

Clearly the platoon performed well in this role, but I am convinced from what I have found that ad hoc D&E Platoon' would be a more appropriate title than 2nd D&E Platoon. I have found nothing to suggest any intention to officially raise a second D&E Platoon in Headquarters Company. Accordingly, the sudden surge of e-mails, suggesting that the existence of 2nd D&E Platoon as a part of the establishment of 1st Australian Task Force has been proved, is incorrect….'

Colmer went ballistic.

On the 13th March 2008, he hit back at Colonel Houston, again using the threat of exposing the atrocities to embarrass the Defence Force:

> *'I am now formally putting you on notice Mr Houston, that I will be immediately seeking counsel opinion, with a purpose of taking vicarious action against you in either the Federal or Supreme Court, and my Statutory Declaration, will be converted to an "Affidavit" under the rules and regulations of that jurisdiction?*
> *I will also now proceed to the Federal Police with a comprehensive "Brief of Criminal Action?" regarding the matters of the 30 May 1969 inter alia!!'*

Ted Colmer was all talk though. Piss and wind. The '200-page brief of evidence' he boasted of having compiled for the Australian Federal Police never saw the light of day. He said he had weapons aplenty stored in and around his home (suggesting 'suicide by police') and made it clear he would be a hostile witness should the police ever drop around to ask him questions about the matter.

No wonder Maj George Pratt retained him in the generic D&E Platoon when the '2nd' was disbanded instead of sending him off to a genuine infantry battalion like most of the rest of us. Just like Major Pratt, Pte Ted Colmer had found his niche.

Whichever way it went, one thing was certain– it was all or nothing. A showdown was looming.

We'd put up, and now it was coming to a head.

As I said, Kevin Lloyd-Thomas had done two tours of Vietnam as an infantryman.

His stint in the 2nd D&E Platoon was a minor part of those tours.

One unit he had served with was the 2nd Battalion, and his platoon-commander in that unit was Lt Vic Adams. Adams was now the office and campaign manager for the Parliamentary-Secretary for Defence– the Hon Dr Mike Kelly MP.

In the background to the public debate, Lloyd-Thomas and Vic Adams had been discussing the ins and outs of the matter and the likelihood of it being resolved. Lloyd-Thomas had a dual reason for pushing for the validation of the platoon– both he *and* his brother Nigel had been at Thua Tich.

Nigel Lloyd-Thomas had been a member of the Mortar Platoon.

It had come as a shock to both of them when they stumbled upon each other outside the gates to the village. It was the first time they had met in Vietnam.

On that occasion they were tackling a cunning enemy; this time they were taking on an even more cunning bureaucracy.

With Anzac Day approaching in 2008 (and Jennie George's submissions on Mike Kelly's table) Vic Adams agreed to meet with us all personally.

He did just that.

At the completion of the march in Sydney that year, we all assembled in Hyde Park– along with Adam Rainford and his camera crew in tow.

Vic Adams listened intently as we rattled off the key points– highlighting the formal announcements by Pratt and Parkin as to the platoon's formal title.

'I'll be making a favourable recommendation to Mike Kelly,' he said, shaking our hands with a wink. 'I think you have made your case.'

Then he and Lloyd-Thomas left for a drink together to reflect on other battles they'd fought in another time.

There was one issue unresolved– *my* whereabouts during the ambush at Thua Tich.

It was a question that aggravated everyone, including me. There'd been some considerable spite surrounding the issue, emanating from Ted Colmer's assertion that I wasn't at Thua Tich at all.

In what was nothing more than sheer malice, Colmer had sent a letter to the Australian Veteran Matters website (and many individual veterans) advising them that I *wasn't* present at Thua Tich, and that therefore my assertions about the contentions that had occurred weren't plausible.

It was sheer malice on his part. There was no evidence to support the contention. Talk about muddy the waters. It poisoned them.

All the time, he knew damn well I *had* been present. He'd said as much in an email to Alan Price, President of the 4RAR Association (QLD) in June, 2009:

'...and yes Jim Riddle, Barney Bigwood; Kevin Lloyd-Thomas; Don Tate, and all others including Peter "Pedro" Allen were involved in the engagements at Thua Tich and elsewhere....'

(Alan Price, incidentally, had never released this fact to the veteran community despite realising its significance, and despite a pretence that he was concerned about the welfare of *all* 4RAR members. Why not? Because he too, was a contributor to the AVM web site, and it suited his purposes in keeping such information to himself. Such is the spite within the veteran community).

But the enmity between me and Colmer had spilled over, and the true nature of the man came to the fore.

The problem for me in handling this was that, over time, the mind had played some curious tricks. So I found myself in a situation where I had a confusion of images and fact and contrary comment in my mind to deal with, and now a damaging comment by a man who had once been an ally.

But the denial by Colmer as to my presence at Thua Tich was compounded by differing opinions from others as to my actual whereabouts during the ambush. One man had me at the listening post; one had me at Arrowsmith's position– and me having no recollection of being at either place, with just those images – as stated earlier – floating around my mind.

It was Robert Enright who gave me some closure when he reappeared on the scene after decades in the wilderness.

His name had cropped up regularly in the early discussions as we sorted out the make-up of the platoon, and determining what other personnel from other units might have been involved.

He was clearly recorded as being an infantryman who had come over from 'D' Company 4RAR (ex-11Platoon) but there had also been a reference to a 'Sapper Enright' from Engineers that threw us for a while.

Eventually, we learned that he had transferred to the Engineers *after* his stint as an infantryman in Vietnam which accounted for the confusion. But despite our best efforts, we couldn't track him down.

As I pointed out earlier, Robert Enright was a significant cog in the story.

He entered the fray quite unexpectedly a day after Anzac Day 2012 when he first became aware of the vitriol about me and Jim Riddle and the others on the off-shore web sites. He immediately sent a letter to them pointing out that their comments were way off the mark.

Enright Letter to the off-shore web site, April 25th 2011 (sic):

> *'I knew the Tate and Riddle guy…and owe them both. I never forget the slight from Tate when he pointed an M60 at me albeit unloaded when climbing on an APC to go to Xuyen Moc……Tate did go out that way and all the tracks (APCs) were at Thua Tich on that particular ambush……I did not see Tate as three APCs*

took off to the east to ambush a cart track and I was aboard one of them while Riddle and some went down the main road and later I was told reported seventy odd noggys on the move and then wham...by the time we got back the sun was up and baking the last body left on the road...I covered Manski as he unceremoniously dragged the unfortunate girl back towards the road arch of ancient where she was tied to an APC along with three others which made four and seven more to be blown up as crows meat...life's a bitch and then you're dead in the blink of an eye...after we took off for Xuyen Moc a light fire team spotted some noggys in the bush on the side of the road and we got five more after a well-executed fire contact by said APCs...the incident spoken of concerning an apc hitting a mine was on the beach road from Xuyen moc and is another story of incompetence, tunnel vision, and ignoring advice from this dumb grunt...'

Robert Enright

In an instant, Enright had validated my attendance at Thua Tich, the treatment of the enemy dead, and the attempted VC ambush of the APC column as we headed towards Xuyen Moc to the veteran community.

In a subsequent email to me, he formally introduced himself (sic):

'hello don, was just browsing on anzac day and found you lot and it seems what a mess you have stirred up... you wouldn't remember me I'm sure because we never spoke ,, but the few I knew I have never forgotten i.e Riddle, Manski, Bann, Ellis, Grant, Whitney, Slattery, especially Slatts, I smoked my first joint in his company and laughed for hours...I've been reading the posts on the avm site...it's a full on shouting match,, and you are carrying a bucket of water to toss at hell on earth but one has to ask why such a vitriolic reaction?... why indeed....after all we were considered no more than a few dumb grunts without a future...and those bodies they desecrated?? I mean so what now... even though years ago I became obsessed with the memory, the dead don't care and the power to be even less...'

...and then made other pertinent observations in a series of vivid images (sic):

'...the shooting at the rice paddy workers who were aghast at the sight of their own (that is, the bodies being towed)... *and just as we turned into the main square of xuyen*

moc I could see the command vehicle which had turned left and the c.o. leaned back to cut the rope to release the done and dusted corpses when a bunch of so called civvy's came running out...such a hero...I never ever thought of you as anything else than switched on...that was all part of your gung-ho nature of wanting to be a professional soldier...'

In that short exchange, Enright had also validated the shooting at civilians; the manner in which Capt Tom Arrowsmith had deposited the bodies in Xuyen Moc; and offered a personal comment about my relative ability as a soldier.

He wasn't a confrontationist, but he wasn't a man to take a backward step either.

The cowards who hid on those off-shore web sites came after him too, as they did anyone who dared present an alternative version of events.

They needed to be careful.

Enright gave me the opinion he wasn't a man to be trifled with.

But the significant aspect as far as I was concerned was that he had validated my presence at Thua Tich– and *that* was all-important.

To this day, I don't know if it was Ted Colmer's threat of initiating federal police action against everyone, or if it was the more detailed analysis of all the facts and evidence presented to Jennie George MP, or if it was Vic Adams' words in important ears, or a decision made privately by Colonel Bill Houston and his Army History Unit after a careful evaluation of the facts– but in April 2008, we got wind that the federal government was close to recognising the platoon.

Or was it because I had informed every politician within earshot that my memoir, *The War Within* would be published that July by one of the country's most prestigious publishers– Murdoch Books, and would contain an outline of the corruptions, and the atrocities involving the 2nd D&E Platoon and its 'disappearance' from the war record. And further, that from that point on, the matter would be in the public domain?

Whatever the reason, on the 29th May 2008 – exactly thirty-eight years to the day that the ambush at Thua Tich was fought – the Hon Mike Kelly MP called us down to Parliament House, Canberra.

And he announced that not only had the 2nd D&E Platoon *existed*, but that it was to be *'forever enshrined in the histories of the war.'*

The Bob Buicks of the world almost choked on their cornflakes.

This was that Statement:

THE HON. DR MIKE KELLY MP
Parliamentary Secretary for Defence Support

Thursday, 29 May 2008   019/2008

COMBAT HISTORY OF THE 2ND D&E PLATOON IN THE VIETNAM WAR

The Parliamentary Secretary for Defence Support, the Hon. Dr Mike Kelly AM MP, and Ms Jennie George MP met today with veterans of the 2nd D&E Platoon who served in the Vietnam War as part of the Australian Task Force (ATF), to discuss the acknowledgement of the Platoon and its history in that conflict.

For many years now the surviving members of the Platoon have been battling to have their record and role in the Vietnam War officially recognised.

Dr Kelly said, "I am pleased to announce that I have been able to bring this long struggle to a conclusion by confirming that the Rudd Labor Government and the Defence Department have been able to determine that the Platoon did indeed exist and engaged in a series of important actions in Vietnam as part of the Australian Task Force."

"I would like to pay particular tribute to the courage and dedication of the men of the 2nd D&E Platoon. They were a team that was effectively born in battle, not having been formally raised and trained as a sub-unit in Australia before deploying to Vietnam, but being assembled in country in response to the particular security requirements of the ATF. They were able to come together as an effective fighting force thanks to the professionalism of the soldiers and in particular the Non-Commissioned Officer who led them, Corporal James Bertram Riddle," he said.

The action for which the 2nd D&E Platoon should particularly be noted for was the successful ambush they executed together with 2 Troop, B Squadron, 3rd Cavalry Regiment, in May 1969 at Thua Tich. This was a ferocious battle that involved the engaged troops taking on a much larger enemy force beyond artillery support and through many heroic individual and collective efforts were able to soundly defeat the enemy without loss. Their success was a tribute to their professionalism and the outstanding leadership and courage of Corporal Riddle whose personal actions ensured the survival of many members of the Platoon who would otherwise surely have been killed.

"I am delighted to advise these proud veterans that their role in the war will be forever enshrined and acknowledged in the Official History of the Vietnam War which is soon to be published. I was privileged to have been able to meet with them personally and thank them for their service to the country and the Australian Army. They served and performed in the finest traditions of the Australian Defence Force and they will have an honoured place in its history. As part of my responsibility for education and training in the ADF I intend to see that our future generations of Army leaders will have the opportunity to not only be aware of this legacy but to have the opportunity to learn from it," Dr Kelly said.

Media contacts:
Mark Sjolander (Dr Mike Kelly):   02 6277 4840 or 0407 102 220
Defence Media Liaison: 02 6265 3343 or 0408 498 664

www.defence.gov.au

CHAPTER 24
THE WAR WITHIN

Then, my memoir– *The War Within* was published.

Another journalist, Paul Ham, gave the speech at the launch.

He is the acclaimed author of the cerebral volume *'Vietnam: The Australian War'* (Harper and Collins); is an established authority on the history of the Vietnam War; is his own man, and doesn't come under the spell of the powerbrokers at the Australian War Memorial.

He also does his homework.

I was quite chuffed that Paul Ham had accepted the invitation. He said,

> *'"The War Within" is an extraordinary memoir- an unadorned, uncensored, unabashed account of one raucous Australian life by a man who has spent much of his life fighting, fighting authority, fighting rivals, fighting a war, fighting perceived injustices, and fighting at times, the enemies of his mind- a man at war with himself. Not all of us contest the inner battlefield with the grit, guts, and impulsiveness of Don Tate, but most of us will recognise the landscape of the mind as he portrays it...'*

It was some rap.
He then referred to my fight to validate the 2nd D&E Platoon:

> '"The War Within" is a memoir that is at once a dramatic, disturbing, sexually charged, often very funny and ultimately moving portrait of a man who has found the inner strength to self-overcome; it is a picture of a steadfast friend; a courageous soldier; but also of a man captive to a volatile character that would sooner leap to attack a perceived injustice than stand aside to discuss the merits of the case. If Don Tate is prone, on occasions, to lunge before he thinks, and think after he lunges, his combative character has served him remarkably well in two celebrated cases, of which many veterans will be aware: his campaign to repatriate to Australia, Jim Riddle, a British-born commando who led Don's unit in Vietnam; and his efforts to secure the official recognition of the 2nd D&E Platoon, in which Don Tate and other veterans served with distinction in Vietnam.'

He then advised the audience that he had made an alteration to his own significant, historical tome by adding the following statement to it (sic):

> '... *a controversial example of this tactical success was the Second Defence and Deployment Platoon, a ready reaction force created in May 1969 with the aim of inflicting lethal incursions into enemy held territory. The platoon performed with exceptional results under its British-born commander, Corporal Jim Riddle, before being unceremoniously disbanded after only weeks in the field leaving no trace of its existence (until July 2008, under constant pressure from Private Don Tate, a former platoon member, when the Australian government formally recognised that the platoon had existed)....*'

We were getting traction.

The formal recognition of the 2nd D&E Platoon by the Hon Dr Mike Kelly MP in May 2008 should have been the end of the matter.

It wasn't.

Journalist, Lisa Whitehead did a great, follow-up story for the ABCs '7.30 Report' which she called 'Ghost Platoon'. It highlighted the facts of the matter and gave the story some considerable impetus. It may be viewed on-line at:

http://www.abc.net.au/7.30/content/2008/s2298141.htm

It didn't help. In fact, the personal attacks, the vitriol, the slander on off-shore web sites increased dramatically.

And I was fool enough to play the same game.

I have always been spontaneous and reactionary, so when the AVM and other web sites began their attacks on me, I didn't hold back.

One of the nation's foremost military men, Brigadier George Mansford AM (a man of some considerable substance) counselled me against doing so. He wrote (sic):

> '...*given your willingness to charge forward I doubt you will heed this advice. But you need to change your strategy. The answer is cease fire. Your enemies thrive in an environment where they can needle you. YOU do not have to prove anything in regards your past military service. The undeniable facts are there for all to see, including official recognition in regards the 2nd D&E Pl. It really does not matter what one or two individuals think, and I doubt that regardless of circumstances that will ever change. (Besides they have a point of view to express regardless of how*

irritating it is to you). Your best weapon is to totally ignore them. It will possibly make them more desperate and indeed frustrated, and no doubt tempt you but you must ignore it. The problem with retaliating is that often there are strong comments made which you might later regret, and worse still, some of your supporters may question your actions. The recent example is where an individual admitted his respect for you but did question your comments. Like it or not, that is a small victory for your arch rivals. If necessary switch off your computer. In conclusion you have climbed what was that unconquered mountain by ensuring your service in the Regiment was recognised, you have proven the existence of the once phantom platoon, you have written a book which is a best seller, and you have been identified with many, many fellow veterans who before never had heard of the name Tate. Don't stuff up such a successful campaign of vindication. Let it go, cease fire, ignore them, break contact, fall back to the high ground and get out of the swamps, whatever....and above all use your evident talents and energy (including the pen) to do far more constructive work than belting your head against a brick wall. Cobber, like all those who wore the uniform, I luv ya, but by God there may come a time when I will have to come down there and remove your magazine and firing pin from your rifle, and if I am not big enough I will bring a bloody RSM with me....!'

Sadly, I didn't heed his advice. Turning the other cheek was never my forte. He was right. My reactions were counter-productive.

The national historian – Ashley Ekins – did not take kindly to the federal government's decision to formally recognise the 2nd D&E Platoon.

He gave evidence at a parliamentary hearing into another vexed military matter on the 15th March 2010. It was a 'Standing Committee on Petitions'– regarding the convictions of 'Breaker' Morant, Handcock, and Witton during the Boer War.

The following exchange between Ekins and my local Member of Parliament, Ms Jennie George who had played a significant role in the 2nd D&E Platoon's validation said much about the intransigent opinion of the historian:

> — Ms Jennie George MP: *'...You spoke about irrefutable facts and the futility of a pardon. You claim there was no evidence of secret orders by Kitchener as if that was a certainty. Yet just in more recent times I have personally on behalf of a constituent had an example where official historians and indeed the Australian War*

Memorial got it wrong as recently as the Vietnam War, where for decades the War Memorial and official historians had written out of existence the 2nd D&E platoon and now the government has recognised that in fact that platoon existed and that records relating to that platoon have proven that case...'

— Mr Ashley Ekins, Historian: *'...Any good historian would be quick to agree with Ms George that of course history is a process of assessment of evidence. More evidence accumulates and interpretations change over time. There is no doubt about that. I am not going to go into the issue of the 2nd D&E platoon, for which there was absolutely no evidence, by the way, and the Memorial still holds to that position. But that is a matter for another time. A number of the people who lobbied Ms George at the time have now refuted the evidence that they put forward and said in fact there was no such unit. But that is a matter for another time and place.'*

This exchange raised two questions:

(a) Ashley Ekins asserted that 'there was absolutely no evidence that the 2nd D&E Platoon existed' and 'the Memorial holds to that position.' Given that the Australian government had been satisfied that enough evidence had been provided to formally recognise the platoon, did the national historian incorrectly advise the Standing Committee?

(b) Ashley Ekins also stated that 'A number of the people who lobbied Ms George at the time have now refuted the evidence that they put forward and said in fact there was no such unit'. Since as far as I am aware, I was the *only* person who lobbied Ms George – and that I had *never* refuted the evidence – did this mean that the national historian misled the Standing Committee on Petitions for a second time?

I just thought to myself, you're kidding. Was there no end to it?

No, there wasn't.

In fact, the publication of *The War Within* resulted in a further upsurge of vitriol from a small element of the veteran community. There was so much malice in it, so much twisting and contortion of facts. Anything I said or wrote (even letters to the editor of a newspaper) was published and commented on.

Idle hands and sick minds can do enormous damage. Some of it was vicious; some, more subtle. Cowards proliferated.

But when you've spent a year of your life in a full body plaster as I did after I was wounded, one needs a strong mind to get through it– and a strong mind was required now to deal with what was coming my way.

Irrespective of the fact that the evidence had been tested by the Army History Unit, and that politicians had validated the platoon (with nothing to gain from doing so) nothing would appease my antagonists.

One of the major figures who attacked me used the pseudonym, 'Fergus Fairfax'. It was such a weak way for men to act.

We never learned who 'Fergus Fairfax' was, although we had our deep suspicions. Some suggested he was a former legal officer from the war who had gone on to become a legal eagle of note; others maintained it was likely to be a former officer of some substance, an author perhaps with a tainted gallantry award and a knowledge of psychology with links to low-life in one particular battalion.

Whoever it was, he had a coward's heart.

One of 'Fergus'' attacks against me went like this:

'NEWS FLASH – NEWS FLASH – NEWS FLASH
Just in case you missed it the first Three Hundred Times.

Don Tate went to war. Don wrote a book. Don got lost in the jungle. Don was a hero. Don didn't get a medal. Don is not happy about not getting a medal. Don got wounded. Don is a Mad Galah. Don is in denial about being a Mad Galah. Don says AWM staff are halfwits. Don hates Army Officers. Don dreamed of a 2nd D&E Platoon. Don is not happy. Don is full of hate. Don does not like Fergus. Don is confused. Don is not a nice man. Don is a good book seller...'

It wasn't the worst of the slander. But sometimes, it got to me, and I reacted. And unfortunately, the reactions were exactly what they wanted. I'd played right into their hands.

But letting the steam out was also good for the soul.

My reaction was (sic):

Subject: FERGUS.YOU GUTLESS PIECE OF SHIT!
Yeah..okay, you've sucked me into a reply Fergus because those you accuse are damned if they don't respond, and damned if they do. Personally, I don't give a

f..what you think, because you're a only a half man, if any part of a man at all. ...I'll answer some of the charges against me publicly..

First, re Jim Riddle. The only time Jim Riddle has entered the book promotion arena, was when I invited him to the Caloundra event. And there again, I was caught between a rock and a hard place. If I hadn't invited him, I'd have been the worst bastard in the world, and if I did, some arsehole like you would accuse me of using him. I'll remind you, you piece of shit, that the plaque erected in Jim Riddle's honour took me years of negotiation, and was all my work. And he's made it clear, that when he dies, he wants his ashes scattered there because I was the only one (up to that point) who had ever positively recognised his worth as a man and soldier. He's not sick because he was "used" as part of my book promotion. He's "sick" because some other gutless wonder bashed him in Brisbane, and it resulted in a stroke- and his 'mates' at the time declined to make it a police matter.

Second..as for using Ted Colmer and others as part of my book promotion, I'll say this- NO ONE coerces Ted Colmer or Barney Bigwood into ANYTHING. They are men in their own right, who stand on their own legs. And I'd rather have a Ted Colmer beside me in a blue than some craven, cowardly squib like you who's not man enough to put your real name to correspondence. Wimp!

The 2nd D&E Platoon matter...get over it you deadshit, people in power have analysed all the evidence..(that's ALL the evidence) and made their decision to acknowledge that the platoon DID exist. Nothing squibs like you can ever have it altered- not even those halfwits in the AWM hell-bent on protecting a few officers at the expense of truth and integrity.

And a member of the "Mad Galahs"?..again, I've never been a part of any such organisation. Haven't got a clue about it, and couldn't care less. As I see it, it's just another piece of the veteran community doing its best to right old wrongs, and look after the newer vets by doing so. I'm not Barry Corse's best mate, and some months ago, asked him to delete me from his email list. That's not out of disrespect for the man or his motives, only because I didn't agree with the manner he writes letters. He probably doesn't like the way I write mine. But again, Corse is an ex-infantry officer who was involved in combat and was never found wanting. He doesn't have to prove himself to someone like you. So I'm hardly a key figure in a movement I know nothing about, and aren't on speaking terms with one of its key personnel!!

And as for savaging George Mansford and Neil Weekes..well all I can say there, is you ought to make a point of meeting those men one day. Shake hands with them. What you'll be shaking hands with- is the best of manhood, not that cringing, spineless example you see in the mirror each morning. I won't defend them any further. Most who know them personally, know those two blokes can walk around with their heads up in any company and don't fear some garden-gnome like you.

And you can say what you want about me 'Fergus', and twist anything to suit your own crude determinations- but there are some things you can never take from me: - on my first day in the jungle, I was separated from the rest of my platoon, and took on a small Viet Cong force ON MY OWN. (That action is recorded in Lt Avery's "In the Anzac Spirit") My platoon commander didn't even know my name that day- but I tell you this, if I was an officer, that action would most certainly have gotten me a medal. After all, others got medals for a damned sight less. And secondly, on my last day in the jungle, I was one of only 3 men from my section who ran into a Viet Cong killing field- knowing that every bloke in the first section had worn it. Two of us got wounded outright- the other one of the three, scored a MM. Whatever you say Fergus- you WILL NEVER take away from me the fact that when the bullets were flying, I wasn't doggin' it behind a log somewhere. I mightn't have been the best soldier (and never claimed to be) but I never ran scared like some did. So shove your web site and your dirtbag comments fair up your Khyber Pass- and go back to playing with yourself.

Don Tate author, "The War Within"

'Fergus Fairfax' replied:

'Although Don is not a nice man, Fergus is happy that Don writes to him. Unfortunately even though Don extols his own virtues with alacrity and passion Fergus is still convinced he is a vicious mercenary ratbag who will say anything to sell his book.

Finally, in case you missed it. Don wrote a book.

Aye, Fergus Fairfax

Our old former platoon commander, Barry Parkin bought into the exchange– the last time he'd enter the fray. He wrote back to 'Fergus', saying simply,

'Fergus…I agree with everything Don Tate said– especially about you.'

Very effective.

'Fergus' never replied to Barry Parkin, but he had another go at me by trotting out his opinion of the 2nd D&E Platoon matter (sic):

'Politicians who declare the existence of a "Phantom platoon" in Vietnam, are also agreeing that very loyal, honourable and competent Army officers of the era were dishonest and corrupt.

A group of in transit infantry soldiers were posted to HQ 1ATF for a period of around six weeks, the Commander HQ 1ATF expanded his Defence and Employment Platoon to accommodate them. The group now has a notion that they were a second Defence and Employment Platoon (D&E Platoon) that was illegally constituted and employed on routine D&E Platoon duties. They now contend that all reference to the creation of this second D&E Platoon has been conspiratorially and dishonestly expunged from all historical records of the time by corrupt Army Officers and Australian War Memorial officials.

Two federal politicians have publicly declared the existence of the Platoon and have stated:

"I am pleased to announce that I have been able to bring this long struggle to a conclusion by confirming that the Rudd Labor Government and the Defence Department have been able to determine that the Platoon did indeed exist and engaged in a series of important actions in Vietnam as part of the Australian Task Force."

The two politicians are Ms Jennie George a leftist NSW politician and the Hon Dr Mike Kelly AM MP, Parliamentary Secretary for Defence Support who is also an ex-Army Legal Officer.

Those supporting the notion of a second D&E Platoon have made the following statements:

"Was there a deliberate cover-up of events at Thua Tich on the 30th May 1969 that resulted in the service records of 39 men being corrupted? Was there a meeting of certain officers in early June (out in the jungle, away from prying eyes) that determined who was going to get the next gallantry medal? Were photographs within the AWM collections falsified to guarantee the platoon commander of another platoon would claim the glory for the actions of the 2nd D&E Platoon?"

"Like it or not (and many veterans don't like it) there is clear evidence of corrupt practices, medal-posturing and grabbing, and falsification of records- and these are currently being investigated by politicians and bureaucrats'?

> *What other skeletons are in the closet? If this could happen to one platoon, what other disgusting practices has the Australian Army been involved in"*
>
> *If, you accept as Dr Mike Kelly and Ms Jennie George have, that there was a second D&E Platoon and its entire existence has been expunged then you must also accept that they assert that Officers of the era were corrupt and that ex Officers and civilian staff at the Australian War Museum are also corrupt.*
>
> *We are not surprised that such allegations would come from Ms Jennie George, but shocked and hurt that the Parliamentary Secretary for Defence Support would make such scurrilous accusations. He has been an Army Officer albeit a Legal Officer without the traditional officer training behind him, even so, he must know that Army officers place honour and integrity above all else. For him to make such an assertion (by default) is very hurtful to the many officers of the era and to the contemporary Defence Force.*
>
> *It is not disputed that a group of soldiers posted to the D&E Platoon in Vietnam in 1969 for a six week period created a "nick" name for their group, and as a group performed as expected by Australian soldiers. Dr Mike Kelly could say as much, but to assert by default that his brother officers of the era corruptly expunged all record of the group is unbecoming an ex officer and very hurtful.*
>
> *The group "nick" named "second D&E Platoon" was always part of the one and only D&E Platoon which was part of HQ 1ATF, Army service records clearly show all those who served in the "second D&E Platoon" were posted to HQ 1ATF as were all members of the D&E Platoon.*
>
> *We have no axe to grind against the Rudd government and believe given the current financial meltdown they are performing well under difficult circumstances; however it is unacceptable that a Federal Government Minister should assert that extremely competent, honourable officers of the Vietnam era have conspired to corruptly alter Military History.*
>
> *We request from The Hon Dr Mike Kelly either give confirmation of his original statement asserting that his fellow officers were generally corrupt or an amendment to the whole notion of the existence of a "second D&E Platoon" and the scurrilous accusation of corruption in the Defence Force of the time.'*

The Hon Dr Mike Kelly MP simply ignored his ramblings.

As for the tone and language of my response, previous– I'll have to claim PTSD as the excuse. But there is only so much a man can take.

The mess we found ourselves in, and the deterioration of our mental health, was nowhere more obvious than in a series of death threats made against me and others by Ted Colmer– he who had been responsible for locating much of the evidence. Not only had he outlined the legal aspects of the atrocities, but had raised them in various correspondence to bureaucrats.

I should have been cognisant of his mental condition when he sent an extraordinary email to one of our most vociferous opponents – Bob Buick – on 14th November, 2008. He wrote (sic):

> *'You are an anally retarded fuckwit Buick, and I'm not threatening legal action arsehole, I have already taken AAT action.*
>
> *No costs will be attributed to me, and why would I spend any real time lecturing a fucking retard!*
>
> *Legal qualification of matters doesn't have any meaning to you, because you are the biggest moron I have ever dealt with.*
>
> *You are absolutely "brain dead" Buick, and who in hell do you think you are??*
>
> *PS: Take this anyway you fucking like dickhead, one anonymous email to me, and I gun for you!!! You're behind every cowardly e-mail transmission. Real heroes Buick [I've met a few] don't act like this. It's your guilt complex isn't it!*
>
> *I'm as aggressive [extremely fit] and can be as violent as I ever was, so just put me to the test. You suck up to the establishment Buick because you have something serious to hide; held within the AWM. This would account for the disappearance of most 6 RAR, AWM Series records. Take a look at AWM290, comprising of 835 Matches, with only 2 records for 6 RAR????*
>
> ***YOU ARE THE WAR HERO BUICK, SO HAVE THE COURAGE TO FACE OFF WITH ME - ONE TO ONE [NO WEAPONS] SOMEWHERE MID WAY NORTH COAST, AND I WILL BE THERE AS FAST AS I CAN DRIVE! I WOULD CONSIDER IT A PRIVILEGE TO GIVE YOU THE BIGGEST FLOGGING OF YOUR MORONIC LIFE, AND I DON'T GIVE A FUCK ABOUT THE LEGAL CONSEQUENCES OF YOUR REQUIRED HOSPITALISATION!'***

Bob 'the bolter' Buick certainly deserved a blast, but one does need to have *some* standards.

I put Colmer's outburst down to drink and a lifetime of acting the tough guy.

But when he saw *The War Within* become a best-seller, Colmer's condition darkened noticeably and abruptly. He began his own offensive against me, piggy-backing the other cowards.

I was in Western Australia on a series of speaking engagements when he began an extraordinarily vicious assault via email, culminating in a series of death threats. I could make allowances for his psychological disability up to a point– but he'd gone way over the line.

I referred Colmer's slander and threats to the NSW Police.

The police were reluctant to act though– trotting out the usual lame excuse of not being able to actually *prove* he wrote the emails. (In cyber-bullying, this remains the biggest stumbling block to police recording a conviction).

However, by detailed analysis of that series of emails, I convinced police that specific comments made in those letters could only have been made by Colmer– and police agreed.

He was placed before Penrith Court in 2010 charged with telecommunications offences, but escaped conviction. He produced evidence to the effect that he was suffering from a mental illness and under the relevant Section of the Mental Health Act, the matter was dismissed.

He'd thumbed his nose at the law and gotten away with it.

But he wasn't Robinson Crusoe in that regard.

Frank Grady, who I mentioned earlier in regards to the construction of the Vietnam Veterans' Commemorative Walk, was one of those cowards who vilified me via pseudonym– 'D371' and 'KD117' (both of which related to his service details).

Time and time again, I referred his slander to my local police, to no avail. Despite his rants being clear breaches of the Telecommunications Act, it was all too hard for the local plods.

But one day, police interviewed him in relation to another matter altogether– and he admitted that he *was* the coward behind the postings on the AVM web site. Trouble was, the police officer – SC Leanne Graham – hadn't warned him of his rights in that regard, so the admission couldn't be acted on.

If nothing else, Grady had been revealed to the veteran community for the fool and coward he really was.

As for my major antagonist– Bob Buick– rather than making empty threats like Ted Colmer had done, I exacted a personal revenge.

By analysing his admissions in his autobiography and letters to me from his former Company commander, Harry Smith, I was able to peel back the layers of lies surrounding Buick's 'heroism' at the battle of Long Tan.

He is now the subject of a federal police investigation into the murder. The wheels are turning slowly. He is the focus of a number of investigations by one agency or another. Storm clouds are gathering. Some of his former associates are ducking for cover as well. Some have already rolled over. Rightly so.

Trouble is, there's nowhere for them to hide.

There were others, too. Little men who had not been involved in the war in any significant way– but who needed to pretend they did for the sake of their own egos:

Men like:

- **Bob 'Bomber' Gibson** (called himself 'NUIDAT 68') had a lot to say for an ex-private who had been unwanted by any infantry units and spent his whole tour out of harm's way in the D&E Platoon. His major accomplishment was to lie his way into the Chicago veterans' 'Welcome Home' Parade as a genuine Australian infantryman

- **Barry Billing** (called himself 'CERTO') and had done two tours, one as a driver, and one as a barman, but told great stories of hand-to-hand heroics against the Viet Cong. A convicted fraudster, he ripped off fellow soldiers and veterans before being exposed

- **Alan Price** (called himself the somewhat effeminate 'BEEBEE') and only managed just over 100 days in the war before tripping over a log and hurting his knee. He had only experienced three minor contacts with the enemy during his time in Vietnam. Price manoeuvred himself into positions where he could rub shoulders with ex-officers, and feel very important. Although I served longer in the war than he did, and experienced much more of the war than he ever had, he wouldn't add my name to his list of 4RAR members, or include my civilian award (the ASM) on his list of 4RAR members who had distinguished themselves in community life

- **Greg Marheine** (called himself 'RUGER357' again, interestingly choosing a somewhat effeminate handgun as his handle) was a vicious opponent behind a keyboard throwing barbs at genuine infantrymen– despite only spending eight months in the war himself, and all of it as an orderly room clerk. He is the subject of an investigation by Queensland Police into cyber-stalking and Telecommunications offences

There were many more.

Just how cowardly Vietnam veterans had become was manifest when I held an Author Talk at Kawana Library in 2013.

Bob Buick (who had steered clear of my author talks on two previous speaking trips at the Sunshine Coast in 2009 and 2011) decided he would 'confront' me.

He brought along a dozen handmaidens to hold his hand.

This is how the 'confrontation' was recorded in local media:

SHOW OF FORCE: Vietnam veteran Bob Buick listens to Donald Tate's presentation of his book The War Within.

The only thing that surprised most veterans was that Buick's former Company Commander, Harry Smith, wasn't there to hold Buick's hand as well.

He's been doing it for almost fifty years. But then, Harry Smith has good reason not to be too prominent. There are a couple of questions many want to ask of him, like: 'Where were you when Buick murdered that enemy soldier? And did you sanction it?'

Another time, perhaps.

CHAPTER 25
APPEAL TO THE MIGHTY

I figured that perhaps an option was to go right to the top.

And they don't get any higher than the former Chief of Army– General Peter Cosgrove OA MC. He'd spent a month in the 9th Battalion back in Vietnam, and the rest of his tour in the D&E Platoon down at Vung Tau.

His service history bemused many veterans. It was often asked why a man who had received a gallantry award within a month in his first unit as Cosgrove had, wasn't subsequently used as a leader of men in a genuine infantry battalion afterwards, instead of the 'dogsbody' platoon in 'pogo' town.

I went to General Cosgrove thinking that surely, a man of his quality would have some answers. I couldn't imagine a fight with military and political bureaucrats would bother him, would it?

Surely not…?

Anyway, I thought I'd chance my arm, and sent him a letter…

> *'Dear Peter,*
>
> *An American diarist of two centuries ago, wrote that: "Patriotism is the last refuge of the scoundrel." Now, I'm not suggesting for a minute that I was a scoundrel (though perhaps, others might have thought so) but patriotism was certainly the reason why I fought in Vietnam..*

...So I volunteered for the army, volunteered for the infantry, and volunteered to get to Vietnam by Christmas eve, 1968. And I was going to get exactly what I wanted when I got there — the full war experience.

But I also marched off to war, as many of us did, with grand notions of the Anzac legend in our hearts— from Gallipoli to Kokoda, and the 'Rats of Torbruk', and found that to some extent it's all a myth. Instead, we found it to be a corrupt, inefficient, insensitive bureaucracy prepared to do whatever is necessary to maintain the 'image' of the military. Where after-action accounts can be falsified to protect the reputations of officers, where ordinary infantry privates became expendable if it advances the careers and the medal prospects of senior officers.

I can say, categorically, that as a consequence of my own experiences, my notions of patriotism have long since evaporated. While I fought alongside wonderful, courageous men— some of whom carried me on their shoulders at times, literally and metaphorically, the aftermath of being wounded to such an extent as I was, and the treatment I received at the hands of the military afterwards, and indeed, the treatment metered out to all veterans with respect to compensation for war wounds, and superannuation, convinces me that this country does not respect, nor even really care about those men who have fought for it.

At best, grandstanding politicians pay nothing more than lip-service to it.

It's just one of the reasons why we veterans remain, to a large extent, alienated and embittered.

But I have had reason to be even more bitter than most men, because I was that patriotic boy, all those years ago. And they did wrong by me.

No more, though.

It's why I'd like to address you sir, a former comrade in arms, about what was done to me. After all, they don't reach any greater heights in the military than you did.

And you were part of it. So who best to address?

Mr Cosgrove, like you, I served in Vietnam, and at about the same time, and even within the same units as you served- though at different times.

I'd like to bring to your attention the years of personal vilification I have received at the hands of some within the military and veteran communities after my memoir, "The War Within" was published and which, as a consequence, has resulted in my alienation from the brotherhood of warriors.

In particular, I refer to my struggle to validate the existence of the 2nd D&E Platoon which operated in Vietnam during 1969, and the corruptions of military *history surrounding it. And, at the same time, to the corruptions of my own service history which has created such angst for me and my family*

I have withstood the attacks and vitriol for many years, but my reputation, my credibility, my achievements, and my family have all suffered as a consequence of it. I don't think you would have any appreciation of just what damage has been inflicted on me- and what the price has been.

I'm sure you are well aware of these matters, since you have an association with a couple of the veteran organisations involved. It's why I'm coming to you directly.

Why you?

Well, to put it simply, because you are a significant person in terms of class, status, reputation, and influence, and you may very well have had some part to play in that vilification these last few years- or at best, stood by and watched it happen.

I write to you as a former Chief of the Army, but more importantly, as a man, and as well as your sense of decency and fair play, it is to your sense of manhood that I now appeal, in particular.

In that light, I am trusting that you might still maintain some notion of care and concern for one like myself- an ordinary ex-Private soldier who went to war with empty-headed notions of war's grandeur and our Anzac heritage- and found it was all manufactured bullshit.

To this letter, I am attaching a Document titled: "Validation of Don Tate's Service History" which includes official army documentation, media pieces, letters from former soldiers, and relevant photographs which do exactly as it says- validates every aspect of my war service- and puts to the sword those claims from armchair experts that my service history is manufactured in any way.

But first, I think a comparison of our relevant army histories makes for interesting reading, simply because although you reached the pinnacle of the Australian military tree, and I remained forever at its roots, it goes some way to explaining why you and I have such divergent opinions about the army, and our military heritage.

Of course, we came from entirely different backgrounds: you entered the army from a privileged family, and became an officer, destined for greatness; I came from a significantly disadvantaged family, socially and financially, and became a Private soldier- always destined to remain so by virtue of the fact that I spent the last half of my military career in a Military Hospital after being wounded in Vietnam.

We were both reinforcements to Vietnam. I arrived a little earlier than you did.

We both served in the 9th Battalion. You served in it for just 39 days, then, despite a recognised act of heroism (and despite the battalion being under-manned) found yourself re-posted to a more sedentary unit; I had served with two other units before arriving at the 9th Battalion, and served with it about 35 days, until being wounded in action and repatriated home.

During our time in that same battalion, you were involved in a very minor contact with just two enemy soldiers at a creek, and for that, and some other relatively minor matter, were awarded a Military Cross- though I must say, there seems to be some serious maladministration even with the dates of those actions; on the other hand, I was one of three men ordered to run into a Viet Cong killing field under heavy enemy fire to support the leading section of my platoon when it was ambushed in a bunker complex- an action which saw one man killed, and ten of us wounded. I didn't even rate a mention in the Battalion's account of that ambush, or get my name recorded in the battalion's history- let alone any gallantry medal for doing what I did- and it was, by every measure, a far more gallant act than either of yours.

We both served in a D&E Platoon, considered by Major George Pratt, company commander of HQ Company at that time, to be a unit designed for men "unfit for normal infantry duties in battalions". In your case, despite your recognised heroism with the 9th Battalion, you spent almost a year in the D&E Platoon; in my case, I was part of a specially-created "2nd D&E Platoon", raised for a specific purpose by Task Force Headquarters- to tackle a large enemy force known to be congregating in the Xuyen Moc area. My unit was disbanded after six weeks, with a significant number of kills up our sleeve, and no losses of our own.

And whereas your official D&E Platoon was always formally recognised, the 2nd D&E Platoon was 'edited-out' of the histories of the war for almost four decades because of certain contentions that occurred in the field on May 29th, 1969.

That was, until May 2008, at which point the existence and activities of the 2nd D&E Platoon was formally validated and acknowledged by the Australian government, and placed back into the history books.

You were never wounded in action, whereas I was severely wounded in action- on July 19th, 1969.

You spent no time in a military hospital; I spent more than two years in them.

You enjoyed a sparkling career in the army, finally being promoted to the premier military position- Chief of the Army; I remained a Private soldier, found myself permanently disabled by my war wounds, and medically discharged from the army as no longer being of use to it.

You had a full working career, and retired with public acclaim and significant superannuation; I had a working life of just 13 years, and received $20,000 in super when I retired as a teacher, following an attack by an assailant with a steel bar.

We both wrote memoirs. You didn't have to work to sell yours, because of your standing in the military and the community; I did have to work at selling and promoting mine, because of my standing in it. Yours was a veneer of the life that was lived- pro-Cosgrove, and pro-military; mine was a self-deprecating, warts and all account of an entire life, and with respect to the Vietnam component, revealed military maladministration, false after-action accounts, medal-grabbing by officers, and corruptions of history.

Veterans loved yours because you said what they wanted to read and didn't interfere with their notion of espirit de corps; mine revealed a different side of the Anzac tradition, entirely.

Since our army days, we have met socially on a number of occasions, as have our wives. Of course, we are in a different social class to you, and were made aware of that.

On one occasion, you agreed to open a "commemorative walk" I had built in the Shellharbour area, (mostly with my own hands) but you were denied by the Council's General Manager, Brian Weir- an insensitive bureaucrat who saw no war service. You took no stand in that minor fracas, despite the personal slap in the face, but I did appreciate your acceptance of the offer to open it.

So we go back aways, Mr Cosgrove, you and I. Walked some similar paths. Which is why your recalcitrance to enter any debate on various issues concerning me and matters I have raised these last few years, has caused me so much angst. Your refusal to assist the lowliest of former comrades-in-arms has been noted by many within the veteran community, including those we both served alongside.

And so to the point of this letter.

Let me be absolutely clear about this- what irks me most, is that you have been well aware of the fact that the maladministration of my service records created significant problems for me during my life, and despite your gallantry medal and your position of influence within the military and veteran communities, never felt inclined to reach down and offer me a helping hand to correct it.

You allowed weaklings within the veteran community to ostracise me for striking out against the military 'establishment', including sycophants leading battalion Associations (Doug McGrath and Alan Price being two of the worst) and *never felt inclined to assist me in validating either my service with 9RAR, or with the 2nd D&E Platoon.*

You sat and watched as an assortment of villainous criminals, cowards, and known paedophiles attacked me mercilessly using off-shore web sites where Australia's weak politicians and useless police forces can't touch them.

How could this be so, Mr Cosgrove? Where were you when a genuine man was needed to stand up and be counted?

What price genuine courage?

Forgive me for this presumption, but one might've thought that a man with your background in the military, with your connections, with your knowledge of military protocol and leadership, might have done something- especially given our common histories.

Yet, and here's the rub, when another veteran (with a sordid past) wrote to you on one occasion requesting that you allow "mitigating circumstances" for an act of paedophilia he committed to be allowed into his service history, you didn't hesitate to act on his behalf, and allowed it.

(I have copies of the Statement made to the Police by the mother of the young victim, the request made to you, and your reply to him).

Of course, it was your right as Chief of the Army to make a determination to this criminal's advantage, and I don't question that right, or your decision to do so. But I must ask this question of you- what was in it for you?

Was it so that that particular individual thus became a slave to the 'military establishment' of which you are the pre-eminent face- condemned to a life of protecting the highest officer ranks from attacks by critics like me? Is he part of that defensive front-line employed by that 'establishment' to vilify those who dare question its integrity- shoot the messenger?

Why would you assist a convicted paedophile in a service-related matter- but not assist a fellow, disabled infantryman trying to validate his service?

Then (and this matter has been a long time in the wings) there is the very delicate matter of Private Peter Allen.

Do you recall the name?

You should- after all, you gave evidence at his trial for murder, back in Vietnam in November, 1969.

And, on reflection, and considering all the variables, your involvement in that matter is intriguing, and revealing.

You were aware, I have no doubt, that prior to his act of murder, Pte Allen had been a member of the 2nd D&E Platoon- that very same infantry platoon I served with- erased from the history books immediately after the contentions of May 29th 1969.

What seemed to escape you was that at Pte Allen's trial, he was unable to use as any defence the fact that he had been traumatised by his involvement in that platoon- because it didn't historically exist!

Imagine that.

And there you were, Mr Cosgrove, kept back in country for that important trial, so that you could give evidence. And what did that evidence amount to?

That he had given you a nasty look at one point. That's all.

A nasty look. Nothing more than that. Could there have been a more significant reason for your appearance at that trial?

Then there are the actions of Bob Buick to consider- the 'hero' of Long Tan, and a darling of the military establishment. It was Bob Buick who led the vociferous attacks against me in the early stages, using his knowledge of army administration to poo-poo any notion that a platoon of men had been created illegally.

It was Buick who announced boldly that he "had support at the highest levels of the government and the military" and was able to operate villainous web sites to vilify me, and which the government and the Federal Police were powerless to shut down.

Or refused to do.

What did you think of the attacks against me by Bob Buick, Mr Cosgrove?

I mean, here was a man who freely admitted to killing an unarmed, wounded enemy soldier after the battle of Long Tan, but received a medal of gallantry instead of being charged with murder. Wasn't it Barrister James Fergus Thomson, a former legal officer in Vietnam in 1966, who wrote (Letters to The Australian, August 2000) that if he'd been aware of Buick's claims of killing those soldiers back in the war, he would've personally prosecuted him for murder?

Of course the question is- why hasn't he been charged, still? I mean, he has admitted to murder

Not only that, but the same Bob Buick managed to score a Long Service and Good Conduct Medal which he had no right to receive, but which he wore for some 20 years before being outed as a medal-wearing fraud

No action was taken against him, yet now, Buick has a free hand to attack any critic of the military with gusto.

Coincidence? I think not.

More importantly, not once, Mr Cosgrove, to the best of my knowledge, did you ever stay his hand or urge restraint.

And finally, I draw your attention to the actions of the Director of the Australian War Memorial, another former general, and a pillar of the military establishment- Mr Steve Gower.

You would be aware that he sent out an email to the veteran community discrediting the valuation of the colour movie footage I had donated to that august institution designed to honour our military history. You would be aware that he chose not to discuss the issue with me personally, but, instead, chose various 'postmen' within the veteran community to disseminate that misinformation- including that very same, sordid individual you have an association with.

Two generals- and both having a connection to a convicted paedophile. Makes interesting reading doesn't it?

I'll ask the question so many other veterans ask- why would men of your standing even countenance such a despicable creature, let alone communicate with him?

Did you ever think to ask Mr Gower why he acted as he did, especially given that I had two official valuations in my possession as to the value of those films? Or is it a fact that Mr Gower shares your concern for maintaining the 'integrity' of the generals of the 'military establishment' and attempted to discredit me further.

After all, the last thing our former generals want is some loose cannon proving that our military history is largely written by historians in collusion and consensus, where historical fact is sacrificed on the altar of self-aggrandisement?

I took the matter to the Minister for Veteran Affairs, Allan Griffin, as you are aware, but he is a weakling, a puppet with no courage of convictions, no strength of character to tackle the major players in the establishment.

But then, nor did you, Mr Cosgrove.

These are just some matters that I need to raise with you.

So I ask you now, publicly, as a former comrade, officer, and as a man, why didn't you ever raise a voice in my defence?

Wasn't it enough that I spent more than two years in hospitals after being wounded? Wasn't it enough that I would be permanently physically disabled as a consequence of that ambush? Wasn't it enough that I would be left out of the 9th Battalion's record of its tour because of incompetent clerical administration?

Wasn't it enough that my actions of the 19th July would be ignored in the history of that battalion, written as it was, by former officers from that battalion who weren't at the coal-face of that ambush? Wasn't it enough that the army corrupted official histories to cover up atrocities in the field by editing the 2nd D&E Platoon from the history books- and to hell with the service histories of the 39 ordinary infantry privates caught up in it? Wasn't it enough that I would be forever alienated from the veteran community because I dared to reveal those corruptions? Wasn't it enough that I had to contend with all that, and to top it off, be denied a full working career, like you were able to enjoy, and had to raise a family of five in relative poverty?

Where were you all this time, Mr Cosgrove?

Where was your heart?

And where was the courage that earned you a Military Cross?

You alone had the capacity to put the jackals to the sword. But where were you?'

He never replied

A couple of years later, on Anzac Day 2012, we both attended the 9th Battalion's function following the march.

I made a point of speaking with him.

I asked him why he had never responded to my letter, and why he hadn't made any attempt to assist us.

'Because I didn't like the tone of your letter,' he said.

I was astounded.

'You mean to say that you didn't extend me a helping hand despite your position, despite your influence, because of the *tone* of my letter?'

'Yes,' he said.

'How'd you ever score a gallantry medal?' I said.

And that was the end of *that* conversation. I'd like to have asked him personally why it was that he hadn't been placed into a genuine battalion as a platoon commander in charge of genuine infantrymen, rather than leading the generic D&E Platoon that operated out of Vung Tau, of all places, the safest place in Vietnam. And I'd like to have asked him exactly what his D&E Platoon *did* all that time, since he didn't spend much time talking about it in his autobiography, *My Story* (Harper and Collins). Probably too embarrassed, I suppose.

Last I heard, he was being mooted as a future Governor-General.

Figures.

CHAPTER 26
THE LISTENING POST

Although the Cavalry had overall authority for the activities of the 2nd D&E Platoon, Cpl James B. Riddle assumed leadership of the infantry contingent.

None of us objected to this.

There was good reason– he had been a sergeant in Britain's Royal Marines and looked every inch a soldier. He was also a deep thinker.

This was his philosophy (sic):

> '……I am a rebel against almost anything that has a taste of tradition and conformity. I do not follow anything. I am a lone wolf and I don't care for non-thinking. I question everything. As far as I am concerned, nothing is fixed and there are no facts or laws of nature. Everything known will change as new findings come to light, and are eventually accepted, in spite of those in the community who have set themselves over us as our leading thinkers.'

Riddle was an experienced campaigner– already the veteran of a couple of previous wars whilst serving with the British Marines, including jungle warfare in Borneo and Malaya. He had reached the rank of sergeant, but had bought himself out of the Marines so as to fight for Australia in the Vietnam War.

'None of us want to go home with more holes than we started with', Riddle said.

Personally, I was pleased about Riddle taking over leadership of the platoon. I'd known him since Corps training at Battle Wing, Ingleburn, gone through the Jungle

Training Centre at Canungra with him, and had served with him in 'D' Company of the 4th Battalion for a couple of months before he was promoted to section-commander and moved to a new platoon.

None of us objected to Riddle taking over the leadership. He was a natural leader of men, and those of us who had fought alongside him in the 4th Battalion, knew him to be astute, ferocious, and fearless– the consummate professional. He had but one flaw– an innate disregard for 'pogo' officers who stayed inside the wire like Major Pratt.

His analysis of what transpired with the creation of the 2nd D&E Platoon was intriguing (sic):

> 'When the 4th Battalion were sent home to Australia, there were a few soldiers who had to remain to complete their own twelve months in-country. I think there were sixteen of us, and we were sent to the Brigade HQ as a defence force. There we met up with 20 more stragglers and formed into a composite infantry platoon, radio call sign "Sabre Two".
>
> This was a novel experiment to have a ready reaction group of Armoured personnel carriers and infantry, all ready to respond to anything that the Brigade Army Intelligence found that needed instant attack. The Infantry battalions and armoured groups who were operating in Phuoc Tuy Province were too big to respond to instant information, and were always too deeply committed to their own search missions to be capable of responding. The armoured units were also independently operating as units with very specific duties, usually only being called for in support of a major Infantry operation. Basically they were all disorganised and incapable of adapting to new situations. The Australians were currently being badly mauled by the adaptable and fast moving VC.
>
> Not having a proper name for this experiment, the infantry had officially become a 2nd Defence and Environment group– the first D&E group being sanitary cleaners of footpaths and toilets, and general dogsbodies.
>
> This 2nd Group was a perfect collection of misfits and rejects who were craving a purpose and a home. I was the only NCO among this new gathering and so I was given the task of Platoon Sergeant. We had several Lieutenants attached to us as commanders, but they were so short in time that they never actually moved out of the brigade camp. This soon left me as the commander and organiser of all who joined our strange band.
>
> I admit that I loved it. Consequently I would be told what armoured unit was going where and when, in a hurry, and I would nominate a part of the 2 D&E Group

to attachment duties. When three ambushes were needed, I would nominate a section to accompany each track unit, and would nominate a section leader and second in command of that section. Then I would pick which outfit I would accompany. The 2 D&E unit seemed to be content with the whole arrangement, as they had someone organising them who spoke their language and was experienced........'

Capt Tom Arrowsmith never questioned Riddle's rank, or his credentials. Arrowsmith, like Riddle, was well respected by us infantrymen as well as by his own soldiers. He had a real military presence about him.

'I was most impressed by Captain Arrowsmith. He was at war with the enemy only, not with his troops or his home life, or office life. He was focussed on the now period, knew what was happening about him, and was flexible in his ability to adapt for ground, weather and any circumstances. He gave a feeling of being seriously capable. He was a rarity.'

The 2nd D&E Platoon was a different animal to the normal infantry platoon.

We were told we would be doing things differently, that instead of barging through the bush like every other infantry platoon, we'd be riding in, and on, armoured personnel carriers. We thought that sounded like a great idea. In the first week or so, we learned new tactics, like quietly rolling out of the backs of APCs as they moved through the jungle, and how to operate with the armour in ambush situations.

Jim Riddle was given the title of 'Sunray' (meaning the leader); and the platoon was given the title, 'Sabre Force':

'The call sign – Sabre Two – was agreed between myself and Arrowsmith on our first Operation. It was based on a misunderstanding by me. I asked Major Pratt (a very aptly named pom) of HQ Coy for my call sign for Sunray Indians of the 2nd D&E Platoon, and he asked the Lieutenant who was our 'behind the lines man'* and he said he thought it was already called "Sword" or "Sabre". Pratt then said, "We shan't change it then, you must stay as 'Sabre' too!' That was it. I don't even know if the other outfit was called Sword or Sabre or Banana, but we became 'Sabre Two."
(* Note: I assume he was referring to Lt Barry Parkin)

The 2nd D&E Platoon was now a platoon of *assault troopers* with a fancy moniker– *'Sabre Force'*, though I must admit, I never heard that term actually used until post-Vietnam.

What official records that do exist of the ambush at Thua Tich on May 29th 1969 pertain only to the Armoured Corps' version of what went down.

The role of the infantrymen of the 2nd D&E Platoon was conveniently overlooked both in Capt Tom Arrowsmith's official, after-action report, and in the interview Arrowsmith gave to ABC radio the next day.

The only recognition Arrowsmith ever gave to the 2nd D&E Platoon was to refer to us as 'scouts' or 'my dismounted elements'. He couldn't bear to use the word, 'infantry'.

For the first time, and to ensure it is now part of the historical record, this is Cpl Jim Riddle's unedited account of the ambush– from *his* perspective at the listening post:

Cpl James B. Riddle in his prime

The Jim Riddle Narrative:

'At 8pm (2000 hours for military bods) I was told of movement on the road and moved forward to the right end of our killing group. On that wing were two diggers in an old crater, about a meter deep. Over the top of their hole was a fallen tree trunk about two feet thick. I crawled into the hole with them and squinted into the darkness and waited for scraping and breathing noises to quiet down. Within moments I saw and heard the enemy. I was out of the hole in silent scramble and dragged the radio over to the front and was keying the switch like a morse key to wake up the armour people. Then, forgetting all military radio procedure I whispered, "This is Sabre 2 . enemy to my front... three bodies moving at walking speed towards you." I repeated without waiting for an answer..."Three Enemy approaching you now" and imagined the panic of a signaller telling Arrowsmith, then Arrowsmith alerting his gunners to man their machine guns... he didn't need to answer me... but I definitely needed to know that he had heard me. so I repeated my message again so there was absolutely no doubt... I hate it when I send an urgent message to someone, only to have them ask me to repeat it so they can believe their ears... so I cut out all that and repeated it 3 or 4 times, very rapidly, before asking for confirmation. It came through from Arrowsmith almost immediately. (Phew. I love that Guy!)

"Alpha Sunray to Sabre 2... OK we're ready"

As short and precise as that. Meanwhile my ambush was alive and alert and 'nervous'. I always get nervous before shooting starts. THIS WAS THE FIRST TIME I NOTICED MY KNEES WERE TREMBLING. I HAD TO HOLD THE RIGHT KNEE TO STOP IT SHAKING MY WHOLE BODY.

It was as if my legs were under some other control. I knew it was fear, but I didn't really feel 'that' fearful. In the dark no one could see my struggle to control my legs. Meanwhile I was taking in all the signs of another blast of killing. Then I had a squeezing sensation in the solar plexus.. Sign that a message was trying to be heard! The three men were wearing white shirts, and talking!! Wrong vibes ! There was something very wrong about this set up. The men were just fading out of sight over the crest to our left, and would be about 200 metres from death... then I knew what was wrong. they were a sacrificial group. They were meant to be spotted. I squinted to the right and nearly stretched my ears into big flaps. and there is was... a very dark and very silent mass.

In the moonlight a column of soldiers came into focus. I was crushing the radio switch and whispering. "Sabre 2. . *DO NOT FIRE AT THOSE MEN... THERES*

LOTS MORE... DO NOT FIRE AT THOSE LEAD MEN, THERE'S LOTS MORE... DO NOT FIRE ON THE FIRST ONES. THERES A FUCKING ARMY COMING UP BEHIND"

Again, I didn't want anyone coming back at me with a disbelieving, "Confirm your last message"

Then I released the switch so that Arrowsmith could reply... and he did!!

No call signs were being used. none was needed...our radio procedure was crap, but the message got through! He just came straight back with a serious whisper,

"OK. what's coming Sabre 2?" I whispered something like, "It's a big column of soldiers, and they're still coming . it looks like a hundred plus. over" He came straight back ."Got it Sabre... do the best you can... we will spring when the main body is here. First group scouts are almost past my location. stand by."

And that was it... 'Intelligence'! had sent us to ambush a courier group of 3 to 5 lightly armed VC. Instead, I could just make out the road to my right was black with a column of bodies which had no end., and still coming.

Some mixed thoughts crossed my mind, first being that it would be a good idea if we just stayed quiet for an hour or so, because to hit this lot with what we were set up for was distinctly nail biting stuff. Oh! Bugger it! At least they won't ALL get away! This is going to be a close run thing... I hope the lads are up for it! Such a nice warm night too!

My group were now pumping adrenaline and twitching with fright. This was bigger than we had expected, and it was about to start... Big Time!

'The column shuffled quietly along the road, not a murmur among them – and so many soldiers! The head of the column went over the crest and into Arrowsmith's killing ground, and still, I could not see the end of the column to my right. It crossed my mind that there were enough fighters out there to sweep us away, even after taking casualties.

It was a worrying thought.

Then, it started. There was a tremendous roar as claymores were fired, and at least four .50 cal machine guns and M60's tore up the head of that huge column.

My blokes expected me to fire our stuff straight away, as soon as we heard the armoured contingent open up, but I could 'see' what was happening with the column who were still on my side of the crest and out of the line of fire from the front. They began to spread out along the crest, as their officers and NCOs started to react and to get them organised. My blokes kept glancing at me, white upturned faces in the dark, waiting for me to react.

I stood beside a small tree, holding an M79 ready, and with my heavy barrelled AR resting against my stomach. I counted to ten, then began to fire the M79 at the main body of troops in the blackness on the other side of the road.

The round exploded high among the heads of the khaki soldiers. This was the signal my blokes had waited for, and now they fired everything they could at the killing ground to our front. Our flares lit up the road and embankment and the claymores blasted thousands of ballbearings into the troops still on the road and this side of the embankment.

And there I saw, for the first time, the enemy in full technicolour- like an awesome three minutes of illuminated war movie. But we couldn't walk out of this cinema; this was real and all our own work. Most of them were in brown uniforms of the NVA, wearing the brown safari helmets and carrying more guns than I had seen outside of a battalion parade. And they were all looking surprised and angry at our little line of gunfire.

I dropped the M79 and pulled up the AR, and fired at the biggest bunch I could see on the other side of the road. I wanted to hit as many as possible while I was standing, because I knew as soon as I had to lie down, I wouldn't be able to fire at the main body behind the embankment. I was surprised now at one enemy soldier to my left, almost on the crest at about 25 metres, who stood upright and fired an AK47 at our position. This one had no hat, and was in regulation Viet Cong black. In the light of the flares I could see it was a female. I brought my AR onto her chest and fired three rounds. She flipped backwards. As it was there was now a great deal of stuff coming back at us and cutting the small trees and bushes into shredded leaves and twigs. The noise was tremendous, and I recall thinking that if this kept up, then someone was going to get hurt.

I lay down and changed clips for a fresh 30 rounds. I was still concerned about the enemy soldiers across the road, now in safe ground from all our shooting, so I collected the M79 and started reloading on the ground – a slow and ponderous process, and then, standing beside the remains of my little tree, firing blindly across the road to explode among the troops, but now without the advantage of the light from our flares.

I was hopeful they were taking casualties, but more importantly, I hoped to keep them confused as to how small our outfit was.

At about this stage, an RPG came into our muzzle flashes and hit just in front of the central M60 and lifted it up almost vertically. The machine gunner was a bit shocked, but sorted it out, and got on with his work. I caught a thump in the face that stopped my right eye working for a second or two. I wiped my face and my hand came away sticky. I then had to wipe my hand carefully on my sweat rag because it was too slippery to change clips.

After too short a time, the flares went out, and in the moonlight and dust, we could see nothing but green tracer and some interesting orange stuff crossing over our heads, zipping off bits of earth at our front. I was now concerned that those enemy remaining out front would have sussed out that we were a small and isolated unit of infantry, and would decide to hook into us from the right flank. That would have been very bad for us, so I grabbed the radio and started asking Arrowsmith for mortar rounds to my front.

At this point I was surprised to find Cecil Ebsworth standing over me. He was standing beside my chest, leaning down and asking if there was anything he could do to help. I told him that lying down would be a good start, as he was attracting some swarms of flicking tracer.

I'd completely forgotten Cecil, and had allocated him a defensive position looking after our rear and manning the radio, but he obviously realised we had an unusually heavy commitment to our front and wanted to help clean things up a bit. So I asked him to take a shooting position to the front left of our ambush, where the heaviest fighting was taking place, and do what he could to thin the enemy out. I also asked him to do me a favour and try to stay close to the ground and move away from his shooting position as often as possible, despite our small and crowded area.

The small area we were in was okay if we only had a small fight, but the enemy now seemed to be almost all around us and making a hell of a noise. All of this shooting seemed to go on for another hour, then started to ease off. I was now concerned that the silence meant planned movement and attacks with grenades from anywhere. We now had sporadic fire coming in, and I had passed the word to hold fire unless attacked in force. I was very surprised that we had no casualties so far, but had to start digging reserve bandoliers of ammunition out of pouches and packs and reclip machine gun belts. No backup mortar fire had yet come down, and it had been an hour since I called... or maybe it was really a month.

A scuffle and there's Ernie again, and he's got the radio. Arrowsmith has organised his mortars and wants me to call his fall of shot. and he's also called for air support in the form of SPOOKY, and it's on the way from Bien Hoa Air Base. I feel a certain relief at this news and I crawl around our position and tell them what's happening, and what may or may not happen, and "Nice Going, I think we've hurt them."

I snaked to the right hand hole to watch for the incoming mortar rounds. I heard the stomp sound of a mortar firing from my left... just so I know it's not the enemy getting in first. Then seconds later the swish of the bomb coming down. It detonates somewhere in the jungle over the other side of the trail... Not very professional! I call in the fall of shot and wait. Another 'stomp' and wait and this one lands miles away down the trail. I hear it but see nothing. Then again another 'stomp' and wait, and this one goes bang somewhere near Singapore. I am now having doubts about calling for close supporting fire. The next bombs land in front of our position and, regardless of where I correct their fire to, they fall ever farther away into the jungle. I ask what's going on with the covering fire and I am told by Arrowsmith that they are chasing possible forming-up points. I ask if there's any point in calling their fall of shot, and there is a long silence. I then tell him that I will remain off the air until something falls very uncomfortably close, and thank you.

As this is going on, there are constant cries from the scattered enemy wounded. One cries out that he wants to Chieu Hoi; part of a surrender programme for VC who want to come over and share rations. Another screams relentlessly close to our position, and in front of Ernie. Others are crawling around our position, unsure now that we aren't firing where we are. We can hear them dragging wounded, who scream, and others who are significantly quiet. I move over to Ernie's position and ask how he's getting on. He is unmoved by the whole thing and points out the shape of the screaming man in front who is having trouble. I focus a moment then realise in the moonlight that there are two others to his flank. I am fairly certain that these are unwounded and trying to locate our position, especially the nearest pit, which is Ernie's. I crawl back and stand up alongside my favourite little tree again for a better downward view, and find that my tree is now only about 1 meter high, so I'm a bit short of the psychological comfort I had earlier. I now stand up quietly in the moonlight and fire a burst into the three soldiers, then fall flat and roll away. And nothing happened except the wounded man stopped screaming. I feel sure that I hit all three.

The contact had started about two hours before by this time, and we now heard the hum of 'Puff the Magic Dragon' coming in from the south.

I had an army torch with red filter, so I dug that out and lying as low as possible I pointed it straight up from a clearing in the centre of our location. I was a little concerned that the enemy would also see this red light and shoot at it, but it didn't happen.

The ground in front of me seemed to suddenly grow into a jungle of brown trees. As the torrent of bullets struck the dry earth, they threw up explosions of soil, each bullet kicked up a 'bush' of earth, and in the orange light of the hanging flares it looked to me, from very close to the ground, that the world was exploding. The leaping ground seemed to run towards us in a wave of loud farting sounds. About this time I had a rush of bodies snaking along away from the direct line- Ernie and Don Tate and Snow Manski, closely followed by two others from the machine gun crew. I think we all pretended that this had been a sort of organised and planned withdrawal, but it was more of a knee jerk panic……'

When Jim Riddle was repatriated to Australia, he was welcomed at various points by men he had served with, as I said. When he arrived in Sydney, some even flew from as far away as Adelaide to welcome him home.

Few, if any of those, had actually lifted a finger to help repatriate him.

It was often said that I was opportunistic in using any opportunity to promote *The War Within* (as indeed, every author is expected to be) but even though it had been me who instigated the clamour to have him return to the country he had fought for, I declined to use it to my advantage.

I could very easily have rocked up with a copy of *The War Within* tucked under my arm for the photo opportunity, but chose not to.

He *was* my guest though, in my home in due course, and later at an Author Talk I gave at Caloundra Library soon after, and ensured that *he* was the centre of attention at both locations. I had no option. If I hadn't invited him I'd have been the worst bloke in the world.

But when I invited him to the Author Talk at Caloundra Library, I was accused of 'using him'.

You just can't win sometimes.

As it was, when he had declined to a point where communication was very difficult, he made one last entry on his Facebook page. It read:

' ..still bloody crook mate...can't walk..chat with you soon my friend...I will go into print about my gratitude....my only honest friend..'

Meant a lot to me, that did.

Sadly, I wasn't his only friend. A fellow veteran, Tex Weston, was. That man gave two years of his life to care for Jim– even accompanying him back to England after he'd been bashed.

Tex Weston was one man I'd take my hat off to.

Don Tate and Jim Riddle at Caloundra

CHAPTER 27
THE END GAME

In November 2010, I advised the veteran community that I would be forwarding a detailed letter about the corruptions of history in regards the 2nd D&E Platoon to Members of Parliament, and key Senators.

Consequently, a series of threats were issued against me. A picture of my house and address was placed on the internet as well as a vitriolic barrage by an old enemy, Frank Grady– the former high-flyer in the Vietnam Veterans Federation who I'd crossed swords with in relation to the tree-planting project years earlier.

On January 2011, following that information being published, I was bashed outside my home.

As bashings go, it wasn't the worst I've had– black eyes, bruising, abrasions etc, but the manner it was delivered and the message that came with it was the most disconcerting aspect.

I'd been rehabilitating from a total knee replacement and was walking short distances each night to strengthen the muscles. This was well known to fellow veterans– I had been corresponding with some about the best methods of doing so, and mentioned that I liked to walk late at night.

Despite the threats, it still caught me by surprise.

I saw a car pull up about thirty metres in front of me, and a man jumped out and sprinted towards me. I thought he had left his wallet behind in the garage behind me, and was running back to get it. But as he approached me, he suddenly veered at me, and at the last moment threw out a forearm and caught me flush across the head.

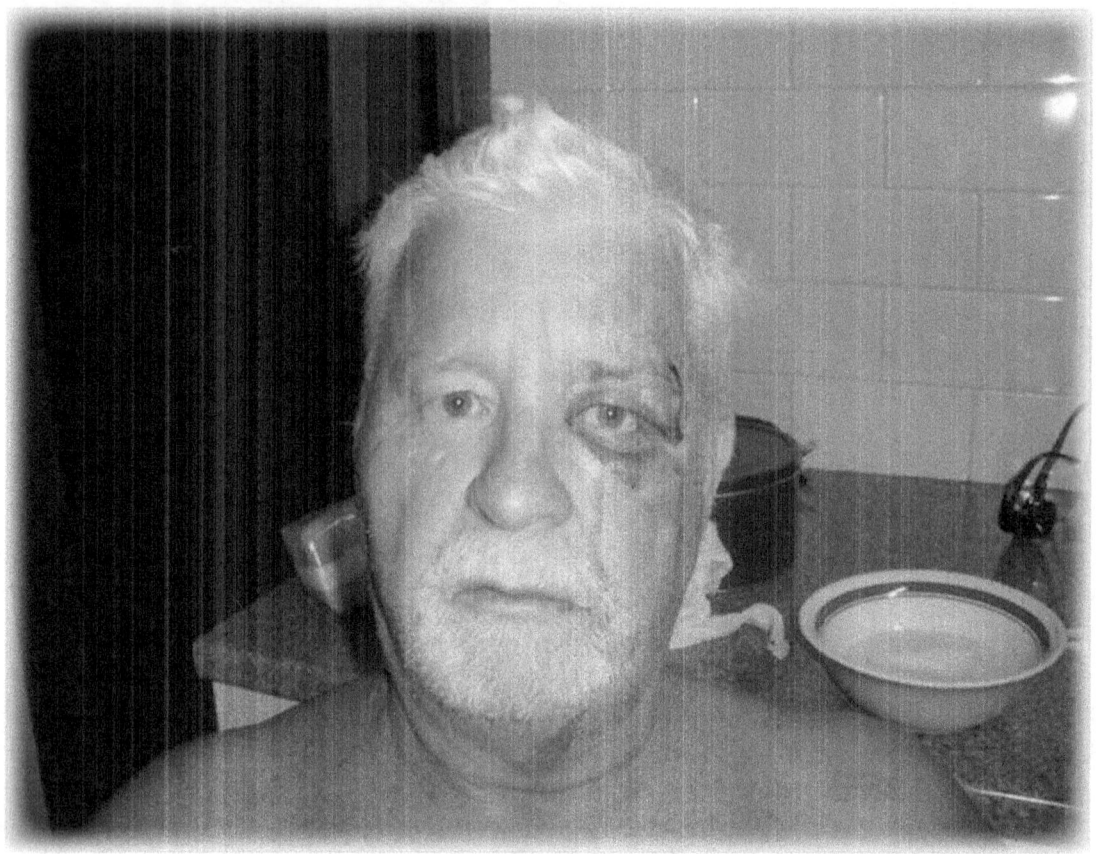

I fell to the ground backwards and my head hit the concrete. I think I was unconscious for a short while because the next thing I knew, he was kneeling over me and striking my face with fists.

As best I could, I defended myself– but with only one good arm available and being unable to stand, life's difficult enough at the best of times.

'This is from the AVM, and *this* is from Fergus!' was all he said, with one good blow to my stomach before running off in the rain.

The local coppers didn't find the assailant– but then, they didn't find the pools of blood on the concrete footpath either.

Now, I really became enraged. It was such an audacious thing to have done– carry out an assault along a national, well-lit highway with some obvious element of planning.

I didn't only get angry. It was time for revenge.

My first port of call was a barrister by the name of Fergus Thompson, or more correctly, James Fergusson Thompson. He was the legal eagle who had written to *The Weekend Australian* in 2000 suggesting that the 'hero' of Long Tan – Bob Buick – should have been tried for murder.

I thought I might lay the matter out for a man with a superb legal mind in the hope that he might be of assistance– especially given that 'Fergus Fairfax' had stolen one of his Christian names and bastardised it. This was that letter (sic):

> *'My name is Don Tate- like you, a veteran of the Vietnam War. It is the only thing we have in common.*
>
> *I am writing to you directly today because I understand that as well as being a former army officer of high standing within the ADF, you a genuine man, a gentleman of good repute, and recognised nationally as a man with a keen and very well-regarded legal brain. But most importantly, I have learned that unlike many other senior ex-officers, you have demonstrated an interest and concern for the well-being of fellow veterans of that most unpopular war.*
>
> *I first learned of you when I read a letter apparently written by you to The Weekend Australian in 2000 concerning the disgraceful actions of the 'lion' of Long Tan, Bob Buick in murdering an unarmed, wounded enemy soldier following the battle- a matter he boasted about in writing. You suggested that he should have been charged with murder in 1966, and that as a member of the Legal Team 'in country' at that time, you would have done so if you'd been aware of it. Many veterans agree with your view. (Incidentally, I've often wondered if your suggestion was ever followed through by any Court, and was there some due process that should have been followed through in that regard?)*
>
> *Buick, as you might know, in recent years, became a strident opponent of any man who criticised the military, and boasted of his connections to high-flying politicians and ex-military types who used him to do their dirty work. Till the veteran community saw through him, that was, and also learned a great deal more about his exploits at Long Tan than he wanted us too. He shut up, very quickly, though many suspect he still is the lap-dog of a military establishment to whom he owes that favour.*
>
> *As I understand it, Mr Thomson, you demonstrate a certain empathy for us less fortunate veterans and volunteer your time and services at the VVF offices in Canberra, and that you are prepared to assist in the welfare of fellow veterans when you are able to.*

So it is in that context that I write to you today. In my humble opinion, there is no man more capable of handling the matters I would place before you. And the matters are such that I intend to forward a copy of this letter to various individuals within the veteran community so that the wider veteran community will be aware of my action, my predicament, and the extent to which I will go to clarify certain issues concerning my service and my integrity.

In the first instance, and by way of introduction in case you aren't aware of me, you should note that I am one of that small percentage of men who was physically wounded in the war (my right hip being shattered by bullet) and subsequently hospitalised in military and repatriation hospitals for more than two years. The fact that I was physically wounded seems to annoy a small section of veterans who, not having been wounded to that extent themselves, prefer to dismiss the consequences of such a wound to a man's life. Even though the wound was received in action, inside a bunker complex (attested to by my platoon commander Bruce Osborne and others, present on the night, and all medical documentation relating to it being freely available) there are those who would still have the audacity to declare that I wasn't wounded. Others mock the severity of the wound. It appears to me that many are embarrassed that I refuse to yield to my disabilities and indeed, have overcome them in ways weaker men couldn't have done.

I realise that as a legal officer you were never involved in combat either, Mr Thomson, and I don't mean any disrespect here, but I'm sure even you might have some difficulty appreciating the actual trauma of having the largest bones in your body shattered during a significant ambush under terrifying conditions. Only men who have experienced such a thing can really appreciate it. But it is important that you try.

I am also the author of an intensely personal memoir- The War Within, published by one of the more prestigious publishers in Australia, Murdoch Books. These were the reflections of a man written from a deliberately limited perspective, and was published in 2008. It sold more than 7000 copies in the first six months of its release (which made it a 'best-seller' in Australia) and is now approaching the 15,000 mark. The second edition has now sold out. In conjunction with its publication, I was engaged to speak at more than 154 libraries across Australia to date (with more yet to go) and have had to refuse invitations to speak at libraries in New Zealand. I have obtained a small number of copies from that second re-print to allow me to complete my speaking engagements.

Those facts are important because there are also those within the veteran community who have seen fit to disparage both the accomplishment of being published, the successful promotion and subsequent sales of the book, its relative literary merit, and certain aspects of my service in Vietnam as I have recorded them in the memoir. I'm sure a learned man such as yourself appreciates that the discipline and integrity of memoir-writing demands that the material should be based solely on the individual's recollections, not on a consensus view- a fact not understood by my critics. In publishing circles, it is a recognised fact that no memoir is 100% accurate- be it that of a politician, a general, or a Private soldier. The human memory is not perfect. You would also be aware that after what has been done to me, books from other war Vietnam veterans are now largely ignored by publishers and the general public (and even by other veterans)- something I've particularly noticed within the last three years as they invariably sink from sight very quickly.

I tell you all this because you inhabit more rarified air than I do, travel in better circles, and might not have been aware of the various contentions that have resulted from its publication, and the vilification I have received from a specific section of veterans- and it is vital that you appreciate those facts in the wider context of the issue I will raise with you later.

It goes without saying that, as well as the controversies arising from publication of my memoir, my travails in recording the deletion of all trace of the 2nd D&E Platoon and its actions in Vietnam from all histories of the war- and convincing the Federal Government and a dubious Australian War Memorial of the authenticity of this battle created heated debate within the veteran community.

The actions (or inactions) of the AWM in this matter have been clearly documented, and the action by one senior member of the AWM in attempting to discredit me and the value of my films revealed him to be something of a fool when the official documentation surrounding the donation of my films to the AWM proved otherwise. (His association with a known paedophile has been duly noted by many veterans, and others of significance).

That debate pitted me against a pack of some of the lowest individuals existing within society, let alone within a veteran community that boasts of its proud Anzac traditions. I refer to a clutch of cowardly, anonymous creatures who preferred the hiding ground of pseudonym and hid within an off-shore website- the AVM (Australian Veteran Matters).

Over a long period, led by two venomous snakes calling themselves "Fergus Fairfax" and "Spartacus", these creatures deliberately lied, slandered, misinterpreted, and obfuscated in a series of missives aimed squarely at discrediting me and my service in that war. In later days, the attacks also focussed on my former employment and family life. (I should alert you to the fact that 'Spartacus' has been revealed to be the paedophile referred to earlier, so his association with 'Fergus Fairfax' and others means they are tarnished with the same brush. Soul mates, to some degree).

There was little I could do about the concerted attacks over the last few years because I was hamstrung by my contract with Murdoch Books (who kept me restrained from overt aggression) and to whom I had a fundamental responsibility to sell and promote my book as best as I could. That's not to say I didn't respond from time to time, as best I could, but it was interesting to note that whenever I provided explanation or proof of any charge against me- the AVM refused to acknowledge or publish it. Invariably, my email replies were bounced by that web site (as have those of other of its victims) leaving some with the impression that I hadn't, or refused, to respond. Yet I always had.

I should advise you now that I did seek legal advice, locally, in respect of these attacks, as well as police action, but to no avail. Defamation laws being what they are, and police powers being what they are, means that cowards in society now proliferate and have the opportunity to operate with gay abandon. But then, a man of your profession and with your experience would be well aware of that- and would appreciate the difficulties any victim faces in such a situation. It is a manifest problem in our society today, and one that the police and politicians are lax in coming to terms with.

Because of limited financial means (I was only able to work for 12 years because of the nature of the disabilities and managed to raise five children in those circumstances) I am acutely aware of the difficulties one has in defending one's self against slander. This is a manifest problem within society- that only those of means have the capacity to defend themselves, and I will come back to that point later in this letter

You might also be aware that in January this year, I was bashed outside my home by someone stating it was from "Fergus Fairfax", and investigations into that matter continue. Currently, there is an internal investigation currently being carried out within the NSW Police Service to explain why the crime scene wasn't properly policed, nor certain other information pertaining to the matter, investigated.

Whether it was 'Fergus' himself who assaulted me, or whether he simply organised it, is for the police to determine. 'Fergus' needs to be very concerned.

That's not to say I was listless in reacting to the various attacks over the years. In some respects, I gave as good as I got.

I did receive certain advice from one solicitor who prompted me to approach professional hackers who, armed with Supreme Court writs, had the legal right to pursue such cowards. I also learned that, for a considerable fee (and without Supreme Court writs) there are those who are prepared to hack for the sport and the challenge. Illegally, of course, and unfortunately, what one learns in such a way cannot be used in court.

But there are many ways to skin a cat- especially 'cats' who dare not put a name to personal emails and slander others from the hidey-hole of gutless pseudonym.

I can advise you that, one way or another (including detailed analysis of syntax and sentence structure by a number of dedicated, decent men within the veteran community) the identities of the hobbits who prefer to hide behind manly aliases like "Shadow" and "Steel" and "Ruger357" and "Certo" and "Action" and "Cicero" and "Mowgli" and "BC" and "Nuidat68" and "Spartacus" and "Cavalry" etc etc., have all been revealed to the veteran community, to various politicians, and to state police agencies.

I refer especially to Keith Tennant, 'Bomber' Bob Gibson, Barry Billing, Peter Mackie, Frank Grady, Kenneth Taylor, Alan Price and Peter Maher. Most disappointingly, at least one one ex-officer, Arthur Clive Mitchell-Taylor, has freely admitted to contributing to the AVM, using a pseudonym. Why a man of his standing wasn't man enough to use his own name is beyond me.

But the most revealing aspect was to find that, almost without exception, most of these 'men' exhibit characteristics of the fringe-dwellers of society- liars, fraudsters, and despicable cowards. Most interesting of all, each is also revealed to be a wannabee- that term they use freely against others. None ever saw any true combat, yet trash those who actually did. Such hypocrisy.

Only the identity of that most pernicious snake- "Fergus Fairfax" remains hidden from view. It appears that the original "Fairfax" left the AVM scene after the site was fully operational (and when his identity was close to being revealed) and others chose to inhabit its skin on its behalf- a common occurrence it seems with the scum who inhabit the AVM.

They change persona from time to time. This has complicated the issue in determining 'Fergus Fairfax's' true identity. (Incidentally, sir, I note that the piece of filth parading as 'Fergus Fairfax' has opted to use your Christian name- possibly an old foe from your days in court, retaliating against you. You might have some better idea than me as to who that 'man' might be. He certainly has a hide).

In case you were wondering, I have, over time, referred all these matters to various bodies and politicians and to a current enquiry presently underway (that conducted by DLA Piper) and have an assurance that all will out, eventually, and those involved in the personal attacks on me and others will be outed, named and shamed well and truly in due course- and revealed for what they truly are.

And to hell with former rank, gallantry medals, professions, and reputations- after all, these cowards never concerned themselves with damaging the reputations of me or those who supported me, even if it was only in a limited way. I refer specifically here to Mr Neil Weekes and George Mansford whose reputations suffered by association with me, despite both men maintaining a distance, and only providing the most limited support. Invariably, they were more concerned with my welfare than my battles- yet, both men were also viciously attacked, nevertheless.

Personally, I believe it says much about the true nature of the Australian military that the reputations of men of the ilk of Weekes and Mansford have been so tarnished. While we love to profess a certain nobility for the Anzac legend, it seems to me that observing the attacks on those two men (as well as against other ex-officers) demonstrates that the Anzac spirit of mateship and honour is really all froth and bubble. It's more about the distribution of "gallantry" medals, promotions, and where such things take a man in life after war, than any notion of 'nobility.'

Luckily for both Weekes and Mansford, both are men whose character and service records can withstand the attacks by mean-spirited, jealous individuals, and while it may be uncomfortable for them to have been attacked as they have been, surely they know that those men they led and served alongside on lonely jungle tracks in Vietnam will not be dissuaded of their opinions by a cowardly element who generally stayed behind the wire all those years ago, and who do not have the courage, all these years on, to identify themselves by putting a name to their slander.

It is entirely my personal opinion that those ex-officers who are behind the AVM web site and behind the attacks on myself and officers like Weekes, Mansford, McGurgan and co are precisely the same sort of men who would have participated in the bastardisation of fellow cadets at Duntroon, been involved in the rape of fellow female cadets, or participated in the homosexual acts performed on fellow male cadets at that infamous officer school. They are the sort of men who either were responsible/ joined in/ watched from the sidelines/ masturbated/ and/or stayed silent as those acts were committed. No doubt, they later marched out proudly in full dress uniform, heads up and chests out, and swords flashing- puffed up with some sense of grandeur and self-importance, but in truth, just hollow excuses for men.

That is the type of man I am contending with, and the type of man under investigation as I write, by DLA Piper.

But that is all background material to the purposes of this letter.

Why I am writing to you is that, given your reputation as a fellow veteran of the same war and being such a man of good will as you are reputed to be, to seek your assistance in validating my service history- and in respect of that, I have attached a document of some length which contains army documents, photographs, media reports, and letters from those I served alongside. I am trusting that you might examine that documentation and report your conclusions.

In particular, you should note that I have been unfortunate in that I was a reinforcement to three different units during my seven and a half months before being wounded, and learned that one of those units (the 2nd D&E Platoon) had been wiped from the history books, and my wounding with 9RAR wasn't recorded (by the battalion.) Those errors of administration have caused me great angst over the years, reflect poorly on the ADF administration, and had significant sequelae for me, as you might imagine. It also meant I was to be denied that sense of belonging to any one unit, and never being able to embrace the notion of espirit de corps like so many of my fellow veterans have been able to do. I have learned that there are many others in a similar boat in that regard, as too, are those who served with other units, created illegally, and which have also vanished from the history books.

You might be aware that recently, a "Septemusprime" validated the matters I raised concerning the 2nd D&E Platoon, and a correspondent calling himself "Cathcart" did validate my service history, but although there was some comfort for me in both, the fact that they too, preferred the robe of anonymity, has detracted from their intentions and conclusions as far as I am concerned, and mean little.

Which is why I am coming to a man of your standing within the veteran community, and the world at large. Some time ago, I also made this request of Mr Peter Cosgrove MC who, like me, also served in 9RAR for a month or so, as well as the more sedentary D&E Platoon for the duration of his tour of duty. Despite the relative parallels of our service, he has chosen not to assist me in clearing my name or the contentions surrounding my service. I was very disappointed by this, we having walked similar paths- the only differences being that he was an officer from a privileged background who wasn't wounded in the war, while I was a Private from a modest family background, who was!

The old CARO was equally reticent in doing so, and if I hadn't recorded significant sections of my experiences in Vietnam on colour film, I may well have been up the creek completely, as they say, in validating my records. Not every fellow veteran seeking to rectify the omissions and errors in their service histories had the luxury of moving film to assist them in validating theirs.

You will note from the attachments, certain facts which are irrefutable, and which I now ask that you validate:

- that I served in three units (4RAR; the 2nd D&E Platoon, as it now officially designated by the Federal Government; and 9RAR)

- that I always served as a rifleman in those units

- that there were no black marks against my name in any of those units

- and that I was actively involved in combat until the day I was wounded

The sole contention relates to my recording of events of May 29th 1969 at the ambush at Thua Tich. In The War Within, I state categorically that I have no recollection of that action or my role in it, yet two of the more significant individuals who were present, Cpl Jim Riddle and Kevin Lloyd-Thomas have publicly recorded me as being present, albeit in two different locations. That I admit to having no memory of the ambush is held against me, yet there are those I have met along the way who were involved in combat who have no problem with admitting that they too, have no recollection of any of it.

I even made the effort to return to Vietnam earlier this month, close to the 42nd anniversary of the day I was wounded, in the hope it might have sparked some long dormant memory. It was a very difficult thing to do with my disabilities, and ultimately, to no avail.

Nevertheless, I did have specific images from that time, and some clear recollections, and was assisted by others, which allowed me to record that ambush as best as possible in The War Within, and was pleased to see that those descriptions of events were validated by Captain Tom Arrowsmith's APC driver well after my book was published. The first manuscript of my memoir was sent to a publisher in 2002 and contained this account in its entirety (long before any other person even mentioned it) but that manuscript was rejected on grounds of length. (I subsequently deleted enough material from it to allow publication of The War Within' and provide the backbone of a second book, currently underway).

You may be aware that in attacking me about my recollections of this matter, the cowards within the AVM cite two individuals as the source of their information. One, supposedly, prefers the comfort of even deeper anonymity than those he corresponds with, while the other is Ted Colmer- a man who publicly declared his state of mental ill-health to the veteran community at large, a condition accepted by a NSW Court. Neither man's comments could be regarded as being valid, or of any substance.

That I have successfully prosecuted the case for the inclusion of the 2nd D&E Platoon into the histories of the war, with the full support of the Army History Unit, when there were no official records or even anecdotal evidence of the platoon should speak for itself. That announcement by the Hon Dr Mike Kelly MP on May 29th 2008 that the 2nd D&E Platoon "will be forever enshrined in the histories of the war" means a great deal to me and those who fought in it, regardless of what the men in suits at the AWM might say.

Anyway, that is the crux of the matter I place before you. Only a man of your stature and substance can clarify the issues pertaining to my service, and I respectfully leave it in your hands.

Secondly, I was wondering if it was possible for you to support me legally should I decide to take action against any of the cowards who have done me so much damage. Obviously, I am unable to afford the sort of fees you might charge, but I would be prepared to pay you from any proceeds that eventuated. I understand such an arrangement is common-place.'

He answered:

'Dear Mr Tate
I have read your lengthy email. You have encountered many problems.
Regrettably, I am just flat out already doing pro bono work for veterans and disadvantaged people.
I simply cannot find more time in the day to assist you.
I wish you well.
Fergus'

To which I replied:

'Dear Fergus
Thank you for that reply.
I must say I'm disappointed that you weren't able to assist me in putting to the sword the questions raised about my service and about the treatment I have received from the hands of a cowardly element within the veteran community.

Might I offer a sincere thank you for at least taking the time out of your busy schedule to read my letter and evaluate it. It meant a lot to me. There were many issues I brought to your attention, as you pointed out, and no doubt men of lesser substance than you might have just disregarded it altogether. After all, I'm really a nobody- just a lowly Private soldier who forced a government to alter the history books and happened to pen a few thousand words to explain why I am the man I am. Many have found the memoir refreshingly honest- especially compared with those of former generals and the like.

(I guess folk are sick of 'memoirs' that only present a veneer of a life that was lived and don't delve into the detail, the failures of character and so forth that are part of all men's' lives. Such memoirs cheat the reader).

Having said that, I trust you'll agree that what this now means is that I have placed the circumstances of my service and all the validating material not only in front of the entire veteran community some time ago, before one of the finest military minds Australia has produced (Peter Cosgrove) and now before one of the nation's most eminent legal minds, and although neither of you were able to assist me, the fact that neither of you found a flaw was of most import.

I'm sure now that most reasonable men would agree that there's not much more a man can do to prove himself than what I've done.

As for that bastard (excuse the language) who stole your Christian name and demonised it by calling himself "Fergus Fairfax" and allying himself with a paedophile, a murderer, a fraudster, a pompous blowhard, a drunk, a wife-beater, a cat-killer and other assorted low life, one can only assume that the giddy merry-go-round of life will catch up with him one day and he'll reap what he's sown.

Just in passing, you might like to know that I <u>know his identity</u>, and that I have planned the perfect revenge for what he and his acolytes have done to me, both in word, and on that footpath close to my home last January. In essence, every shadowy aspect of his life will be revealed, at a time of my choosing. He will never know when the axe will fall, and that's the beauty of it. There will be the most precise time to exact that revenge, and it'll be one that only I will determine, and in the event of my untimely demise, left in the hands of trusted media men and friends to carry out.

I can assure you that the damage done to me, my wife, and my family by 'Fergus' and his cohorts will pale by comparison with what I have in store for 'Fergus's' family. His reputation, his achievements- all will be taken from him.

Oh, by the way, I note your association with VVF in Canberra and was wondering if you have ever heard of Frank Grady? He was a big shot in the VVF for a long time and put in place the template the VVF and other veteran associations use to score TPI's for those who don't deserve them. It involved fake suicide attempts. Grady was good at them.

And perhaps you're aware of the fraudster, Barry Billing- currently about to face court again.

Grady and Billing are cogs in the AVM pig-pen that 'Fergus' heads up.

Not that this is of any interest or importance to you, I suppose. But you'd have to agree that it makes for interesting discussion at least.

Anyway, I don't want to waste any more of your time. None of it is your concern.

I just wanted to thank you.

For now, the various matters are in the hands of DLA Piper, and in front of a couple of politicians and media men. I doubt "Fergus Fairfax's" tentacles can stretch that far. ..'

Aye'

I wondered if he was smart enough to have read between the lines.

So, over time, I had placed detailed explanations of these matters into the hands of two of Australia's most celebrated men– the Chief of the Army, Gen Peter Cosgrove, and Barrister, James Fergusson Thomson.

You do not get any higher than that.

And it goes without saying that one would not have done so, nor made the submissions public, had there been even the slightest fraud in respect of my service, or my version of any of these things in that correspondence.

CHAPTER 28
RUN, RABBIT...

It's a few days after the ambush at Thua Tich.

The ambush is history; the atrocities are done and dusted.

We're harbouring up in Xuyen Moc where the village chief seems pleased to have us hanging about. It was the first time any of us had ever spent time in a Vietnamese village. Mostly, we were in and out as quick as possible.

But for the 2nd D&E Platoon and this combined armour/infantry force, everything about our operations was a new way of doing things, and it was an interesting night. As Des Blazely put it (sic):

> '... the D&E Platoon was invited to be guests at a dinner hosted by the village chief of Xuyen Moc. As we had no officers in our platoon I clearly remember being briefed by Jim Riddle on behaviour, respect and etiquette required at that dinner. We did Australia and ourselves proud at that dinner. At Xuyen Moc the D&E Platoon was accommodated in a solid concrete walled room. I did not feel safe as one RPG or grenade lobbed in there would have caused many casualties.....I remember Normie Rowe playing a guitar and singing in one of the cafes......I noticed that Capt Arrowsmith carried a non-military sawn-off shotgun sort of weapon and after hearing a shotgun blast was told that he had shot one of the villagers dogs that had encroached into their harbour position. Our good infantry behaviour at the village chief's dinner had all been undone by Arrowsmith.....'

Meanwhile, not that we knew about it at the time, all hell was breaking loose within the military hierarchy about those events that had transpired on May 30th 1969. The only whiff we got about it was a relatively innocuous remark by Cpl Jim Riddle to the effect of, 'Arrowsmith is going to get a kick up the date. There goes our medals.'

For infantry Privates, it was neither here nor there.

It was down time. There was precious little of that for infantrymen.

But we got an inkling that something was up when Capt Tom Arrowsmith and his Troop of APCs disappeared the next day without a farewell, and never to be seen again.

At Nui Dat, word of the atrocities was spreading quickly. And back in Canberra, photographs were landing on desks.

Brigadier Pearson was feeling the heat. One minute he'd been celebrating a very successful operation that had defused what turned out to be a planned attack against Baria (maps and documents taken from the bodies at Thua Tich had confirmed this) and was expecting a pat on the back and probably another medal to add to his collection– and the next, he was under pressure to explain the photographs showing degradation of bodies at the ambush site.

He'd been instructed to enquire into the atrocities and report back to Army Headquarters in Canberra.

As per protocol, he duly ordered Major Ron Rooks, OC of the Armoured Corps to undertake an enquiry since it was an Armoured Corps officer who led the combined force.

The results of that enquiry have never seen the light of day.

Indeed, until I began to pursue this matter, no one knew anything about that enquiry or about any of the events that had transpired at Thua Tich, or afterwards. *All* reports and enquiries seemed to have disappeared into a black hole within the military bureaucracies.

It took me years, but eventually I located the most significant document of all. It was titled, 'ATROCITY ALLEGATIONS – SOUTH VIETNAM – 3 CAV. REGIMENT'.

I found it in the National Archives.

To the best of my knowledge, the documents contained within that plain Defence folder constitute what is more colloquially referred to as that long-lost 'Major Pound Enquiry'.

It contains six pages of telegrams which were sent by Major Gordon Pound to AHQ in Canberra following his 'interview' with Robert Enright, and four, hand-written pages which I assume is Pound's summation of the whole matter.

As far as those pages of telegram are concerned (and just to add to the intrigue) Robert Enright has confirmed that he did *not* provide all the information contained in those telegrams– and suggests that Pound must have 'collected' much of that material from other sources to 'bulk up' the report.

The summary has not been typed up as one would expect such a Defence Report to be. There isn't even a signature present– but they do confirm most of what we had always alleged:

– that the combined armour/infantry force *was* operating outside the range of artillery, but contingency plans had also been made in case we had been overwhelmed (including 'Spooky' being available; tanks from Tango Force on stand-by; and artillery, which had been instructed to be ready to move from Nui Dat to a position where they could have provided support......all further evidence of just how aware the brass had been of a likely major encounter)

– that bodies had been 'destroyed' (with the exception of those regarded as being 'not too badly cut about')

– that bodies *were* strapped to the backs of APCs, and subsequently 'dragged'

– that a light Fire Team (helicopter gunships) was instructed to accompany the force into Xuyen Moc with the imminent risk of ambush existing

– that machine-guns *were* fired at villagers who were collecting grass outside Xuyen Moc and had their hands up

Our allegations were proven, with the exception of whether or not a woman and child had been killed on the outskirts of Xuyen Moc.

In respect of *that* issue, it is important to note that it had happened as the troop was travelling at speed, had only been carried out by a few of the troopers, and that at no point did we stop to actually see the results of that indiscriminate shooting.

I have included all those pages from the Major Pound Enquiry in the *Attachments*.

In quick succession, I lodged formal complaints with the relevant authorities.
First– to the Australian Defence Force to explain the historical corruptions:

Department of Defence
Defence Legal – DOIL
CP2-3-082
PO Box 7911
CANBERRA BC ACT 2610

Dear Sir or Madam

You are aware that I am the author of *The War Within*- a memoir which includes two chapters concerning the actions of the 2nd D&E Platoon in South Vietnam in 1969.

I write in reference to the matters concerning that Platoon- and specifically refer to the revelation by investigative journalist Frank Walker (author of *Ghost Platoon*) that he had unearthed evidence proving that atrocities had been committed in Vietnam by a combined armour/infantry force of which that platoon was part, in 1969, and that that evidence had subsequently been 'buried'.

I am aware that the Directorate has stated that it enquired into the allegations previously, and declared that the 'enquiry' by Major Gordon Pound had found no evidence to substantiate the allegations.

I am also aware the ADF and the AWM have both declared that they were unable to provide copies of that 'enquiry'- which allowed them to wipe their hands of the matter, and Major Pound now professes no recall of ever conducting it. (Because he didn't! He called not one witness to it.)

I am now aware that a file exists within the National Archives titled: *"Atrocities- South Vietnam- 3 CAV"* and that it clearly states that Brigadier C.M.I. Pearson, Task Force Commander of the day, had been made aware that atrocities had been committed, and not only took no action (as he was required under international law at the time, and remains) but rewarded the miscreant responsible with a Mention-in-Dispatches.

You would be aware that I have been the recipient of years of vilification and slander as a consequence of pursuing this matter, received death threats on many occasions, and a physical bashing in January this year- and all the while, the truths of this matter have remained closely guarded secrets.

No longer.

I formally request you open an investigation into why the 2nd D&E Platoon was erased from records of the war, why the atrocities of May 29th were not acted upon by C Pearson, which senior officers have been complicit in various cover-ups to do with the matter (including the extent of historian Ashley Ekins' involvement), which senior officers set up the Australian Veteran Matters website (which was used to try and silence me), which legal officers were utilised to moderate and administer that web site, where did the funding for the site come from, and what role did the AWM play in this cover-up.

You should be aware that the erasure of this platoon has caused me and many others great anguish over the years, and I will not rest until a full enquiry of some sort is held, and those responsible are called to account- regardless of their reputations or standing within the ADF or society.

I fought for my country willingly in a time of war, and sacrificed my health in circumstances which any soldier would normally be proud of. But the bastardisation of my service history has detracted from that, at great personal cost. And some bastards are going to pay.

In the likely event of another whitewash, or this letter being 'lost', or ignored, I intend publishing it far and wide. There will be no place to hide for those who are complicit in this matter.

It's time to do the right thing by the 39 infantry privates, sir- and to hell with protecting the officer ranks.

Yours Sincerely

Phantom force secrets

Vietnam's grave request to reveal war atrocity

By MATTHEW BENNS

Sun-Herald 12/7/09

AUSTRALIAN soldiers dragged corpses behind armoured cars in a Vietnam war atrocity that officials have spent 40 years denying ever happened.

Now a request by the Vietnamese Government to locate the bodies of Viet Cong soldiers killed in action may finally uncover the truth of what happened in the villages of Thua Thich and Xuyen Moc in May, 1969.

Don Tate, now 60, was a member of the 2nd D and E platoon when the atrocities were committed.

"Mate, this has been a bullshit cover-up for 40 years and it is now finally coming into the open," he said. "They will never find the graves because there aren't any."

It was only after Mr Tate's book, *The War Within*, was published last year that the phantom 2nd D and E platoon was finally acknowledged as even having existed. Parliamentary secretary for defence support Mike Kelly confirmed in July that the platoon had not been formally raised but had been born in battle.

Mr Tate, from Shellharbour, south of Wollongong, said the phantom force of 39 Diggers ambushed a much larger number of Viet Cong in May 1969 in one of the war's biggest platoon-sized battles. Official reports claimed the bodies of the dead Viet Cong were wrapped in green ponchos and buried.

But Mr Tate, who was a private in the platoon, said the bodies were dragged into a crater filled with claymore mines and C4 explosive and given an "engineers' burial" – they were blown up.

"There are no bodies left for them to find," said Mr Tate.

Another five bodies were tied by the ankles to the back of an armoured personnel carrier and dragged to a local village as a warning to Viet Cong sympathisers.

In his book Mr Tate wrote: "Eventually the remaining bodies were dumped in the centre of Xuyen Moc, headless. They'd been banging around at the back of the APC till they fell off. God knows where the heads ended up."

Photographs taken at the time show the horrified reaction of villagers as the bodies were dragged behind the APC.

Following Mr Kelly's official acknowledgement last year, the Vietnamese Government approached the Australian embassy in Hanoi and requested help in locating the burial sites of all Vietnamese soldiers killed in action.

The Australian embassy's defence attache, Colonel Stuart Dodds, contacted members of the 2nd D and E Platoon and requested information on the location of the graves.

Mr Tate said the Australian soldiers had been acting under orders. "To cover that atrocity up the military establishment has wiped the official record of 39 Australian Diggers, denying some of them access to war pensions. Finally the truth can come out."

The driver of the APC, Allan Stanton, who was from a different cavalry unit, earlier this year published a book, *Before I Forget*, that confirmed the accounts of the 2nd D and E Platoon members.

Vietnam veteran, retired Brigadier Neil Weekes, a member of the Prime Minister's Advisory Council on Ex-Service matters, said he was aware of the issue but could only offer a personal view. "I think there seems to be some controversy there and it needs to be resolved at a pretty high level," he said.

Brigadier George Mansford, who was a captain in the Australian Army Training Team which won four Victoria Crosses in Vietnam, advised against looking for the graves. "Some things are best left alone. If what we hear is true then it will certainly be rubbing salt in the wound," he said.

A spokeswoman for the Australian War Memorial said there was no "official view" of the "successful operation" at Thua Thich. "The operational records and veterans' accounts indicate conflicting views over the manner of disposal of enemy bodies," she said.

'There are no bodies left for them to find.'

No more lies ... Don Tate, holding his controversial book *The War Within*, says it's time the truth came out about his platoon in Vietnam. Photo: Adam Rainford

Shocked ... Xuyen Moc villagers watch in horror as bodies of Viet Cong soldiers are dragged behind an Australian APC vehicle. Photo: Australian War Memorial

Help to locate the last missing Australians

AN archaeological dig is under way to find the bodies of the last two Australian servicemen missing in Vietnam.

Flying Officer Michael Herbert and Pilot Officer Robert Carver were returning from a mission in 1970 when their Canberra bomber crashed in Quang Nam Province.

A Defence spokeswoman said the Vietnamese Government was assisting with the search.

The media was always an ally.

The newspaper story on the preceding page, published in the Sun-Herald (one of NSW's largest papers) put the matter squarely into the public domain.

And then, because of the vitriol I had endured and the recalcitrance of senior officers to open their mouths, I followed Richard Bigwood's suit and referred the entire matter to the Australian Federal Police (via the Attorney-General's Department) and requested they investigate whether or not international or Commonwealth law had been broken.

My letter was quite detailed, and contained all the relevant evidence, as reproduced in this narrative.

The Attorney-General, the Hon Brendan O'Connor MP, replied:

Dear Mr Tate

Thank you for your correspondence dated 2 September 2009, to the Attorney-General, the Hon Robert McClelland MP, concerning alleged incidents that occurred in Vietnam during 1969. As this pertains to matters that fall within my portfolio responsibilities I am responding to your correspondence.

The Australian Federal Police (AFP) has advised me that you also hand delivered additional documents to AFP Headquarters on 9 September 2009 concerning the same alleged incidents. The matters you have outlined are deeply concerning issues.

The particular concerns you have raised are the direct responsibility of the Department of Veterans' Affairs. They are very important concerns and as such my office has forwarded your correspondence to the office of the Minister for Veterans' Affairs, the Hon Alan Griffin MP, for appropriate follow-up action.

I trust this information is of assistance to you and thank you for taking the time to write in relation to your concerns.

Yours sincerely

Brendan O'Connor

And finally, I lodged a series of claims with the Defence Abuse Reparation Taskforce (DART) – set up by the Minister for Defence, the Hon Stephen Smith MP – into the maladministration, the falsifications, and the corruptions of my service records, and into the abuse I had received from fellow veterans via the AVM and ANZMI web sites.

In particular, it is my hope that the DART Enquiry will have the powers to identify those cowardly men who hid behind pseudonyms to do their dirty work. Independent investigations have already revealed a number of significant players– about 300 hundred entities in total (many of whom have multiple personalities).

But private research is one thing; legal, professional investigations are more compelling and may result in the retrospective legal action promised by the initial investigating team– the DLA PIPER Review.

It is my understanding that there will also be compensation, although no amount could ever compensate me for what I have endured.

Whatever, as long as there *is* justice of some sort.

The vexed question as to the relative capabilities of the men and commanders who served in the D&E Platoons has been a matter of great contention within the veteran community. The opinions I have expressed earlier have been those given to me by the likes of Maj George Pratt and Jim Riddle.

It would be fair and honest of me to present an alternative view, written by John Burrows, who was one of the D&E platoon commanders during 1970:

> *'Please be aware that the opinions contained within are my own and if I embarrass or offend anyone then I apologise.....*
>
> *When I arrived in Vietnam in February '70, I was OC 12Pl, D COY 7RAR.*
>
> *In mid-year 1970, I was interviewed for the job as D&E Platoon commander. I was told by the CO 7RAR that Brigadier Henderson, CO of the Task Force 1ATF was looking for a competent Platoon commander to follow on from Lt Peter Cosgrove. At that time, I was told that D&E was being used as a ready reaction Platoon and spending some time in the field.*
>
> *Apparently Henderson wanted to develop D&E Platoon's capability along the lines of a reconnaissance Platoon and involve it more in operations .*
>
> *I was duly "detached" from 7RAR and "attached" to HQ 1ATF and assigned to D&E PL, 7 July 70. During my time in D&E which I found to be very satisfying and professionally rewarding, we positioned a number of highly secretive intelligence audio and ground sensors around the province, started the demise of the Chau Duc*

VC unit, participated in Operation Massey Harris (the destruction of enemy crops in the Mao Tay Mountain region) worked a lot with 7RAR and had a couple of good contacts with the enemy. Further to that we often followed up SAS and intelligence information, were on standby as the Task Force ready reaction force when in base and had a very interesting time.

It should be noted that when I took over D&E PL, I found that the officers of HQ 1ATF including Maj Peter Bool (Cosgrove's OC in HQ Coy) and the soldiers in D&E also spoke very highly of him and many have continued to do so ever since.

As you are well aware the utilisation of the respective D&E Platoons at 1ATF fluctuated and they were committed to a variety of tasks. On occasions the Platoon was very active, and yet there were periods when there was a low operational commitment with the Platoon mainly being confined to Nui Dat.

It is my understanding that the use of a D&E Platoon was, and has been, very much at the direction of the respective Commanders and/ or Operations Officers. I believe that under Brigadier Weir (Henderson's predecessor) D&E Platoon HQ 1ATF spent a lot of its time in the HQ/ base area.

I'm not sure why COSGROVE doesn't make much of his time with D&E Platoon. His non-attendance at HQ COY 1ATF reunions has been disappointing and saddened a number of those who he served with in the Platoon.

Perhaps his reluctance about his time in D&E may relate to an unwarranted perception/ stigma that all D&Es have had over time, not only long prior to, but during and after Vietnam. In my view (and from numerous discussions that I had) the basis of the stigma/ inappropriate attitude towards the Platoon hasn't been helped by the fact that it has often been seen in an insipid light, and uninvolved.

With the D&E Companies (at Divisional level) and Platoons (Task Force and Brigade levels) being a part of main HQs throughout many conflicts which have included Task Force/ Brigade/ Divisional and the odd Force HQ's, they have often been labelled as "pogos" and on occasions "bludgers".

I think that a number of these perceptions/ stigma's are applied "willy nilly", without appreciation and often with very little knowledge of the reality of the situation. In many regards they are no different to a lot of irrelevant and sometimes intra/ inter unit/ formation rivalry/slanging/ bad mouthing which is perpetuated in many forms and forums but can be easily scotched by leaders and a positive outlook and the good record of the "ostracised/ defamed" unit/ group.

(As you are well aware the 2nd D&E Platoon led by Jimmy Riddle is a prime example).

Despite some fairly derogatory comments at the time of being the D&E Platoon Commander and since, I found the Platoon that I commanded to be professional, brave, resourceful, a great team, larrikins, very capable, and respected as "doers".

In regard to D&E Platoons being a dumping ground for some "bad eggs", the answer is YES. But during my time I don't think that D&E PL HQ 1ATF was any more a dumping ground than a number of other units of the Task Force.

Whilst in HQ 1ATF, I became aware that the posting ("shipping out") of "incompetent/bad eggs" infantrymen not only involved D&E PL but occurred within/ between BATTALIONS, ARU, D&E HQ 1ATF , D&E PL 1ALSG, D&E PL HQ AFV Saigon and on occasions, other non-infantry units within the Task Force.

I came to believe that soldiering is a great leveller with some better than others but the reasons for the difference can be very wide and complex. For example I believe that leadership, training, knowledge, equipment and environment are very significant aspects of the performance of infantry soldiers and their respective teams.

I was extremely happy to be involved, serve with and lead either and would do so again.

Regarding Maj George Pratt's comments, I'd be very reluctant to put any credence to his words about the soldiers in D&E. Like all soldiers in units throughout the Army during those days they all did their share of "kitchen duties". I only knew Maj Pratt by his reputation, and I don't believe (in view of that reputation) that his words should be given the credence that perhaps you'd like to think they should. Furthermore to make a relationship between the comments he has made about the soldiers of D&E Platoon Nui Dat and its officers (particularly about their possible involvement in "kitchen duties") is in my view naive, inappropriate and seriously questions the reason/ motive behind it?....'

John Burrows is entitled to his opinion.

The problem is, like most things military, it all comes down to perspective and timing. No private who served in the D&E Platoons at any time wants to believe it was anything but a hot-shot unit, and no officer who ever led one wants to be considered as any less of a man for having done so.

And the fact is, the way D&E Platoons were regarded and subsequently used by various Task Force commanders varied from man to man.

Given my relative lack of military experience, my opinion is purely speculative and irrelevant.

And the documentary by Adam Rainford?

Well, like Ted Colmer's fanciful 'brief of evidence', it never eventuated.

He pulled it together, but it lacked the finesse required. And after I was bashed, he got an insight into the inherent madness of elements of the veteran community and opted to put his own health and the welfare of his family first and abandoned the project.

I didn't blame him.

There are more important things in life.

So I'm the last man standing. That's how it should be, too, since I'm the only one who had the gumption to fight this battle for all these years.

Mind you– the 'establishment' plays dirty now. It's on the run.

The last thing they did to me was hack my website: **www.dontate.info** and render it inoperable. Or 'inert' as one of my major antagonists, Greg Marheine boasted in an email to me, mockingly.

I'm still waiting for 'good men' to stand up and be counted, and start asking questions too.

It might be a long wait.

'Good men' *do* exist– but they are scarce in the veteran community.

POSTSCRIPT
THE LEGAL SITUATION

I have no legal expertise, but my pursuit of this matter required me to understand and appreciate the legal aspects of these matters to some degree– after all, if a crime was committed, then I was party to it.

I needed to know where I stood.

And my layman's appreciation is that Ted Colmer was right. There is no statute of limitations when it comes to war crimes.

Of course, whether or not the events that occurred all that time ago might be classified as 'war crimes' would be for men of greater learning and substance than me to answer.

But on the 'balance of probabilities' I have no doubt that a case could be made that the officers who ordered the destruction of bodies, the strapping up of bodies to the backs of APCs with toggle ropes, and the indiscriminate shooting at civilians which resulted in the death of at least one woman have hard questions to answer.

There appears to be a conclusive, evidentiary chain of evidence to support the contention that atrocities *were* committed, as well as factual, corroborating statements by primary witnesses at each step of the way.

Some might argue that individual photographs only *suggest* a crime being carried out– and are not definitive, clinical 'evidence' per se. But when placed into the 'chain of evidence', the criteria is fulfilled.

That 'chain of evidence' is:

- that a successful ambush was carried out on May 29th 1969 which resulted in a number of enemy bodies being displayed for photographs on the road to Thua Tich
- that a photograph shows the bodies *in situ*
- that there are soldiers standing at the scene, observing said bodies
- that some of those soldiers are infantrymen from the 'non-existent' 2nd D&E Platoon and have been identified as such– substantive, irrefutable proof of their presence
- that two of those soldiers are dragging bodies along the road
- that one of the said soldiers has given a sworn Affidavit that he was one of those men dragging the bodies into a bomb crater
- that one of those soldiers also swears that he and another soldier tied bodies to the back of the APC belonging to the commander of the combined force– Capt Tom Arrowsmith
- that a number of soldiers will swear that those bodies and weapons in the bomb crater were then wired up with explosives
- that some soldiers will attest to hearing the bodies being blown up, to seeing a pall of black smoke behind us, and attest that Engineers carried it out
- that an order was given by 'Seagull' (Major David Chinn) that some bodies were to be transported into Xuyen Moc for 'propaganda purposes'
- that en route to Xuyen Moc the combined force was ambushed and a photograph taken which shows a member of the 2nd D&E Platoon heavily involved (Cpl Len Ellecombe) as well as other photographs showing the involvement of Capt Tom Arrowsmith's Troop (including one of the APC which was hit by RPG)
- that some bodies were loosed from the back of Arrowsmith's APC during the second ambush and subsequently dragged headless into Xuyen Moc, and this being further evidenced by another photograph showing the shocked reactions by villagers to the sight
- and that the bodies were cut from the APC and deposited in the village square where another photograph shows the villagers congregating around the scene, inspecting the bodies
- and most importantly, that the photographic evidence of Brigadier C. Pearson and other members of the 'high brass' on the ground (with 2nd D&E Platoon members) is evidence that command physical presence existed– and compromises them

A statement by the Australian War Memorial that the bodies were, indeed, 'transported' to Thua Tich (which conflicts with their earlier stand that all the bodies were buried elsewhere) was a critical, and fundamental link in the evidence.

When the photographic 'chain of evidence' is complimented by extracts from the Narratives, LOCSTATS, after-action reports, and written corroboration by the men involved, it is a damning indictment on the Australian Defence Force and its conduct of the war.

Villagers in Xuyen Moc swarm to view the headless bodies cut from Capt Tom Arrowsmith's APC

Frank Walker spent more than a year investigating the whole matter before he wrote *Ghost Platoon*. He spoke to almost every man involved– across all units. He spoke with senior officers, including Brigadier Pearson. He even travelled to England to speak with the crippled Jim Riddle.

The only significant individuals who wouldn't grant him an interview were Dennis Manski (who had been a section-commander in the platoon); General Steve Gower of the War Memorial; and the historian, Ashley Ekins.

Two of the men who had fought to validate this platoon with me– Ted Colmer and Richard Bigwood allowed themselves to be interviewed, but did not want anything they said, or any document they had located to be used in his book for fear of inciting further abuse. They had done the same when journalist, Matthew Benns of the *Sun-Herald*, was writing up his story (see page 276).

After coming so far, and then pulling up stakes so close to the end, I considered to be cowardice in the extreme.

In the end though, Walker validated much of what we had always said, but of most significance, agreed that senior officers of the Australian Defence Force had engaged in a cover-up of the facts which continues to this day.

Most tellingly, Walker was scathing in his assessment of the Army brass. He wrote:

> *'Instead of supporting their former diggers who had risked their lives fighting for their country, the Army dismissed their concerns out of hand…Instead of choosing to properly investigate the claims by Riddle, Tate and others, top-ranking generals and taxpayer-funded military historians all chose to pull the shutters down and hide behind bureaucratic semantics…….it appears the Department of Defence, the military establishment and a core of veterans are more intent on trying to preserve the glossy image of the bronzed Anzac; the irreverent larrikin who fights honourably. The myth serves the military well.'*

After Ghost Platoon was published, Ashley Ekins attempted to degrade the book and the research conducted by Walker, even though Walker was an experienced investigative journalist and had spoken with every key individual. Ekins wrote that it was, *'…riddled with factual errors and unfounded assumptions and interpretations'*. But neither Steve Gower nor Ekins ever thought it would be a good idea to ask Walker to put his evidence on the table and discuss any aspect of it.

It would be easy to conclude that I have a poor opinion of my fellow veterans. There would be some truth in that. The fact is, I fought alongside some of the most decent, courageous men one is ever likely to meet– men like Jim Riddle of the 4th Battalion, and Andrew Ochiltree MM of the 9th Battalion.

And it's been a pleasure to meet many former veterans of the war as I've travelled Australia speaking about *The War Within*– men who have demonstrated true grit and sensitivity to my situation. They include: Garry Heskett, Tony White, Ben Morris, Jack Babbage, Bill Dobell, Terry Westerway, Brian McKenzie, Allen Peterson and Robert Enright.

These are men who'd have your back in a fight.

But the reality is that the great majority of infantry privates weren't exactly the cream of the crop back then, me included, and for many of those it's been downhill ever since.

I'm referring to the low life who have contributed to the ANZMI and AVM web sites– men who obviously never aimed too high in life, and still fell short. The sort of man who hates to see anyone rising above the herd.

But there *are* some men who stand apart, like Brigadier Neil Weekes and men of that ilk, as the following comments indicate:

First, by Brigadier George Mansford AM (one of Australia's most celebrated senior army officers from the war). He wrote:

> *'..I have noted part of the hate traffic and as always am very disappointed with it all. It is simply beyond me to understand the spite and lack of logic that elements of our vet community demonstrate. More to the point I am always angry and certainly saddened at the attacks on your efforts to find justice and recognition.*
>
> *Let me say at the very beginning that I am very much appalled at the treatment you have received, not only in recent times but the whole sad story of total negligence and questionable leadership you experienced in Vietnam. I certainly do not support or justify your critics, however I think I understand some of their thinking and resentment. First there is no doubt that some of your critics are in denial, and nothing is going to change that but those I think I understand simply do not want to hear criticism of their beloved units/regiments/corp and leaders they readily identify with. (For example, Sandy Pearson was and is loved by many)*
>
> *Some would feel a touch of shame/guilt that a wounded soldier could be so easily divorced from his past regardless of the circumstances of evacuation. (and although I was not part of your unit or even in Vn at that time, it includes me) and why is that? I will answer my own question... Because our ethos and brotherhood has been so strong, it has always been our centre of pride, and has been the very base of our strength when things have not gone well or when we tried to find courage to overcome whatever the obstacle was before us. Many often use it as support to negate the nightmares and ghosts we try to forget. Thus there can be an instant reaction of resentment because someone they don't know appears out of a past they are not familiar with, nor can they comprehend such neglect could happen and above all, they see it as attacking their beliefs, their personal experiences, their past.*

(Nevertheless I have noted with interest your campaign in regards wounded has not been lost on the Battalions, the Associations and indeed the Chief of Army). Could I also add that some of your critics are old comrades who I have the highest regard for but do not necessarily agree with their comments.

This is a time to remind all that when wood is chopped splinters must fly and it stands to reason there will be mistakes in a busy and intense environment. Equally I am of the view that public slanging of such proportions does demean all Vietnam Vets and who can deny that it was a magnificent force comprising both regular and magnificent conscripts who came from all walks of life. I would argue it was one of the most disciplined forces to leave our shores. I would also argue that it was a time of immense commitment, Borneo and Vietnam and continuing increases of strength in Vietnam plus expansion of the Army with new units etc and the need to rotate troops and replace casualties. I emphasise it does not excuse poor leadership or major stuffups but I think it does demonstrate that the Officer and NCO Corp could not have been that bad and of course it also meant our soldiers were nothing short of brilliant no matter where or when they served and no matter what they did or did not do. In short we are getting old and its time to reflect on what a great team it was. It was a time of trust, of sharing, of giving, and looking after each other, (thus the embarrassment of such cases as yours) But how can we describe such ethos when we have such slanging matches.

So far I have not given any advice. Let me try.

First, do not be confused about what you have pursued. Your efforts have been very honourable and you have demonstrated much courage in pursuing recognition and justice for your comrades, as well as pointing out some of the serious shortcomings in regards reinforcements and casualties. I have no doubt your personal efforts will help future vets.

Accept the fact there are those if given the opportunity will continue their attacks. They are in my view very much a minority and should be totally ignored.... Finally let me say without hesitation, if you are ever in my location on Anzac day I would be bloody proud to march alongside Don Tate. I have no doubt all those I know well, and those I think I know would agree..'

And this from Kevin Bovill, ex-SAS, and ex-infantry:

'It does appear to me that over the years your detractors (of which there are many) have always attacked you personally and have never ever at any point proved you to be factually wrong.

They are all enraged that you have pulled scabs off old wounds, exposed frauds and wannabees, shattered more than a few reputations and generally told it how it was for you without fear or favour. This has enraged these geriatric defenders of democracy whose outraged bleats of indignation have more to do with concealing the truth rather than exposing it.

You will never be brought to trial because there is no evidence to convict you but in the eyes of these paragons of a "fair go" you are guilty without the benefit of due process.

This has divided the veteran community to the extent that old mates no longer talk to each other, cannot rationally discuss your situation without violent disagreement and are polarised and radicalised into either camp.

Pretty bloody sad all-round, and all a bit childish. I would have thought that grown men who in many cases are now grandfathers would have a more mature and objective view of things. Passionate-yes but not bound by blind bigotry and ignorance.

No one, least of all yourself, could ever have imagined that following your psych's advice to write a couple of pages a month as a therapeutic tool could have led to this. (He may be a little bit more circumspect about who he offers that advice to in future.)

There are many who have good reason to hope that past misdeeds remain buried in the past, many who have previously been proud of their service to the nation are now questioning whether or not it was all worthwhile. Some will no doubt go to their graves carrying a burden of guilt and others will die still too arrogant to admit that they failed.

Even our greatest war historian CEW Bean sought to play down or understate certain events but I believe that future generations are entitled to the raw, unvarnished truth, if not, how else will they ever learn the futility of war and the duplicity of our politicians and senior commanders?

We must accept the failings and frailty of human nature in all our endeavours but warfare is the one endeavour where we can least afford it. We must learn that lesson at least for future generations.

I suspect that DLA Piper will rock the Anzac community to a far greater extent that you have thus far and I look forward to many, including yourself, having your day in court (in the witness box of course)'
-*'Kevin 'Kiwi' Bovill (ex-SAS)*

And from Robert de Haas...(a former officer, admonishing Bob Buick):

'Whether the "2nd D&E Pl" had that name officially or not is not particularly relevant to the overall situation. Don Tate and the members of that "group" were pulled together in such a "group" by the then TF COMD - as was (essentially) his right as you explained some time ago. However, as there were no records of that "group" being formed for whatever specific tasks they were given or carried out, the lads have not had access to the "compensations" of war that the rest of us may have had - through DVA or any other statutory authority. They (the members of that "group" - in platoon-type configuration) have individually and collectively been accused of "making up stories" for whatever reasons - even by their very own children, as no "official" proof of their formation, their tasking, their method of operating, or their results (good, bad, or indifferent) could be found. And, when it was found, no-one wanted to validate it or admit to it!

Unfortunately the benefit of doubt never went their way.

The lads strove tirelessly over very many years to collect any evidence they could to substantiate their claims, and suffered intolerably the abuses of others who really knew no better themselves and who seem to have been unable to accept that the stories might actually have been factual. Rather than assist in actually and properly investigating the stories, many resorted to verbal abuse and derision - based on nothing more than what I would call "self righteous indignation", i.e. "what right do these upstarts have in proposing such tall stories as factual.., etc". And, let's face it, many people never want to admit there may be another "truth" different from their own version, even when it stares them in the face.

Issues such as these are always highly emotive, as peoples' perceptions are always different. To persist in being pedantic about actual names (e.g., 2nd D&E Pl) does nothing to calm emotions - as you would well be aware from your experience and in the teachings to attain higher rank levels. As far as Don and his mates were aware, they were (then) an iteration (a copy) of the already existent ATF D&E Pl. Whether such a name as "2nd D&E Pl" was actually given to them or not does matter. Perhaps such a name was "alluded to" at some stage. Who cares! What was important was that all of that "arrangement" was not recorded. Why it was not recorded may well be the subject of further investigation. The most important aspects now are that they have all been recognised and "legitimised". And, unless any of us specifically are aware of any information that remains to the contrary, we should be happy for the "group" and their families to finally be "at peace" - within themselves and within the "official" circles, the veteran community at large, and even within "history" itself.

I personally don't believe the story finishes here. I don't know where it will end up, but I have a gut feel that there is still a lot more to be uncovered. Perhaps we can all learn from this past experience and approach whatever needs to be uncovered in a more methodical manner, devoid of emotion and personal criticisms.

Perceptions can be completely out of whack where emotions are involved, and emails are probably notorious for not presenting correct emotions - thus distorting perceptions. Can't see the face in front of you, can't hear the tone of voice, can't read the body language. Emails are not a good medium of "fair" discussion - but they are quick to write, quick and cheap to deliver and receive, and are usually all most veterans have to rely on when attempting to communicate and even pass the time. If an emotion is stirred by someone's wrong turn of phrase, it can elicit any number of different responses which are hard to retrieve once sent! We (as the entire Veteran group) really are (as George Mansford suggests) a bunch of "mad galahs". But "mad" here also has many appropriate meanings - not just "larrikin-like". Mad also means "angry", "bitter", "suspicious" - all very common in the Veteran community.

We all went through varying degrees of personal and collective experiences many, many years ago. We all have to accept that our memories of events back then may not be a sharp as they should be. Some have memories of events that are distinctly different from fact (perhaps because of traumas that were experienced) - and the events these memories portray are very real to those that have them. Others have no memory or recollections of certain events at all. Such are the results of the passage of time and the afflictions we may have.

Can we put our emotions aside and get on with the job of investigation, and of righting wrongs to the entire Veteran community of the past, so that our young veterans of the present and future can benefit, and learn from good example, rather than bad?

Perhaps we can't put our "emotions" aside entirely.. But we can TRY to not let them influence our efforts to work together for the common good!

- Bob De Haas

And then, just before this manuscript was in the final stages, there came a last slap in the face.

It came via Dr Brendan Nelson– the new Director of the Australian War Memorial who had taken over from General Steve Gower. I wrote to him asking why it was that the Memorial hadn't accepted the decision by Dr Mike Kelly MP and the federal government that the 2nd D&E Platoon *had* existed.

He wrote back on 5th April 2013 with the ubiquitous but condescending statement, *'acknowledging (my) service to our country during the Vietnam War, and thanking (me) for (my) contribution to our nation's security.'*

But then he stated:

> *'In the absence of evidence that proves otherwise, the Memorial's position remains unchanged: there was no 'Second D&E Platoon.'*

I sent back the statements from Major George Pratt and Major Barry Parkin who both stated publicly a contrary view– that the platoon *had* existed.

The final word?

Nelson wrote back by email on May 16th 2013 saying simply: *'I'm sorry Mr Tate, but the Memorial's position remains unchanged.'*

Apparently, the word of two Australian Defence Force officers (Major George Pratt and Major Barry Parkin) isn't worth much. There is probably good reason for that.

Round and round we go.

**The War Within is available in hard copy direct from the author.
Contact Don at: warvet_69@yahoo.com for details.
It is also available from Amazon Books (on-line)
in both hard copy and Kindle eBook formats.**

Attachments

(a) the Roll Book pages of HQ Company 1ATF for May and June, 1969

(b) the Defence document titled: 'ATROCITY ALLEGATIONS – SOUTH VIETNAM, 3 CAV.' which contains the following:

1. the six-page telegram sent from Major Gordon Pound to AHQ Canberra following his interview with Sapper Robert Enright into his allegations of atrocities at Thua Tich (which Enright says is 'padded' to some extent) and

2. four, unsigned, hand-written pages purporting to be the results of Pound's investigations

Don Tate

Anzacs Betrayed

[Handwritten attendance register - rotated 90°. Contents include columns for Army Number, Rank and Name, Attendance for Month of May, Attendance for Month of June, and Remarks.]

Army Number	Rank and Name	Remarks
215533	PTE MOSS D.R.	M/O 9RAR 18.6
14825	PTE MILLAR A.E.	M/O 9RAR 18.6
216644	PTE O'GRADY D.J.	
2411720	PTE PATERSON S.F.	Posted 9 RAR, 9 Jnr bn moved 15.6
53326	PTE ROSS S.A.	Posted 6 RAR
2145496	PTE RICKERT R.T.	AWOL IN AUST. T OPS
19531	PTE PLUMTREE I.R.	M/O 9 RAR 8 JUN 69
211589	PTE RIDDLE J.B.	M/O 9RAR 18.6
212661	PTE RENNIE B.	R+R Aust M/O 9RAR 22.6.69
216677	PTE SCHULER O.W.	M/O 9RAR 18.6
1202845	PTE SIMPSON D.H.	
213601	PTE ELLIOTT L.	
7121	PTE SECRETT R.S.	M/O 1RAR 15.6
20707	PTE TATE J.B.	Posted 9 RAR, 9 Jnr bn moved 15.6
14275	PTE WILLIAMS G.C.	M/O 1 RAR 26.6.69
216632	PTE WHITNEY W.H.	Posted 9 RAR, 9 Jnr bn moved 15.6
2202044	PTE BROWNING H.A.	
215664	PTE BELL G.W.	MEDEVAC
57066	PTE ARNOLD J.L.	Posted 9 RAR, 9 Jnr bn moved 15.6
14636	PTE SLATTERY R.J.	Posted 9 RAR, 9 Jnr bn moved 15.6
215609	PTE MANSKI D.W.	M/O 9RAR 16.6
215602	PTE CAIRNS R.T.	M/O 9RAR 18.6
2184472	PTE BELGROVE R.S.	Posted 9 RAR 9 Jnr moved 15-6
120685	PTE ROACH A.T.	M/O 9 RAR 18.6
1206833	PTE FAHEY C.J.	M/O 9RAR 18.6
13863	PTE SEYCHELL A.R.M.	M/O 9RAR 2.6.69
44041	PTE FLEER J.C.	PRE-EXT
3723691	PTE BRYANT R.F.	PRE-EXT
1085636	PTE CRANDUS R.T.	PRE-EXT
3411663	PTE McCAULEY J.B.	M/O 1ARW 18.6
63730	PTE FELAPPA A	
3793903	PTE WALKER T.C.	
2130504	PTE BOWDEN C.P.	
2789004	PTE DEGUARA J.J.	H.S. 29 MAY 69

PRESENT — Available for Duty
ABSENT — Detached — Hospital, School/Course, Detention, etc.
On Leave
AWOL
TOTAL
Number PRESENT — Rationed

Not available — Rest Day, Sick, Light Duty

Don Tate

AR 5 (1975)	Department of Defence		File Number			Fo 1
			A138	3	5.	

DETAILS OF INFORMATION ANALYSIS

Security Classification: CONFIDENTIAL

*NOTE: Please print all entries clearly.

REGISTRATION

Title: ATROCITY ALLEGATIONS — SOUTH VIETNAM — 3 CAV. REGT.

Mark to: DGOP (Name or Designation)   G (Location)

Cancel File No .... and inform Movements Section.
Close File No ....
Cross reference this file with: ....

SUBJECT INDEX

Posting	Precis	Initials
C57.2 ~~ARMY~~	AS TITLE	

NAME INDEX

Heading	Precis	Initials
STH. VIETNAM 3 CAV. REGT.	AS TITLE " "	

LOGGING

Originator	Originator's Reference	Date	Initials
		/ /	

Information Classifier: J Woll   10. 6. 76

```
                    CONFIDENTIAL

                        220 9 14 AM '76


        H
   VV (DRA535)     HH
   PP RAYWFF
   DE RAYSND 395 2200832
   ZNY CCCCC                              4RAR - DE   14 May 69
   P 070825Z AUG 76                       DE - 9RAR   5 Jun 69.
   FM MILDIST DARWIN
   TO DEFARM CANBERRA
   BT
   CONFIDENTIAL
   OPS 1172
   DEFARM FOR DGOP. ATTN BRIG BUTLER
   A. TELECON COL HINDS/MAJ WILSCHEFSKI OF 06 AUG 76
   B. TELECON BRIG BUTLER/MAJ POUND OF 06 AUG 76
   1. RECORD OF AN INTERVIEW WITH EX 1202112 SPR R J ENRIGHT.
   INTERVIEW RECORDED BY 311513 MAJ G G POUND, HQ 7 MD ON 07 AUG 76.
   ENRIGHT ASKED TO TELL INTERVIEWING OFFICER DETAILS OF STATEMENT MADE
   BY HIM (ENRIGHT) TO THE PRESS. STORY TOLD BY ENRIGHT IS AS FOLLOWS
   QUOTE. I DECIDED TO TELL MY STORY OF WHAT I SAW AND DID IN SVN
   AS A RESULT OF HEARING MR KILLEN ON THE ABC PROGRAMME AM LAST
   FRIDAY MORNING. THE THINGS HE SAID MADE ME FEEL PISSED OFF AND
   WHILE I WAS AT WORK I KEPT THINKING ABOUT IT. I ASKED FOR AN HOUR
   OFF AND RANG THE NT NEWS AND ASKED TO SPEAK TO A REPORTER.
   THE GIRL PUT ME ON TO A MAN AND I ASKED HIM IF HE WAS INTERESTED
   IN A STORY ABOUT VN. HE TOLD ME TO WAIT THEN PUT ME ON TO A
```

PAGE 2 RAYSND 395 C O N F I D E N T I A L

REPORTER NAMED MRS TERRY DAHLENBERG. I STARTED TO TELL HER THE STORY AND SHE ASKED ME IF I COULD COME INTO HER OFFICE AND BRING SOME SORT OF EVIDENCE THAT I WAS IN VN. I GOT MY DISCHARGE PAPERS FROM HOME AND TOOK THEM IN.

I TOLD HER ABOUT A CONTACT INVOLVING UNARMED WOMEN. IT WAS A RIVER AMBUSH WHICH MY PLATOON INITATED. I SAID THAT I WAS IN 7 SECT 12 PL, DCOY, 9 RAR. I COULD NOT REMEMBER THE NAME OF THE RIVER BUT I COULD POINT IT OUT ON A MAP. I SAID THE CONTACT HAPPENED IN ABOUT AUG 69. I SAID I WAS THE M60 GUNNER IN THE SECT. THE PL COMD, LT DALEY WAS NOT WITH US ON THAT OP. THE CSM WAS IC THE PL. I CANNOT REMEMBER HIS NAME. WE GOT TO THE RIVER AND THE CSM LAID OUT THE AMBUSH IN A GOOD SPOT. WE WERE THERE FOR 4 OR 5 DAYS AND MOST OF THE BLOKES WERE PISSED OFF. ME AND MY NUMBER TWO WERE STANDING UP STRETCHING A HOOTCHIE OVER A BUSH. THE NUMBER TWO (I CANT REMEMBER HIS NAME) SAID LOOK BEHIND YOU. I SAW A BOAT LOAD OF NOGS ON THE RIVER. I GOT BEHIND THE M60 BUT THERE WAS A TREE IN THE WAY. THE BLOKE ON THE BACK OF THE BOAT WITH A STEERING OAR TRIED TO TURN AROUND AND PULLED TO THE MIDDLE OF THE RIVER WHERE I COULD SEE HIM. I OPENED UP AT THE BLOKE IN THE BACK THEN RAKED THE BOAT. SOME-

PAGE 3 RAYSND 395 C O N F I D E N T I A L

BODY ELSE USED A M79 WHICH SANK THE BOAT AND THE SURVIVORS SWAM AWAY. 8 SECT OPENED UP AND DECAPITATED SOMEONE SWIMMING. I ALSO FIRED AT THEM.

I TOLD TERRY DAHLENBERG THAT I TOLD THE CSM HOW MANY WERE IN THE BOAT AND THAT I WAS A BIT EXCITED. 9 SECT MOVED AROUND TO OUR FLANK AND FIRED UP RIVER. THE CSM ASKED A BLOKE CALLED IRISH WHO WAS NORMALLY OUR 2IC (THE SECT IC WAS AWAY) HOW MANY WERE IN THE BOAT. HE SAID 2 MEN AND 4 WOMEN. A CHOPPER CAME IN, I DONT KNOW WHY. WE GOT INTO SOME ASSAULT BOATS AND PATROLLED DOWN RIVER. THE 9 SECT MACHINE GUNNER SMELT SOMETHING AND WE FOUND THE BODY OF A WOMAN IN A SMALL TIDAL CREEK. THE CSM CHECKED OUT THE BODY AND I WENT TO LOOK. THERE WERE SIX OR SEVEN BULLET HOLES IN THE SIDE. WE LEFT THE BODY THERE, NOBODY WANTED TO TOUCH IT AND THE CSM THREW UP. ONE SOLDIER DID A BODY SEARCH.

WE WENT ON DOWN TO A BEACH AND CAMPED. THERE WERE MORE BODIES FOUND ON THE BEACH BUT NOT BY US.

I ALSO STARTED TO TELL TERRY DAHLENBERG ABOUT ANOTHER THING I DID NOT LIKE. IT HAPPENED WHEN I WAS IN D AND E PL OF HQ 1 ATF. I WENT OVER AS A REO FOR 4 RAR AND THEN WHEN THEY WENT HOME I WENT TO D AND E BEFORE GOING TO 9 RAR. WE WERE WITH SOME CAV AND

PAGE 4 RAYSND 395 C O N F I D E N T I A L

THEY AMBUSHED A TRACK NEAR TUI TIC. I WAS AT ANOTHER AMBUSH NEAR BY AND WAS PIQUET ON TOP OF AN APC. I HEARD THE SHOTS AND HEARD DETAILS OF THE AMBUSH ON THE RADIO. ABOUT 70 VN FROM XUYEN MOC WERE ON THE TRACK AND ABOUT ELEVEN WERE KILLED. A SPOOKY CAME IN AND WENT AFTER THE REST WHO HAD SCATTERED. WE WENT BACK TO THE MAIN AMBUSH SITE IN THE MORNING.

THE BODIES WERE LEFT OUT UNTIL THE AFTERNOON THEN WE HAD TO DRAG THEM INTO A BOMB CRATER. WE PUT THEIR WEAPONS AND AMMO IN AS WELL AND THE SAPPERS BLEW THEM. AN APC DRAGGED, I THINK IT WAS FOUR BODIES BY THE FEET ON THE END OF A ROPE BACK TO XUYEN MOC. THE BODIES INCLUDED A YOUNG WOMEN WHO HAD HAD A NEW AK 47 AND A MEDICAL PACK. WE WERE AMBUSHED ON THE WAY AND KILLED FIVE VN. THE AMBUSH HAD BEEN SPOTTED BY A LIGHT FIRE TEAM. ON THE WAY THE APC FIRED AT VILLAGERS IN THE FIELDS WHO RAN AWAY AT THE SIGHT OF THE BODIES. THEY FIRED UNTIL THE VILLAGERS STOPPED. I THINK THEY FIRED OVER THEIR HEADS.

BY THE TIME WE GOT TO XUYEN MOC THE BODIES WERE IN A BAD WAY. WE LEFT THEM IN THE MAIN SQUARE. WE WERE TOLD THE BODIES HAD BEEN DRAGGED AT THE REQUEST OF THE VILLAGE CHEIF. THEY WERE DRAGGED FROM TUI TIC TO XUYEN MOC.

PAGE 5 RAYSNE 395 C O N F I D E N T I A L

I DID NOT TELL TERRY DAHLENBERG ALL OF THE LAST STORY, SHE STOPPED ME AND SAID SHE WOULD DO THE FIRST STORY FIRST BUT SHE TOOK SHORTHAND NOTES OF THE PART OF THE SECOND STORY I TOLD. SHE ASKED ME WHY I CAME IN AND I SAID IT WAS MY OWN CONCIENCE. I HAVE KNOWN ABOUT IT EVER SINCE IT HAPPENED AND IT HAS BEEN WORRYING ME FOR THE LAST COUPLE OF YEARS. I TOLD THE STORY BECAUSE PEOPLE HERE HAVE BEEN SAYING THAT SUCH THINGS DID NOT HAPPEN, I SAY THEY DID.

I TOLD HER I WAS A SIX YEAR REGULAR BUT DID NOT FINISH MY TIME. SHE ASKED ME IF I WOULD APPEAR AT AN INQUIRY AND I SAID YES. WHEN I WENT BACK LATER SHE WAS ON THE PHONE. I WENT INTO THE OFFICE AND SAT DOWN. SHE SAID I CANT TALK ANY MORE HE HAS JUST COME IN. I SAID DID SHE WANT ME TO GO OUT AND SHE SAID YES. I WENT TO THE OTHER END OF THE OFFICE. SHE THEN ASKED ME IF I WANTED TO SPEAK TO A BLOKE FROM 2UE, I SAID I WOULD. HE SAID HIS NAME WAS GREG GRANGER. HE ASKED ME IF I WOULD RECORD AN INTERVIEW AND I SAID YES. HE TOLD ME THAT HE HAD SET UP A TAPE RECORDER AND I TOLD MY STORY. I HAD TO TELL IT TWICE BECAUSE HE SAID THE FIRST ONE HAD MESSED UP. SJERRY DAHLENBERG GOT BACK ON THE PHONE AND ASKED HIM NOT TO RELEASE THE STORY UNTIL AFTER THREE OCLOCK

```
PAGE 6 RAYSND 395 C O N F I D E N T I A L

ON MONDAY AFTERNOON WHEN THE NT NEWS COMES OUT.

TARY DAHLENBERG SHOWED ME TWO COPIES OF WHAT SHE HAD WRITTEN FOR

THE PAPER.  I SIGNED BOTH COPIES.  IT DID NOT INCLUDE EVERYTHING

I HAD TOLD HER ONLY ABOUT THE CONTACT, KNOCKING THE BLOKE OFF THE

BACK OF THE BOAT, THE M79 SINKING THE BOAT AND THE WOMAN FOUND BY

US AND NOT BURIED.  THEN THERE WERE MY PERSONAL PARTICULARS.

UNQUOTE

BT
```

> THIS MESSAGE WAS RECEIVED BY THE ARMY
> FIXED COMMUNICATIONS SYSTEM COMMCEN
> CANBERRA. A.C.T. Contact telephones:
> Queries relating to this Message : 65 4045
> General Communications Queries : 65 4100

CONFIDENTIAL

On the night 29/30 May 1969, 2 Tp B Sqn 3 Cav Regt (Commanded by Capt T Arrowsmith - now major), with under command the D9E Pl HQ ITF, was sighted in ambush position around THUA TICH and on a destroyed tank kp to the North of XUYEN MOC district. 2 Tp HQ was located near the old gates to THUA TIC and elements of the D9 E Pl were sighted several hundred yards South on Route 328.

At 2030 hr the D9 E Pl reported a large number of VC marching North along Route 328. Several minutes later the leading elements of the VC party passed in front of 2 Tp HQ. The Troop leader allowed the scout group to go past and then initiated the ambush with machine gun fire and claymore mines, on the /main body of the VC party. The D9 E Pl ambush was also sprung. The VC party was later estimated to be well in excess of 50.

2 Tp was operating well outside of artillery range and although they had a section of mortars under command HQ 1 TF took the following precautions:

    a. A SPOOKY aircraft armed with mini guns was tasked to give fire support to the troop.

    b. TANGO Force (elements of the tank squadron) which was operating in the adjacent district of DUCH TAN was put on notice to move to help 2 Tp if that proved necessary.

    c. A section of 105 mm gun was warned to be ready to move from NUI DAT base to within gun range.

The fire support from the SPOOKY was effective and it was not necessary to move TANGO force or the section of 105 mm guns.

The next morning the troop, which had been in five separate ambush positions overnight, concentrated at the entrance to THUA TIC and conducted several clearing patrols or sweeps to check the general area of the ambush. Comd 1TF (Brig Pearson now Maj Gen retired) and OC B Sqn 3 Cav Regt (Maj R.E. Rooks now Col DARMD-A) flew in at approximately 0900 hr to examine the ambush results at first hand.

2 Tp was ordered to move to XUYEN MOC as soon as possible in case the troop was attacked by the remainder of the VC party. Because of the strong possibility of the troop being ambushed on Route 328 on their way to XUYEN MOC OC B Sqn 3 Cav Regt tasked a Light Fire Team (helicopter gunships) to overfly the troop during its move.

At 1020 hr HQ 1TF received a radio request from the District Chief of XUYEN MOC to have the bodies delivered to XUYEN MOC. This request was approved by the SO2 of HQ 1TF.

At 1352 hrs 30 May 1969 (a day of   ) 2 Tp was ambushed on Route 328. Supported by the Light Fire Team 2 Tp countered the ambush. A further 7 VC were killed and an additional three weapons were captured. During the fire fight one of the APCs was hit by³ an RPG 7 rocket at very close range. Because of the nearness of the VC to the APC the RPG 7 rocket failed to detonate

2 Tp continued on as quickly as possible to XUYEN MOC. As they left Route 328 another group of people were sighted in long grass. The Troop Leader was not certain that they were VC so machine guns were fired over their heads. The group turned out to be women and children from XUYEN MOC collecting grass.

Throughout the three contacts no casualties were suffered by 2 Tp or the D & E Pl.

Sometime later (Col R E Rocks is not sure when) OC B Sqn 3 Cav Regt was told by Comd 1 TF to investigate how the bodies had been carried to XUYEN MOC. Col R E Rocks cannot remember why he was asked to carry out the investigation except that it was related to bodies being towed by APCs.

OC B Sqn 3 Cav Regt interviewed the Troop Leader who provided the following information:

   a. Because he wanted to leave THUA TIC as quickly as possible to avoid being attacked he destroyed all bodies and equipment of use to the VC, except for about four bodies which were not badly cut about. The bodies not destroyed were tied onto the 4th back of the APCs. The captured weapons were not destroyed but placed inside an APC.

b. The bodies had not been dragged from THUA TIC. ~~XUYEN MOC~~

c. During the ambush on 30 May 1969 the tactical moves of the APCs caused the bodies to fall off the APCs.

d. The Troop Leader was not prepared to risk the lives of his men to lift the bodies back onto the APCs. The troop was still at considerable risk of being ambushed again.

e. The bodies were dragged for the remainder of the move to XUYEN MOC.

OC B Sqn 3 Cav Regt repeated the Troop Leaders explanation to the Comd 1TF. No further action was taken except that OC B Sqn 3 Cav Regt who had only been in command for 21 days issued orders to his squadron that:

a. VC bodies were not to be carried on APCs without his personal approval, and

b. in future all VC bodies were to be buried.

www.ingramcontent.com/pod-product-compliance
Lightning Source LLC
Chambersburg PA
CBHW060310240426
43661CB00059B/2719